P9-DUK-456

DATE DUE

SUBJECT TO OVERDUE FINES
CALL 465-2330 TO RENEW

5/19/07	

LIBRARY
COLLEGE of the REDWOODS
DEL NORTE
883 W. Washington Blvd.
Crescent City, CA 95531

LC 151 .M25 2001
Martin, Rachel.
Listening up

·················listening up

listening up

reinventing ourselves as teachers and students

rachel martin

Boynton/Cook Publishers
HEINEMANN
Portsmouth, NH

Boynton/Cook Publishers, Inc.
A subsidiary of Reed Elsevier Inc.
361 Hanover Street
Portsmouth, NH 03801–3912
www.boyntoncook.com

Offices and agents throughout the world

© 2001 by Rachel Martin

All rights reserved. No part of this book may be reproduced in any form or by any electronic or mechanical means, including information storage and retrieval systems, without permission in writing from the publisher, except by a reviewer, who may quote brief passages in a review.

The author and publisher wish to thank those who have generously given permission to reprint borrowed material:

Excerpts from *Worker Writers* by Meridel Le Sueur. Copyright © 1982 by the estate of Meridel LeSueur. Printed by permission of West End Press.

The poem, "On the Question of Race" used by permission of Enrique Aviles and Michelle Banks.

Library of Congress Cataloging-in-Publication Data
Martin, Rachel.
    Listening up : reinventing ourselves as teachers and students / Rachel Martin.
      p. cm.
    Includes bibliographical references and index.
    ISBN 0-86709-387-0 (alk. paper)
    1. Literacy—Social aspects—United States.   2. Postmodernism and education—United States.   3. Psychoanalysis and education—United States.   4. Critical pedagogy—United States.   5. Poststructuralism—United States. I. Title: Reinventing ourselves as teachers and students.   II. Title.

LC151 .M25 2000
370.11'5—dc21

                                       00–062086

Editor: Lisa Luedeke
Production: Lynne Reed
Cover design: Jenny Jensen Greenleaf
Cover photograph: Hakim Raquib
Manufacturing: Louise Richardson

Printed in the United States of America on acid-free paper
05   04   03   02   01   DA   1   2   3   4   5

For Tom and Nomi

Contents

Acknowledgments

Many thanks to the writers of *Neighbors Talk in Roxbury, Dorchester, and Jamaica Plain, United Youth of Boston*, and *Survival News*, especially for the risks we helped each other take. Extra appreciation goes to Dolores Pickett, Celena Castillo, and Cathy Horne, members of the *Neighbors Talk* publishing committee; and Betty Reid Mandell and Florence Miller, two of the movers and shakers behind *Survival News*.

Susan Lytle expects her students to search for their own questions and won't let them get away with only responding to someone else's; she helped me find mine. Valerie Walkerdine then pointed me toward some answers. It was my respect for Valerie, as someone working to further radical change in the world, that made me hang in with difficult readings on poststructural and psychoanalytic theory, about which I was initially skeptical, if not suspicious! A special thank-you for the many crises she sparked in me over one tumultuous, six-week period at the Ontario Institute for Studies in Education.

Much love and appreciation go to the friends who read this manuscript and who nourish my life. Andy Nash, who loves to argue as much as I do, let me know when I wasn't saying enough here so that she could. Alison Jaggar, who pushes things beyond their seeming limits, shows me how I might, too. And an extra thanks to Sukey Blanc, whom I depend on to raise one more issue just when I think things are finally settled, and who lovingly didn't when she knew that, at last, this manuscript had to be finished. She pushed me to turn the "I think"s into "I know"s and told me I had something to say.

Mindy Noble made long-distance phone calls that always warmed me up. Lisa Schachter gave me unwavering insight and the Cape Cod Bay. I continue to depend on the ideas and challenges I receive from Erica Foldy. And I first learned what grassroots education is about from Blair Mooney and the East End Alternative School in Cincinnati.

In addition, the following friends and colleagues provided invaluable feedback on this manuscript: Catherine Anderson, Gary Anderson,

Tom Brouillette, Sara Freedman, Jaime Grinberg, Mira-Lisa Katz, Susan Roberta Katz, Lisa Luedeke, Barbara Neumann, Marcine Pickron-Davis, Susan Rosenblum, Ruth Salvaggio, and Deborah Weiner.

And to my partner and friend Tom Brouillette, thank you for the magic you create for Nomi and me.

One

Introduction
Teaching in the Space
Between Action and Reflection

I think of myself as a teacher of language: that is as someone for whom language has implied freedom, who is trying to aid others to free themselves through the written word, and above all through learning to write it for themselves. I cannot know for them what it is they need to free, or what words they need to write; I can only try with them to get an approximation of the story they want to tell.
—Adrienne Rich, *On Lies, Secrets,*
and Silence (1979, 63)

Poverty in an age of affluence is being unable to write and having others write about you.
—Sister Stanislaus Kennedy,
Dublin, Ireland[1]

During my first years of teaching, I thought that it was through collectively telling our stories and then reexploring them in the light of new knowledge, about ourselves and the world, that individual and community change occurred. I believed that what Adrienne Rich said lay at the heart of radical literacy teaching. More recently, I've come to see that the stories we need to tell are more likely those we create, rather than those we simply uncover. And I've come to believe that

1

publishing them—for a wide audience—is as necessary as the telling. At bottom, this work represents the changes in my view of myself as a teacher, and it explains why I now believe it's Sister Kennedy's thoughts about the importance of articulating one's own situation that lie closer to the heart of radical change.

To chart these changes, this book becomes a look at the Freirian ideas that guided my early years of teaching, the classroom experiences and the poststructural and psychoanalytic theories that urged me to question those ideas, and the work toward a new pedagogy in which I'm currently involved.

Following a route typical of literacy, writing, and ESL teachers, I have taught in many places over the years, always piecing together several part-time jobs. Here, I draw mainly on five of those teaching situations: a neighborhood women's literacy program in Philadelphia; a large community college in Boston; and three Boston-based community writing and publishing projects—a neighborhood book project, a newspaper published by welfare activists, and a citywide youth newspaper.[2] My story is a record of one teacher's movement back and forth between theory and practice, one constantly causing the other to shift. As such, it's meant as a tool for curriculum development, as well as for expanding theoretical ideas of what we do when we teach. I believe that one person's thoughts on making her practice come into line with her goals—what's working, what isn't, and what there is yet to try— can be of use to other literacy workers immersed in the same process.

At the same time, this book is grounded in a particular, if evolving, view of what constitutes *radical* and what constitutes *change*. One of my goals is to demonstrate when a poststructural perspective is meaningful and useful in a classroom. Poststructuralism is a way of looking at the world that recognizes that the categories through which we define people, things, and ideas—including those central to this book, such as identity, truth, and voice—are not fixed and eternally stable. It sees categories as fluid and suggests the danger that comes from assuming the world is composed of binary oppositions, either/or constructions, in which there is *always* an Other. Through poststructuralism, we deconstruct how we come to think what we think, and see what we see, making it possible to think, and see, and create the world differently. One of the central themes I return to at various points in these chapters is shifting perceptions of race and experiences of racial identity. I'm a White, Jewish woman from a middle-class background currently living in New Mexico. The people with whom I work are teenagers and adults; the majority are people of color from poor and working-class backgrounds. Both the tensions and the excitement we find in simultaneous, and sometimes shifting, sameness and difference can be seen in these chapters.[3] Along with poststructural ideas, I look at why our unconscious fears and desires, as viewed by psychoanalytic theories, need to be considered if we are to create effective change. The specific techniques for reading, writing and discussion offered here share the goal of opening up new conversations to pave the way for reinventing our ideas about ourselves and the world.[4]

In early drafts of this introduction, I wrote that this book looks at classroom practice and at the same time uses theory to raise questions about and expand that practice. But what I need to add is that the various descriptions of my practice included here are themselves the stories I create, as much as my students do theirs. What I choose to include necessarily excludes; what I highlight also silences. As Jane Flax (1993) writes, "Much material must also elude my awareness, including the excluded content of and unconscious motivations for my story" (4). As I hope to make clear, poststructuralism refutes the idea that the knower and the known can ever be separated from each other.[5]

Many teachers are working in their individual classrooms to develop a practice consistent with their goals, but few of us have published accounts of what we're doing and how we're thinking about it. In an essay she titled "The Pedagogy of the Distressed," Jane Tompkins (1990) wrote, "No one ever talked, really talked about what they did. Oh, there were plenty of success stories and the predictable remarks about a discussion that had been like pulling teeth but never anything about how it really felt to be up there day after day" (655). One of the intended outcomes of this book is to encourage all of us to create more opportunities to document and distribute what we're seeing in our work, how what we see is forcing us to change our ideas, how our ideas are compelling us to change what we "see," and how it really feels day after day.

The Handbook That Refused to Be One

Something happened to me midway through writing this manuscript. I set out to write about my practice and the theory that grounds it. When I stood back and looked at my early drafts, I realized that the theory I was articulating held out promises the practice didn't deliver. One problem was that my goals as a teacher, a large part of anyone's theory, had gone through tumultuous change since I had first written a grant proposal to do a teacher "handbook" for a community-based organization, a project that turned into this book. At the time I actually began to write, I was just beginning to rethink my teaching to help me achieve these newly forming goals.

I write about the changes in my goals here. I also still write about my practice. I'm confident that the way I teach literacy is on the right track. Many of the people in my classes engage with reading and writing, beginning to enjoy both, and I think that's an important grounding for whatever else we do. The literacy activities described here are meant to facilitate engagement with classroom discussion and vice versa. And they acknowledge that reading is no more unambiguous, writing and voice no more unidimensional, than categories are fixed.[6]

Teachers in workshops I facilitate frequently ask how to deal with "multi-level" classrooms. My response rests on a belief that what students are able to do has little to do with their supposed level of reading or writing ability. The techniques suggested in these chapters will help you ask students to read and write things you may have thought they were incapable of engaging with before. That engagement will come most easily, of course, when the content of what they're reading or writing is compelling. But I believe that neither the technique nor content will work unless grounded in a belief that the meanings our students make of a reading, and the writings they create, will inform us. Much of this book centers on the effort to put this latter belief into practice.

Here and there are ideas I'm toying with that are suggestive, not fully developed. There are inconsistencies in theory and contradictions in practice. But if I ignore the incongruities, then I marginalize those things that don't fit into the categories I've created. And it is those very anomalies that urge me to question my underlying beliefs. At first I tried to hide the contradictions as I wrote, ultimately finding, of course, that they wouldn't stay hidden. In the end, I gave up trying to disguise the contradictions or force the inconsistencies into a coherent theory that is not yet there, and may never be in a form one would think of as final.

Lucy Lippard (1990) says she writes in what James Clifford has called "that moment in which the possibility of comparison exists in unmediated tension with sheer incongruity . . . a permanent ironic play of similarity and difference, the familiar and the strange, the here and the elsewhere" (5). I found the same thing as I wrote this manuscript. Incongruities sneaked out of neat comparisons; similarities were always interrupting differences; the familiar emerged out of the strange. Teaching holds within it a similar tension between knowing and not knowing. The knowing means being aware of and sharpening the rationale, or conviction, that underlies the everyday decisions we make in the classroom. The not knowing means questioning those convictions at the very same time:

> To put our beliefs on hold is to cease to exist as ourselves for a moment—and that is not easy . . . We must learn to be vulnerable enough to allow our worlds to turn upside down in order to allow the realities of others to edge themselves into our consciousness. (Delpit 1988, 297)

Included in Chapter Two is a description of the places where I have taught, an overview of the issues that have arisen, and a look at my current goals. Chapter Three is a look at the writings of Paulo Freire and the curricula he has inspired. It also examines the classroom experiences and poststructural and psychoanalytic theories that urged me to take a second look at critical pedagogy, and it offers thoughts on developing alternative ideas and practices. Encouraging engagement with reading and writing forms the basis of the following chapters. Chapter Four highlights the practical implications of multiple voices and identities for the teaching of writing and argues for the publication of what I call community writing, while Chapter Five turns to the integration of reading and writing. In each, I hold suggested techniques up for scrutiny against the goals I'm wanting them to achieve. Additional activities for reading and writing are offered within Chapter Six, which focuses on theme-based curricula. Here, I'd like to say a bit more about what this book is, overall, and what it isn't.

A Focus on Teachers

Over the last few years, my work has focused on community writing and publishing, based on a belief that self-definition is vital to self-determination. In line with that, I write here more about those changes I've undergone as a teacher, and those I still look forward to, than I do my speculations about the changes students experience. I get frustrated reading academics' interpretations of their students' or "subjects'" lives, when what I always want to know is how the latter would have themselves described their situations.

A letter from a social work student following the publication of her professor's article in the *Women's Review of Books* points to a danger in analyzing our students. The professor had written:

> These students, working in women's traditional occupations, are finding their voices, identifying ruling relations, and discovering how they are oppressed. But at the same time they see how their work implicates them, too, in ruling practices. This is an empowering stance both for them and their clients. These students, as they start to make these connections for themselves, are learning how a struggle for change might begin. (Tracy & Campbell 1993, 4)

The student wrote in response:

> How does she know that I am finding my voice? I didn't know I had lost it. How does she know that I didn't understand ruling relations and my oppression before coming into this program? How does she know my work implicates me into ruling practices? How does she know I am *starting* to make these connections? (Tracy & Campbell 1993, 4)

The professor then answered in a letter of her own that she should have qualified her statements by saying "many" students. But at issue is more than overgeneralizing. What the professor wrote were her analyses, her interpretations, and her conjectures, presented as truth.

A further reason to focus on teaching here is that so much of adult education locates the root of classroom and programmatic difficulties in the behavior of the students. A common assumption, for example, is that women on welfare are late to class because they haven't yet learned the importance of punctuality. This problem is then addressed in the job readiness class—the class that also reminds women to wear deodorant and refrain from chewing gum during a job interview. Aside from its obvious condescension, this response ignores the possibility that the women, in fact, may not have complete control over their time. Even more importantly for my purpose here, it ignores the possibility that the women are late because they aren't enthused about what's happening in class. Maybe, as William Ayers (1990) suggests in his review of *Among Schoolchildren*, it means we need to look at us, not "them":

> When Chris [the teacher] moves Felipe's desk because he is "chattering too much," what is he chattering about? When she keeps a group of children in from recess for failing to do their homework, what had the homework been? And when she sets as a goal getting the troubled Clarence not only to "do his work," really her work, but to "like school and schoolwork someday," what is there about it to like? (3)

What most interests me here is, as Ann Berthoff once wrote, "thinking about my own thinking and interpreting my own interpretations." Just as more and more researchers, particularly feminists, have stopped writing in the passive voice—instead acknowledging their role in the shaping of research results—so can we as teachers acknowledge the ways we influence the life of a classroom and the ways it influences us.[7]

A New Look at Critical Pedagogy

Up until a few years ago, I would say I became a teacher because I thought people needed to think more critically about the social conditioning of their personal experience, to look underneath the myths that obscure our vision of what's going on in our lives and the world. I wanted people to see that getting injured on the job is more often the result of safety hazards than personal carelessness, that not acquiring reading and writing skills is often due to a setup by the school system itself and not a function of personal failure, that the "true stories" of tabloid TV shows *create* a view of the world in which our streets are made safe from African American and Latino drug dealers by police officers. Critical pedagogy provided the theoretical base to my teaching when I began.

But this notion began to raise a problem for me because the women where I worked very often did view reality with a critical consciousness; they quite often saw the social conditioning of their lives. In *Drylongso*, John Gwaltney (1980) wrote, "principled survival . . . is a preeminently analytical process" (xxx). Several years ago, a woman in one of my classes talked about how you have to lie to your caseworker to squeeze what you need out of welfare, but that having to lie in front of your children "takes away your freedom." Many other students have since raised the same point. Deciding which to trade off—your right to demonstrate your real integrity to your child or being able to get her a decent-looking coat—knowing that your freedom hangs in the balance, is a "preeminently analytical process."

I also began to realize that within the framework I'd used, there wasn't a place for me, as a teacher, with which I was comfortable. The role it left me was that of a facilitator whose consciousness was already raised, helping other people raise theirs. I was beginning to see that I couldn't reconcile that idea with the reality of who the people in my classes were. I also started to see how that premise didn't fit with the fact that my own awareness of some issues still needed heightening or that even when my awareness is high, my actions don't always match it. In sum, I couldn't reconcile this role with the view I wanted to have of myself as a colearner, a term used again and again in conferences and writing about radical education. When I've asked other teachers what they perceive they are learning in the classroom, the responses have invariably been linked to learning about poverty—what it's like to live in a public housing development or to buy groceries on a welfare budget.

A passage typical of this representation of teacher as colearner comes from *Celebrating Community Voice*:

> The tutors' role in a participatory curriculum is . . . (to) catalyze the learners' ability to reflect on their everyday reality. As concerns are identified, the tutors re-present them to the class and guide students through an exploration process, contributing linguistic expertise while learning from the students about their reality. This approach equalizes the roles of "learner/educator" and "educator/learner" (Paulo Freire). (Albuquerque Literacy Program 1994, 12)

Our consciousness raising is almost exclusively seen as a process of learning about our students' lives. Ira Shor, coauthor with Freire of *A Pedagogy for Liberation* (1987), echoes this in saying that the way teachers change in the process of "critical" or "liberatory" teaching is that we become "more student-centered as . . . the teacher learns how to existentialize philosophy while the students learn how to philosophize experience" (156).

While I, too, have learned important things about the lives of the people with whom I have worked, there's something more I want in my role as a colearner. I think there's something we as teachers can be learning about our own lives and freedom, about our role as teachers within a movement for social change, and about what we really are and aren't accomplishing in that role—in short, new ways to philosophize *our* experience. This book describes how I am feeling my way toward such a pedagogy. In doing so, I needed to take a second look at critical pedagogy—at its theory, as developed by Paulo Freire and further articulated by others in this country; at the ways it is commonly practiced, as described in Freire-inspired curricula; and at my own experiences with it.

Cornel West (1993), among others, pays tribute to Freire for his unique "fusion of social theory, moral outrage and political praxis" (xiii). As Jeanne Brady (1994) writes, Freire "makes the concrete central to struggle without ever sacrificing the importance of theory and analysis" (151). I want to honor that tradition in this book by pointing to the practical problems to which a theoretical reliance on Freire has led us as radical educators in the United States. I do so with the awareness that new discourses can emerge thanks to the many seeds Freire has sown.

My second look at Freirian pedagogy, as it is often called, was stimulated by exposure to poststructuralism—a political theory that helps illuminate our own complicity with power and also helps us subvert it, by showing how it works through a web of relations, rather than via a deterministic force—and by radical attempts to use psychoanalysis, representing a departure from classical Freudian ideas. I had begun to perceive a dissonance between my earlier assumptions and what I saw in my practice; these readings made the gaps even clearer. Both poststructuralism and psychoanalysis helped me think in new ways about how power works. They allowed me to see how my own needs, fears, and desires might find a place in classroom investigations, as I also came to see how our relationship to domination is not simply a matter of complete acquiescence on the one hand, nor absolute resistance on the other. While the goal of meaning making has become an overall guidepost in radical teaching, I'm aiming now in the direction of a pedagogy that places me in a position of colearner as my students and I together question how these meanings are shaped.

As I've said, this book was initially intended to offer classroom methods. As I wrote, I found I also needed it to show that progressive classroom methods work only if grounded in attempts to move beyond often unperceived beliefs, held by both teachers and students, that impede their implementation. The book takes a critical look at my role, both ideal and real, in the production and questioning of the meanings we make.

This is as much a book on theorizing as on theory itself. It describes the processes I've gone through and am going through still as I leave behind the certainty I brought to my early years of teaching, yet still find ground on which to make pedagogical and political decisions—and act.

Notes

1. From a postcard produced by Spellbound Postcards, Dublin, Ireland.

2. While I have taught some GED and ESL classes, most of my teaching has been in what's referred to as basic literacy, pre-freshman composition, and what I call community writing. The GED and ESL teachers who have come to workshops I've facilitated have often found more common ground with literacy and writing teachers than they'd recognized before, while I learned at the same time some of their distinct needs. I hope that as you read, you will recognize the links that tie us together as teachers of language, even as you find the moments when your work demands a unique perspective.

3. Leslie Roman (1993) points out that the term *people of color* "still implies that White culture is the hidden norm against which all other racially subordinate groups' so-called 'differences' are measured" (71). I continue to use this term in workshops and classes for now and find that talking about its very difficulty opens up useful dialogue.

4. I began my political life twenty years ago in the feminist movement. I taught women's studies and worked in a rape crisis center, a battered women's shelter, and a women's peace organization. At one point I decided I needed to develop a career. I knew I had enjoyed teaching more than anything else, and I knew I wanted to work in a neighborhood setting. I began teaching in literacy programs, returned to school, and, disturbingly, found myself thinking less and less about gender, somehow feeling I was leaving feminism outside my graduate school door. Even now, I think about race most often—whether I'm teaching in a multicultural class or a homogeneous one or examining my role as a member of a mostly African American youth/adult alliance—and I'm sure there are times I miss key insights about gender.

But what I now see as I write this book is how much it, and I, are informed by feminism(s). (It is becoming more common to use the plural *feminisms* in recognition of the many theories of feminism, shaped differently by varying positions of race, culture, class, and sexuality.) If I stand back far enough, I can see the feminist lenses I've come to take for granted. The consciousness-raising group, community women's newspaper, and other feminist projects I participated in during the 1970s taught me to value the collaboration I now assume as central to learning. I also learned to trust that the collaborative process of dialogue would itself lead to new understandings and decisions. And it was, of course, feminism, long before I read any educational theory, that taught me to see the personal as political. I've realized that those early years may have also contributed to some of the problems I faced when I first began teaching. If, for instance, all contributions to a discussion were to be validated, how did we challenge those we opposed?

Most importantly, I realized that it was from feminism that I learned to scrutinize both my work and the way I think about it, through a tacit understanding of the influence of my own various positions in the world. Even as I would like to make gender relations more central to my future thinking about what's happening in my classrooms, I realize that in a very real way, feminism underlies my teaching and this book.

5. Like a lot of teachers, I have often been isolated from coworkers. The Women's School in Philadelphia, where I first began teaching literacy, had only two teachers most of the time I was there. I taught during the day; the other teacher at night. Working at a large community college, I arrived in time only to make a dash to the copy room before meeting with students and then my class. While there are friends I rely on for an ear and critique, what I've longed for is to be a part of a group of teachers who meet regularly to help one another think and write about our work together. Clearly, if I'd worked collaboratively, my thinking about my own work would have taken directions I couldn't have imagined alone.

I left the Women's School to move to Boston before I began this book. Not only is the Women's School the place I worked the longest; it's also one of the places where I learned the most. Each step of the way, I've thought about what it would have meant to write while I was still there. An integral part of our classes was examining ourselves as writers, readers, and participants in discussions. We self-consciously looked for the ways our ideas were either changing or becoming stronger through these activities so we could hold on to the changes and build on them. I was also becoming more conscious of my particular role in each of these activities. The next time I write, I want to write with a group of teachers and participants to create additional lenses on my experience and theirs, challenging each of our individual perceptions in the process.

6. Among the methods discussed here for engaging people with reading and writing are things I've done in my own classrooms, different ways of doing them that I have thought of while working on these chapters, and ideas from other teachers that I haven't yet tried. Few of the methods I use are completely original. Like all of us, I borrow ideas and then make them my own through the way I use them in my classes. I've credited the source of ideas wherever I could. But there were times when readings, conversations, workshops, and spur of the moment experiments blurred together so that I wasn't sure where an idea came from. My apologies for any omissions.

7. In Chapter Four, however, I do offer ideas on why, at a given moment, pens moved in a writing classroom. Sometimes I know because I've asked the students; at other times I'm only guessing.

Two

From the Women's School to *Neighbors Talk*
What We've Got Going For Us and What We're Up Against

An itinerant teacher for many years, I have taught many places, including a school of office technology; two art colleges, one for women and another for Native American students; and two community-based Latina ESL projects. More recently, I taught at a New Mexico community college vastly different from the one I describe in this chapter. Small and located in a rural county with a majority of Chicano students, it's a place where I sang in the college choir and felt more a part of the college community. While references to each of these sites crop up here and there in the chapters that follow, it is the five situations described in this chapter to which I refer most often, providing a classroom context for the theories and practices detailed in later chapters. These include the Women's School; a community college in Boston; and three community writing and publishing projects: *Neighbors Talk*, *Survival News*, and *United Youth of Boston*. I offer a further context by looking at issues such as teaching conditions, the creation of classroom communities, some of what it means to work in multicultural settings, my role in classrooms, and the impact on our work of the prevailing image of "illiteracy."

11

The Women's School

The Women's School was housed in one room on the second floor of a neighborhood activist church, with an adjacent balcony for bookshelves and a couch. While I've worked in several adult literacy and ESL programs in which I had classes of only women, this was the only school explicitly for women.

The students ranged in age from seventeen to sixty-eight and shared experiences as poor and working-class African American women living in West Philadelphia. Some had graduated from high school with tentative literacy skills, but the majority had dropped out.[1] Some had become pregnant or gone to work. Many—because they were hungry, or were cruelly teased for the way their clothes looked, or were undone after maneuvering their way around gangs to get to school, or had tuned out because they knew the teacher preferred the light-skinned kids— had a hard time paying attention, got labeled mentally retarded, were put into "special" classes, and were ignored. Several of the older women had grown up in South Carolina in sharecropping families, so they went to school only when it rained and they weren't needed for work.

A few people who read early drafts of this book said sometimes I made classroom practice sound too easy. That was at a point when I was writing primarily about the Women's School, and I realized that, in many ways, it *was* easy for me there because of what I now know was an unusual situation. The homogeneity of the students—all women who lived in the same neighborhood—and the fact that there was no large administration setting administrative rules, and no large funders dictating the kinds of tests we used, made conditions for teaching ideal. The reading and writing classes were not too large or small; for the most part, the same women stayed together for at least nine months. This structure stands in sharp contrast to the community college where I taught writing and reading.

Community College Teaching

The community college where I taught in Boston is the most traditional place I have worked. Something that happened one fall illustrates why it was also the most draining: It was the third week of the semester. After a summer away from the college, I walked around the halls feeling excited and proud to be a teacher again, as I do each fall. But when the third week of the semester came and went, and I still had no desk at which I could meet with students and no phone where a message could be left, I began to feel like a fool for seeing myself as important. I began to internalize the administration's view of me: a part-time instructor in a no-credit course, that is, as someone with little prestige, to match that attributed to my students.

The college was also a difficult place to be because of departmental requirements that put teachers in difficult positions. For some readers, the following description will be all too familiar. The department required students to write a one-paragraph essay—two paragraphs were not allowed—in order to leave my class in developmental studies and enter freshman composition. The paragraph could have no more than one fragment, comma splice, or run-on sentence. Essays were judged on the use of transitional words, unity, development (eight to ten sentences, one hundred words, movement from general to specific), and the existence of a topic sentence. Whether or not it had something to say was not considered. When I raised the possibility that we do consider it, several faculty agreed the exam might produce "banal" writing, but said that's what they want in developmental courses, to "control for mistakes." These were the topics students could choose from:

- Explain the risks of buying a used car.
- You are what you eat. Explain.
- A dictionary is a writer's best friend.
- What I enjoy most (least) about winter is_____.
- Each group of immigrants that comes to the United States has something special to contribute to society.[2]

Where essays are evaluated on how closely they stick to topics such as the ones above, I suggested at a department meeting that a student who manages to play with the topic—to alter it in order to make it more answerable—be rewarded for her strategic creativity. I advocated for more leeway on syntax for the student who manages to say something in response to such topics. Another instructor—in part, perhaps, responding to the self-righteousness I project—said he couldn't imagine his students "saying anything complex." The "more intelligent students" don't take his course, he said. I know that he's not alone in thinking this. Faculty often speak with a thinly veiled racism about how some students will never be writers.

When I first talked of moving to Boston from Philadelphia, people told me how racist they'd heard Boston to be. "But so is any place I've ever lived," I responded. After my first year there, I knew there was something different going on. Unlike many parts of Philadelphia, the boundaries between White communities and communities of color in Boston are seldom crossed. That means a White person who grows up in Boston could live his or her life and virtually never communicate directly with a person of color—not on a city bus, not in a movie theater, not anywhere. The reverse is less possible for people of color, who may well interact with bureaucracies that are entirely White. Like many of the White faculty, most of the White students who attended the college while I was there lived their entire lives in segregated working-class Boston neighborhoods. That was the first time they found themselves not only in an integrated situation but in the case of "developmental" students, in the minority.

While more than 60 percent of the students at the college were White, the overwhelming majority of the students in developmental courses were people of color, including African American students and students who immigrated from Haiti, Puerto Rico, the Dominican Republic, and Southeast Asia. I once heard someone say, "The term *basic writer* is a euphemism for a minority student."

There is an ongoing debate in such places as the Conference of Basic Writing over whether there's a need for developmental courses. I'm drawn to the idea of abolishing them in favor of changing the way we teach Freshman Composition. Positioned on the margins of the university, in a noncredit "remedial" no-person's-land, some students' perception of themselves as "slow" is reinforced. My own experiences convince me that this self-perception, coupled with the disrespect they experience, create the largest obstacles to learning.

Before registering for the semester, students took a computerized test that determined whether they would take developmental studies courses. My class then appeared on some schedules a few months later. Students had to pay tuition for the class, but they received no academic credit. Most of the students were financially stretched to the limit, and this is not what they wanted to see on their printout. When I greeted them the first day, some were angry, some were confused as to why they were there, and some felt humiliated; one young woman wrote, "Last September, I felt at first that the school had made a mistake with the placement. Then I thought because I was placed in this class that I was stupid."

Faculty members themselves were not treated well. Among the demands being considered for the bargaining table by the unionized part-time instructors were such basic needs as paid office hours, access to telephones and copy machines, and the establishment of maximum class sizes. Even full-time faculty members had no offices. Their desks were placed on raised tiers in rows located along the large hallways outside the classroom doors; eight desks shared one phone. Wages were extremely low. Jane Tompkins (1991) might have been speaking of this community college when she wrote, "In order to see the value of one's students, one has to feel one's own value first, not feel so beleaguered. This isn't easy, given the way the system works" (603).

Community Writing and Publishing Programs

One thing African Americans have learned the hard way is if you don't tell your story, someone else will.

—John Edgar Wideman[3]

The history of indigenous people cannot be written from within Western culture. Such a story is merely the West's story of itself.

—Haunani-Kay Trask,
From a Native Daughter (1993, 157)

When someone else is telling your stories, in effect what they are doing is defining to the world who you are, what you are, what they think you are and what they think you should be.

—Lenore Keeshig-Tobias, Ojibwa[4]

Radical teaching depends on the idea that as we read and write, we create the world differently, as opposed to simply discovering it. That's why reading is a constructive act, not something we do in order to "get" an unambiguous meaning. Roger Simon and Don Dippo (1987), citing Michel Foucault, write that "no experience is simply given. How we think and talk about our world shapes our understandings of why things are the way they are, which images of 'that which is not yet' are possible and desirable; and what needs to be done for things to be otherwise" (109).

There really is a dialectical relationship between what's real (or truth) and something or someone that explains it. Our understandings of what the world is now, and our dreams and strategies for changing it, are shaped by the ways we have of describing it. And now we overwhelmingly rely on the written descriptions of people with the means of getting their words in print. Seldom are the visions and strategies of poor and working-class people written down and distributed, to become part of the way the world is described and possibilities for change are considered. This is one of the ways dominant discourses prevail and power is maintained.

Publication is also a way for people to construct their own images in public discourse. In an article discussing his work with AIDS patients in a New York City hospital, Andrew Krivak (1992) found that it wasn't the "horrors" of AIDS that people longed to share:

As I searched for a way to make my presence with the patients relevant, I found that many were best reached, in fact, longed to be reached, through the stories they had to tell. They were not necessarily the stories of how one contracted the virus, or the horrors of where they lived; that was information that went under "risk factor" or "housing status" on the admitting form. The stories these people told were about where they grew up, what they had always dreamed of doing, how they were determined to spend the next year, or 10 years, of their lives. (472)

I've become clearer about what my role is and is not in the communities in which I work. I want to help people publish what they want to say and at the same time avoid, as Lucy Lippard (1990) puts it, the paradox of "speaking for the people whose voices I am hoping to make heard" (10). In Chapter Four, I'll look at why avoiding that paradox is so tricky.

Neighbors Talk

The self-made images in *Neighbors Talk in Roxbury, Dorchester, and Jamaica Plain* create vibrant pictures of neighborhoods that are more often described in language of despair and desolation by the newspaper reporters who live outside of them. As one contributor to the book wrote, "Here are stories, poems, raps from people in my community that speak to our survival skills, our spirit, and our visions for the future. There are people who need to read from us that we're still here and we ain't leaving" (Martin 1993, 16).

To generate the writings for *Neighbors Talk*, I facilitated nine-week workshops in community organizations in which people wrote about themselves and their neighborhoods. Once the pieces were completed, a multicultural editorial board from each community, made up of workshop participants, created a narration, categorized the writings into themes, and wrote introductions.

All kinds of people come together in *Neighbors Talk*: teenagers as well as people who've lived in their communities for more than sixty years; women from the Dominican Republic and from Haiti; Native Americans who move back and forth between Boston and the Micmac reservation in Canada. More than eighty people participated in the book. Community residents defend rap with "a touch of pizzazz jazz" and rejoice in neighborhood victories. They drop in at popular hangouts, reminisce about those that have closed, and pass teenagers in Dudley Square who are forced by police to lie with their hands behind their backs, automatic suspects. They find common ground in speaking out against housing practices that similarly discriminate against immigrants from the islands and women on welfare. They speak of tensions—and alliances—among cultures. In addition to challenging the image of the community created by the media, *Neighbors Talk* furthers a dialogue within the community.

When I talk about this work, it's often difficult for people to understand how it's different from oral history. In fact, often people assume I mean oral history. With a few exceptions, the contributions to *Neighbors Talk* are written stories, different from oral histories in that the writer has had a chance to move her words around and change her meaning. Sometimes, in the process, she found a story she'd never thought about before and a message in it she never quite knew. As Dave Morley and Ken Warpole (n.d.), the authors of *The Republic of Letters*, have said, "Spaces [need to be] made to listen to people—not the conditional space of the interview but spaces in which they can develop what they want to say" (72). Just as important, the story a writer creates in a workshop may well be different because it's influenced by those of other people in his community, rather than being mediated only by an interviewer who may represent the outside.

I want to tell the story of one young contributor to *Neighbors Talk*. I realize I risk sensationalism as I do, and I mention him for a very specific reason. Less than a year after writing a piece for *Neighbors Talk* as a member of a youth group, he was involved in a shooting, and he ended up killing two other youths. I found out about it one morning as I read the newspaper while eating breakfast. It was the first time I thought about the *suspect* in a neighborhood shooting, not only the victim, and of the suspect's family's grief, not just the victim's. My first thought was that the fifteen-year-old I knew was not a monster. His writing had been a quiet and thoughtful piece about police harassment. As I sat in a community meeting about the shooting that evening, I thought about the young man I knew as a victim of a world that tells him he has no value and offers him little opportunity to make his mark. Showing his multiple sides through his writing is one of the critical reasons for publishing a book like *Neighbors Talk*.

I believe there is a difference between community publications and the published writings of adult literacy students.[5] One way to explain what I mean is to relate the history of this project. Because as important as *Neighbors Talk* itself is, the story of the community control needed to bring it to publication.

The public library had received a grant to publish the writings of adult literacy students in the neighboring communities of Roxbury, Dorchester, and Jamaica Plain, Massachusetts. I suggested instead a book in which anyone in the three neighborhoods might be represented. There were two reasons for this. The first was to avoid further stereotyping Area B—the Roxbury police precinct often given a spotlight in the media for crime, which then–mayoral candidate John Silber referred to in a highly publicized speech as "drug-infested"—this time as illiterate. The second reason had to do with the fact that many adult literacy programs around the country publish student writings. But very often only the students' first drafts are printed. The writings are as undeveloped as anyone's first drafts would be, and so they project an image of the writers' thinking as undeveloped as well. And although some writings do say something important, readers often applaud the books simply because the writers could write at all, ignoring what they are *saying*.

The library was happy to agree with this approach. There are participants from adult education programs in the book, and there are also experienced writers. There are community activists, youth leaders, hairdressers, retired cafeteria workers, social workers, and tenant organizers. But as the manuscript neared completion, the library's administration began to promote the book, and an exhibit we made for it, in a way that perpetuated at least two of the very stereotypes the book was meant to contradict. The first press release from the library's downtown public relations department emphasized "violence, fear and despair." Above all, this book is not about despair. The impact of violence and drugs is there, but so are barbecues, friends, tenant organizing, and Nelson Mandela's visit to the African American community. As Donna Finn writes, while the pieces "speak to the problems we face—problems faced by women alone, by people who are in the minority in our community, by people new to our country or isolated—they also speak to the strengths of women and men needed to solve these problems. The Dorchester chapter is dedicated to organizations like 'We Care,' 'Free My People,' and 'Gang Peace,' and all the others who won't give up on our communities" (in Martin 1993, 42).

In addition, the same press statement, and a subsequent one, implied that the writers in the book were all adult literacy students. We soon found out that the library wanted the book's publication to coincide with its budget negotiations with Boston City Council. It wanted to invite the mayor to the publication party and have his endorsement on the back cover. We began to see that the library wanted this book to show what they, and the mayor, were doing, not just for poor people in the inner city, but for poor *illiterate* people.

Many of the writers in the book, supporters in the community, and representatives from the National Writers Union became involved in attempts to make the library accountable to the community in its promotional activities. These efforts were extensive, and they failed. We then created a publication committee including three contributing writers and myself. The committee contacted all of the writers in the book and asked that they sign a letter denying the library permission to use their work. With advice from Volunteer Lawyers for the Arts, a new title, and a new introduction, the book became the community's, and we raised the money to publish it ourselves.

In the end, what *Neighbors Talk* is about is expressed by some of the people involved, speaking at meetings held throughout the book's creation:

Dudley Station was the place I met my first girlfriend. The idea was to get here early to see the girls going to the Burke. . . Your mother would send you to Blue Hill Avenue for milk. The only place still there is Eddie's . . . These things I'm recalling, there are more now reading this book.

—Hakim Raquib

These stories remind me of where I grew up in Brooklyn . . . My husband working at the Jewish synagogue. . . They remind me of the stories Nandi told after her visit to El Salvador. Poor people all over the world are treated the same way, but they don't want us talking to each other. That's what I like about this project.

—Dolores Pickett

All kinds of voices need to be heard. A lot of people have a lot to say. Who knows? Maybe something that could cure something. Or help someone else who's grieving the same thing.

—Diane Appleberry

Nobody can say they know from the outside.

—Zelletta Mae Hunt

Survival News

Survival News is a Boston-based newspaper produced by and for low-income women. Distributed nationally, *Survival News* aims to reframe the public perception of social services and the people who receive them by providing a forum for low-income people to publish their articles, poetry, and graphics.

The paper also facilitates a dialogue among welfare activists. Most of the board members are present or past recipients of some form of public welfare assistance. The paper is distributed through subscriptions, as well as drop-offs to homeless and battered women's shelters, welfare offices, neighborhood health clinics, public housing developments, and state and community colleges. More than half of the subscribers are on welfare and the remainder are advocates and allies.

The first *Survival News* project for which I was a writing workshop facilitator, came out of a collaboration among a community-based Latina adult education program, a project for African American women in recovery from substance abuse, and an advocacy center for homeless and formerly homeless women. The idea was to produce a special issue of the newspaper on race. The words of poet Audre Lorde had served as inspiration for the project: "Do not let your differences pull you apart. Use them, examine them, go through them." For five months, I and eleven low-income African American, Latina, and White women came together to talk and write.

As the project progressed, producing an issue on race came to mean publishing articles based on discussions and writings of what poverty looks like in Roxbury, a community of color in Boston; Saugus, a White suburb; and Santo Domingo, Dominican Republic. Articles described how malnourished children beg for food from the tables of outdoor restaurants in Honduras and how malnourishment here takes its toll more slowly. Articles reflected the way common themes are experienced differently by African American, Latina, and White women. They described the feelings of helplessness that come from knowing you can't turn to authorities for protection, when your abuser is your husband and a member of the local police department, or when you are cheated out of your life savings by lawyers you hired to help you gain legal immigrant status. The collaboration meant coming to grips with the tension that developed when Latina women felt discriminated against by Anglo women who didn't take the time to really listen when they spoke English very slowly and the exclusion felt by an African American woman eating lunch with three women speaking Spanish. We wrote in the introduction to the paper, "None of this came easy, but we confront more now and we laugh more than ever" (*Survival News* 1992, 2).

Two of the central themes that emerged in the group were (1) the social services purportedly designed to help poor people instead make them feel their lives are constantly under scrutiny and (2) more and more often, the public sees a woman's poverty as making her unfit for motherhood. Within this climate, the women talked across their differences and published their stories in order to change the meanings ascribed to their lives:

Florence: When you're on welfare, no one says, "Good job, your son's looking *good*." But let my child go in raggedy sneakers and they'll say, "Oh, she must be on drugs," and someone will report you to D.S.S.

Julia: If someone walks into a middle-class person's house and it's messy, they'll say, "She must be very busy." But let them come in my house and they'll say, "Lazy-ass welfare mother."

Florence: But *then*, if you look nice and your house looks nice, something must be wrong. Everybody's like, "Where'd she get the money to do that?" (*Survival News* 1992, 19)

For the majority of the women who produced this special issue, both writing itself and participation in a multicultural group were new. Below are excerpts from the introduction to the paper, taken from notes of a conversation some of the writers had as we neared publication:

On Being in a Multicultural Group

Florence M: You know, I'm not shy, but even those of us with our *boldness* wondered how it would work at first.

Laura: There was a holding back at first.

Diana: I was afraid. I had to speak more English, meet people from other cultures. I was afraid I won't understand what other people say.

Leslie: I thought, "I'm not going to be a friend with this lady, I'm never going to be her friend." So, now I am hanging out with people speaking English— broken English, but I am!

Florence M: Even in my building, it's mixed, but it's not like here, one-on-one. All my life I cleaned offices and homes. Now I started thinking about how, like Constanza says, it's a lot of Spanish-speaking people.

Laura: In the beginning, I think more things were different between us. Now it's like, yeah, some of us may have a job, and others don't. But we may not have it tomorrow. Maybe the boss won't like our accent. (2)

On Writing

Leslie: I thought, "OK, girl. This is a big mess you put your foot in."

Laura: Maybe everyone was a little hesitant when we started. I mean, I learned defeat for most of my childhood. I hated to write all those years. Then it was like, "Hey, I'm going to writing class at 10:00 today." And it was a comfort zone.

Florence T: Reading each other's words, you find out things you wouldn't normally know about each other. I myself wrote things I don't always feel comfortable telling people up front. Maybe we all did. Violence was one of our biggest categories when we started grouping the articles together.

Julia: My way of dealing is to distance. I mean especially when you're on welfare, if you deal with stuff every day, it's overwhelming. I don't want to say there's no hope for change, but you're up against so much. Distance is one way of surviving. So writing about something close was hard.

Florence M: We try to disassociate because it hurts too much.

Florence T: But sitting home crying about my brother being killed is one thing. Writing about it is different. It was like my mind was *running*. The pen sometimes kept going. I got so much more *out* on this paper.

Florence M: Yes! I was feeling guilty about my son's drug use. Writing about it made me realize it wasn't me.

Florence T: Once I started to write and I said, "Read this," I didn't feel like I was so alone.

Dottie: There's very little written about poverty from our perspective. About the things you're forced to do, like lying. Other people assume they know what we have to go through. But it's not authentic.

Leslie: I'm sending the paper to Honduras and New York and telling them, "I wrote this in the United States!"

Dottie: We talk about needing success stories for the paper. This *paper* is a success story. (2)[6]

Youth Workshops

My role in the *United Youth of Boston* project was to facilitate six- to nine-week writing workshops for teenagers, whose work was then submitted to the newspaper. The workshops were held in neighborhood after-school programs, a girls center in a South Boston public housing development, a health careers program at a large city hospital, and residential detention centers.[7] One of the most important things about youth publishing may be that, here again, the writing repositions the writer as authoritative:

> Some people say "youth are the problem." There's not enough discipline nowadays; young people are the ones dealing the drugs, mugging, shooting up the community. Stop them, search them, send them to boot camp, to prison. Shave their heads, pull their pants down in the streets; go after the casual user. Put inner-city Black children in orphanages . . . Build more jails.
>
> There are a second set of people who view youth as the victims. "How does this crisis make you feel?"
> "Well, I think . . . "
> "No. How does it make you feel?"
> An increasing number of adults are interested in young people's emotions about the situation. Are we sad, scared, confused, or angry? But while they want to hear about our feelings, they do not want to hear our analysis of the situation. They paint us as the victims—helpless, hopeless, passive, pitiful . . .
> We say youth are the *answer*; we are on the front lines of this struggle. (deLeón 1990, 1)

Even though I have avoided speculation on what the act of writing and publishing might mean to the writers with whom I have worked, a remark by Sharon Cox, a poet/writer in Roxbury, makes it difficult to resist here. "Kids are being told, 'You're expendable.' It's hard to get to be twenty-five and be a person with dreams" (R. Martin 1991, 6). Yet it's often dreams that lead to resistance. I thought about this when I did workshops in a detention center. The teenagers shot rubber bands across the room, they wrestled with each other, papers and pencils flew in the air . . . yet for the five short minutes they were writing, there was silence. They were telling their stories—about being "committed," about being "state property," about the possibility they would be "bound over"—and they knew the stories would be published and read. It was the time in the week when the focus was not on group therapy—what *they* needed to do to change—but on how the world needed to change. Their words were not expendable, and it seemed like while they were writing, they knew that.

The Working Conditions of Teaching

Increasingly, adult literacy teachers find themselves feeling the direct effect of welfare policy in our classrooms. I ultimately left one GED program because I felt the structure, dictated in part by the welfare department, undermined my ability to do something nontraditional in my classroom. Not only were new students frequently assigned to my class without consultation with me, but I was given no notice prior to their walking through the classroom door. I got the message that the administration didn't really care about what we were doing in the classroom; certainly, it couldn't think anything very serious was going on. In this same program, the administration asked me to comply with a policy that denied entrance to class to anyone who was more than thirty minutes late, unless he or she first went to see the program coordinator for a pass. The women received child care and advocacy services as a result of their participation in the program. The administration felt that students should pay back the program through their participation—participation upon which the program's funding was dependent. The administrative staff expected the women to feel grateful. I felt more and more that I was being asked to take on the role of punitive caseworker. Even when I refused, the influence of this framework entered through the walls of the classroom. My leaving was a recognition that sometimes the conditions of our work make it extremely hard to create something new, especially when we are trying to do it alone.

But leaving a job isn't always an option when there's rent to pay, and it does nothing to create change where change is needed. In a few cities around the country, adult educators are organizing for more control over the conditions of their work.[8] Some are specifically addressing the increasingly tight relationship between literacy programs and welfare departments. As much as we talk about theory and practice, it's clear we need to simultaneously grapple with the underlying material conditions that sometimes make doing what we think is right so difficult.

What a Community Provides

For me, successfully using the techniques suggested in the following chapters depends on helping to create a community within which to study, teach, and learn. It's the primary reason I don't teach one-to-one. In fact, I've come to believe, as Jean Paul Sartre put it, that one of the things that's basic to writing is believing that there are readers willing to "collaborate with you in the production of the work" (in Rich 1979, 64).

It's within this framework that people begin speaking aloud thoughts not completely expressed before, relying on each other's expertise, perceiving of themselves as authoritative writers, and taking on some of the authority previously thought to be held only by me. I think what often makes reading and writing so difficult for participants in literacy programs and community college classrooms is that they are expected to find words outside of such a community.

I know this was true for me the summer I spent in a graduate seminar in Canada, where I suddenly raised questions I'd never raised before. I was in a class where the students shared a basic assumption about the need for radical change in the world. I talked more, thought harder, and worked more intensely on new ideas than I had in my previous graduate school experience.

I want to be clear that contrary to the prevailing image of adult literacy students, many of the people in my classes already belong to a community aside from the one we make in the classroom. That which we create together becomes for them what it is for me: a different place to explore ideas in a different way. Creating the community I felt we became at the Women's School certainly had to do with the fact that we were all women and with the intimate nature of the things we talked about. For example, one of our themes for reading and writing was AIDS, and talk once turned to oral sex and dental dams.[9] But we had to develop an atmosphere within which we could begin to talk about such things, and not insignificant to this was the spontaneous way we worked together to make the school more comfortable. Mildred brought an extension cord for the space heater when others complained about the church's unpredictable heat. Mattie would make a coffee cake one day and the next day someone else would pick up doughnuts. We fell into the habit of sharing the responsibility for replacing the coffee, tea, sugar, and cups when the supply ran low. People arranged to meet each other on street corners to walk to class. And when Salina needed to practice hairstyling for her beautician license, several women volunteered themselves and relatives. It was the interweaving of these acts (the social) with the classroom agenda we established collectively (the intellectual) that helped make us a group.

Teaching in Multicultural Classrooms

There are ways my experiences both intersect with and diverge from those of the people in my classes. There were times at the Women's School—when talking about safe sex or the neighborhood in which we all lived—when I recognized how our lives were similar. There were other times—when someone talked about the frustration of sleeping with her baby on her mother's couch because she couldn't afford her own apartment—that I remembered how they were different. After reading the words of the children in *White Teacher*, by Vivian Gussin Paley, Lisa Delpit (1994), an African American educator, surmised that "several of the Black students had been exposed to the philosophies of the Nation of Islam and carried some of those discussions from home into the classroom" (132), something Paley had apparently not seen. As I will discuss in Chapters Four and Five, living on the overlapping edges between the cultures I grew up with and those that influence me now has had an impact on the way I teach reading and writing.

One thing I am beginning to understand are the ways I have contributed to a polarization in multicultural groups by at times aligning myself with students of color while alienating White students and failing to engage common class and gender interests. Adrienne Rich (1979) could not have been more right when she warned, "There is the danger that, paradoxically or not, the White middle-class teacher may find it easier to identify with the strongly motivated, obviously oppressed, politically conscious Black student" (62).

In every class at the community college, there was at least one young White man who sat against the back wall of the classroom and treated me with disrespect. It was always a young White man. Is it because, as Rich suggests, "the white students have as yet no real political analysis going for them; only the knowledge that they have not been as successful in school as white students are supposed to be" (63)? As I mentioned earlier, the White students are in the minority in developmental courses. Maybe out of their own racism, they react even more against their placement in this class. Or maybe they "act out" because of my own stance against them.

At a friend's suggestion, I took a look at how I had widened a growing polarization within the *Survival News* group. Without intending to do so, many of my interventions had positioned the participants by race in some ways, limiting the ways they might write and speak from the multiple identities they held—as mothers, neighborhood residents, women fighting breast cancer, poor people . . . When I began using activities in small multicultural groups, the polarization began to ease.

As I facilitated workshops for *Neighbors Talk,* I found myself in situations in which I heard Latinos express prejudice against African Americans or Haitians against African Americans and Latinos; where African Americans would complain when workshops were facilitated bilingually in Spanish and English. I eventually figured out that when participants expressed such comments, the best thing I could do was to ask the speaker or writer to simply say or write more; the "more" always revealed a deeper knowledge, another truth.

Eliane Poindujour, who is Haitian, had written in her first draft of a work that everything in her building was fine until the Spanish moved in on the fifth floor, possibly reflecting Haitian-Dominican tensions on the island. But when she continued, she revealed a fear that she and her neighbors shared:

> In the fifth floor, the only people who used to live there were Spanish. Tell you the truth, I didn't know their nationality, but I knew they speak Spanish. People are scared of each other there. The only thing they say to one another is "Good Morning." If you are going out and you hear a noise in the stairwell, you can see that the person who meets you is frightened, and you are feeling the same. (in Martin 1993, 75)

At one ESL program for which I facilitated a series of workshops for *Neighbors Talk*, a small class of four Latino students had expressed the idea that African American mothers in their neighborhood let their children run in the streets, not caring for them or caring if they were home at night. Then they read a short piece written by a participant at another literacy program in which a mother discusses her fears for her children. All four students assumed the author was Latina and afraid of African Americans. When I told them Charise was African American, they then assumed she was afraid of other African Americans. I asked them to turn their assumptions into questions for Charise and the others in her class, and the two groups began an exchange in which, once again, more complexity emerged than was initially evident and available to us to examine. The African American students wrote about the way the media shapes new immigrants' perceptions of their Black neighbors; Puerto Rican students wrote about their lack of equal rights as citizens; women in both groups wrote about their role as neighborhood protectors and the way they rely on each other; and Latino men like José Rivera wrote about the projection of White fears onto them:

> When a white person sees a Latino man on the street, he thinks maybe he has a knife. When your skin is darker, like for Black people, it's a bigger problem. A Black man can understand my situation better than a white man. (in Martin 1993, 52)

In another exchange, women from an African American literacy project read the writings of the women from a Latina ESL program, who expressed their disappointment over the "welcome" they have received in the United States, typified by city bus drivers who pass them by. In response, one African American woman compared this experience to her own move to Boston from the South. From there, the exchange moved into writing about the relative isolation of living in Boston.

Luisa: In Santo Domingo, three or four friends come to your house to see the soap opera, and from the front of your house you can speak to your neighbor. (Martin 1993, 24)

Finally, two Latina women began to address racism and prejudice in Santo Domingo, though unfortunately, it came too late for the African American students to respond:

Luisa: Here, Hispanic people and Black people from the South have two problems. One is discrimination and one is being alone. But in my country there is racism, too. The Haitians come to cut sugar cane in Santo Domingo. They pay a low, low salary—one or two dollars a day—and put them to live in very poor conditions . . .

Arelis: Even between Dominicans, there is racism. If one Dominican is more white, they don't like someone who is more Black. (24)

My Role in the Production of Meaning

Many teachers have suggested that we need to acknowledge how our role in a class is different from that of our students. After reading a draft of this manuscript, a friend suggested that what I brought to the classroom was the fact that I'd learned to take myself seriously intellectually and was encouraging people in my classes to do the same. That was a helpful frame for me—it's not that I've figured out all the answers to the issues that get raised in my classes, but that I'm serious in my effort to keep pushing to find them. I was reminded of something Karsten Struhl (1979) wrote about his students:

> My experience has been that working-class people . . . are by no means totally taken in by bourgeois ideology as are many of their middle-class counterparts . . . At a gut level, they know that the deck is stacked against them; and while they often think of themselves as anticommunists, they also know that their interests are not the same as the interests of their bosses. They know, in short, that something they often refer to as "the system" is out to screw them, and they deeply crave the intellectual tools with which to understand their own oppression. (13)

I will talk later about the tools I'm working to develop and would add to Struhl's thoughts only that I need these tools as much as my students do.

Keeping an Issue Alive

Someone once pointed out that Velma, a character in Toni Cade Bambara's *Salt Eaters*, plays the catalytic role of keeping people arguing with each other. I've begun to see how important a role that is.

One of my goals is to bring to the surface what we already know and dig deeper into it. I see my role as not only keeping us focused on analyzing our object of study but also articulating when and how I'm doing that, encouraging others to take on that responsibility, too. One woman in a *Neighbors Talk* workshop said that it's the police who will protect her community from drugs and violence. Oftentimes when someone says this, someone else in the room will bring up the role the police play in keeping the drugs coming in or the hopelessness that lies in the belief that one's community has to be policed by people outside. In this class, no one did. I decided to simply keep the issue alive. Among other things, I took one student's writing about the police and asked people to portray the characters and keep the story going through a role play. This exercise didn't "work" in that the role play itself didn't seem to lead us anywhere. But after it was over, I asked everyone to simply write whatever was on his or her mind at that moment. By staying with the topic, we brought out contradictions; for example, some knew the police were not helping, yet they still hoped they would because they didn't know what else to believe in. The same woman who advocated for police protection wrote, "I used to be a mother who wanted her son to be cops because I thought it was a noble profession. Now I'm afraid of the cops, for me and for my sons."

Knowing Ourselves

Another role I see for myself is to bring us back again and again to struggle with the contrast between what we know to be right for ourselves and the world, on the one hand—articulated in our discussions and writing—and the actions we take, on the other. I'm coming to think of "empowerment" as expanding our understanding of ourselves.

The obstacles to such empowerment are maintained through dominant discourses—the ways the world is described—our own internalized view of ourselves, and certainly the material conditions with which we live. It's this framework that gives me a new handle on an alternately funny and painful discussion we had at the Women's School about the use of condoms. Already convinced of their need to use them as protection against AIDS with male partners, several of the women faced the conflict of what to do with men who refused. This conflict was never deeply explored by the group. As I think about it now, I believe the three-part framework that follows might have helped.

The first thing we might have done is explore the discourse on birth control itself, with which we've grown up and still live, using Carol Snyder's (1984) framework for classification, adapted from the ideas of Michel Foucault. Thus, we would have asked ourselves the following questions regarding acceptable methods of birth control:

What is included in this classification?

What is excluded?

Who does it privilege?

Who does it disadvantage?

Who devised this classification?

When did it come into being?

Where? (Adapted from Snyder, 212–14)

The second idea would be to figure out what investments we had made in a situation that made it difficult to demand safe sex, even in the face of possible death. Psychoanalytic theory helps us get a handle on the internal fight within our multiple class-, gender-, and race-positioned subjectivities. The distinction between *subjectivities* and *selves* is one I will explore in Chapter Three, along with psychoanalytic ideas. A teacher I know once said, it was a pretty tall order to expect to unravel these complexities. Maybe all I want for now is to do a better job of trying.

Third would be to talk directly about the material conditions that would have to be met before each of us could unequivocally demand safe sex—things that might include financial independence, for example, or freedom from the threat of physical abuse.

If we view one of our main goals as deconstructing how we come to know what we know, it may help make moot the question of whether we impose our ideas of social change, a question that so often preoccupies discussion of radical education. Besides, why isn't it assumed that the people in our classes can accept, reject, or debate our ideas just as anyone else would, especially in adult education classrooms, where we don't hold the power of the grade? Seen in this light, the suggestion that we are imposing our ideology seems belittling. Furthermore, it's in giving voice to our ideas, allowing ourselves to explore them with our students, that we expose them to change and begin to change ourselves.

Images of "the Illiterate" in Traditional and Radical Constructions of Literacy

An early statement by the United Literacy Workers reads, "We recognize that the working conditions we face mirror the status accorded our students . . . The jobs in our field are not viewed as 'real jobs.'" I've seen my own status change. When I used to mention I worked for an international women's peace organization—at a party or my high school reunion, for example—people would usually perk up and ask questions about the work or the organization. Now when I say I teach literacy, I hear comments such as, "Isn't that nice? Is that your paid work or do you volunteer?" as though I'd just said I was a candy striper in a hospital. I believe that attitude comes from the prevailing image of "the illiterate."

> It's hard for people who can't read to believe in happy endings.
>
>   Subway placard, Commonwealth Literacy Corps

> Twenty-seven million Americans can't read a bedtime story to a child . . . Functional illiteracy has become an epidemic . . . that has reached one out of five Americans. It robs them of a decent living . . . of the simplest of human pleasures, like reading a fairy tale to a child. You can change all this by joining the fight against illiteracy. Volunteer Against Illiteracy. The only degree you need is a degree in caring.
>
>   Ad Council Coalition for Literacy

Poor workers and poor parents, deprived of human pleasures—the image of people with minimal literacy skills invoked here is constantly recreated in newspaper and magazine articles, literacy program descriptions, TV documentaries, sitcoms, and made-for-TV movies. If we were to believe them, we'd believe that scores of mothers are giving their children poison instead of medicine because they can't read labels, that thousands of people are afraid to leave their homes because they won't know which restroom to use. The reality, of course, is that you don't live your life without developing strategies for reading labels and identifying bathrooms. What's happening is the portrayal of people with minimal literacy skills as childlike, dependent, unable to function—at bottom, stupid. Literacy programs are set up, volunteers and students recruited, funding granted and pedagogy designed to help people become more functional. Tests that assign students a 0–5 grade level, funders who tout their efforts to help "misfortunate illiterates," and links between literacy programs and welfare offices that regard students as social service recipients, all position literacy program participants as childlike, helpless, and needy. Knowing that the majority of people with less developed literacy skills in this country are poor people, we can see how the construction insidiously justifies the condition of poverty. Why *was* literacy Barbara Bush's favorite cause? Possibly because she could claim illiteracy as the root cause of nearly every social issue imaginable, avoiding the need to address the more significant roots of poverty, unemployment, and child abuse.

> When my husband decided to run for high public office, I knew I would have a chance to call attention to an important cause. I thought about all the problems that concerned me: poverty, crime, unemployment, teenage pregnancy, drugs, the economy, high school dropouts, neglected and abused children—the list is endless. Yet, it occurred to me that education was a factor in every one of those issues and that there wasn't a pressing problem that this nation faced that couldn't be helped if more people could read and write. (Bush 1989, 6, 22)

Bush elaborated:

> Billions of dollars are lost annually to *related* problems like crime, un-employment, unrealized tax revenues, worker error, and low productivity. Frighteningly high percentages of minorities and imprisoned Americans are illiterate. (22, emphasis mine)

Sometimes when I facilitate a workshop with teachers, I pass out artifacts of the literacy field. These have included articles and photographs from the mass media, literacy program newsletters, publicity pieces for literacy campaigns, and fund-raising appeals. They come from all over this country, Canada, and England. I then ask the participants to list the adjectives that come to mind that describe a person with minimal literacy skills, as conjured by the documents they have before them. Here are the responses:[10]

damaged	slipshod	degraded
poor	restricted	uncertain
dangerous	timid	inadequate
alone	needy	afraid
passive	foreign	outcast
discouraged	rejected	aimless
lazy	subordinated	backward
confused	undependable	lost
despairing	despondent	insecure
resentful	careless	limited
powerless	diseased	unhappy
irresponsible	unfulfilled	dependent
unproductive	unmotivated	stunted
hopeless	animalistic	at risk
antisocial	fatalistic	doomed
inhuman	deprived	delinquent
criminal	shamed	violent
isolated	incompetent	defeated
frustrated	angry	slow
dim-witted	shabby	childlike
dazed	ashamed	lonely
uncultured	depressed	cautious
helpless	other	

Also included in the materials we look at are student writings themselves:

Students Praise Their Tutors

My tutor inspired me more than one time. He has given me so many written compliments that I think I don't deserve them. He has taken a very important place in my destiny. He has opened a door that was closed before. (Perez 1989, 2)

I Was Lost

The Council was one of the nicest gifts that I have ever received in my life. It's a gift I can use forever. There are not many gifts like that. I never knew how to work a crossword puzzle, when to put a period or a question mark at the end of a sentence or how to find answers to my questions.

Life is so much more exciting and new to me. I thank God for the help I have received and the nice people that made it happen. I was lost and now I know I am on the right path.

Thanks again and again.

J. K., *Greater Pittsburgh Literacy Council Newsletter*

Variations on the same theme appear around the country: "I was no one until I came to (fill in the blank) literacy program, and now thanks to God and my tutor, I am someone." I believe these writings, just as the media focus and outreach materials do, reflect not who the students are, but who we in the literacy field position them to be.

This is not the first time in history in which illiteracy has been used to prove or disprove humanity. As J. Elspeth Stuckey (1991) points out, we need illiteracy. If it is a barrier to achievement, it is because we construct it as such. When I was reading Stuckey's *The Violence of Literacy,* the United States began an occupation of Haiti. Over and over in media accounts, Haitians were portrayed as unable to govern themselves in a country overrun with "Haitian on Haitian" violence. An article from the *Los Angeles Times* described huge piles of garbage "full of human excrement," and how "all day long, men, women and children in rags and bare feet had been pushing forward to see the miracle of 20th century American know-how that the Marines had brought with them to this Caribbean island: a garbage truck." A Marine is quoted as saying, "How can you feel anything about these people? They made this mess, and now we've got to clean it up . . . We can help them. But we can't do it all, and they've got to help themselves, and I don't know if they can."[11] Coinciding with these descriptions in news reports was nearly always a reference to Haiti as a nation of illiterates.

In the United States, adult literacy students are often assumed to need drug abuse prevention classes. Responding to the availability of federal funds, an adult literacy funding agency in Boston granted money to programs in public housing developments if they offered such classes, using a curriculum developed by a local hospital. While one might imagine a curriculum that looks at the reasons drugs have taken a heavy toll on individuals and communities, the focus of this one was on simplistic methods of prevention that assume individual answers, and massive ignorance. Most offensive is the assumption that because one lives in a housing development and is taking a literacy class there, one needs to be told how to avoid substance abuse. A similar attitude can be seen in a 1990s federal mandate that all Department of Public Welfare literacy programs include HIV/AIDS education.

I am not the first person to point out the image of the illiterate as Other. The "dysfunctional" image of literacy students has been well documented. But what has remained unexamined are the reasons for its persistence. Why is it even radical educators who condemn it end up perpetuating it? I will return to this question. But first, consider the following scenes:

- The podium of a critical pedagogy conference in New York, where a staff member of a labor union literacy program speaks of the honor she feels in being asked to introduce Paulo Freire. She says she wouldn't be where she is were it not for her students, and that's why she has asked two of them to join her on stage. The men stand behind her, arms behind their backs, legs apart, silent.

- The overwhelming number of times students' self-esteem is assumed to be low in both traditional and radical writings about adult literacy. Not only have all of us, no doubt, had students who appeared to have a perfectly healthy sense of self-esteem, even more important is that self-esteem is not a constant, independent of context, for any of us.[12] A ubiquitous reference to literacy students' lack of self-esteem further positions them as Other.

- The frequent use of creating community and decreasing isolation as criteria for evaluating the success of literacy programs. This assumption of loneliness/lack of community grates against the actual lives of many of the people in my classes, whose communities include those within their churches, their choirs, on their blocks, among their family and friends . . . This is more true for some than others, to be sure, but the prevalent assumption of isolation doesn't fit.

- Adult literacy fund-raising appeals. Characterizing adult literacy students in a way similar to the common portrayal of women who receive welfare, these appeals ask readers to help the illiterate contribute to society. A quote from a literacy student in one foundation's letter states, "We have something worthwhile to contribute to society. We just need the chance."[13] The discourse is similar to that of magazine ads that implore the reader to feed a hungry child, who also deserves a chance. The more one looks, the more one sees these implicit, as well as explicit, links between the world of social service and that of adult literacy. One example is the Mentoring Project in Massachusetts, which was funded by an agreement between the Department of Education and the Department of Public Welfare. A volunteer tutor/mentor is matched one-to-one with a woman receiving AFDC. "Mentors are trained to work with learners on mastering not only academic skills, but also *life skills* such as communication, goal setting and assessing community resources" (Massachusetts Adult Basic Education Directory 1993, 180, emphasis mine). There is something dangerously condescending in the prevailing assumption that neither women who receive welfare nor students in adult literacy classes possess these skills.

■ A passage from an Association for Community-Based Education handbook:

Promoting Learner Participation

Personal Development: Learners, who take on new roles in the program develop not only their reading and writing skills, but also other important skills and attributes. These include interpersonal skills, general problem-solving skills, self-confidence, self-reliance, and an interest in life-long learning.

Social Change: Learners who are given real responsibility and authority within a program will learn to take charge, set directions, analyze obstacles, and act collaboratively. This is what is needed if the learners are to effect the social changes necessary to gain the education, power, and wealth that they have been denied. (1988, 81)

There has always been something that seemed a little bit patronizing in the emphasis on learner involvement in running literacy programs. I am certain the author of the ACBE passage would himself deplore the dysfunctional image of literacy students. Yet here he assumes they need to develop interpersonal and problem-solving skills, self-confidence, and self-esteem. They need to learn how to take charge, set directions, analyze obstacles, and act collaboratively. He believes it is the lack of these skills that has been the barrier to students achieving power, and they need to be involved in the literacy program in order to attain it. Furthermore, the emphasis on student involvement rests on an assumption that students in adult education programs see one of their primary identities *as* students. Interestingly, of the fifty writers in *Neighbors Talk* who were adult literacy or ESL students, none defined her- or himself as such in the book's "Contributors' Notes." Among the identities listed were housing activist, beautician, Christian, lesbian mother, West Indian, factory supervisor, father of six, lover of peace. Who is doing the defining in this field?

The Barriers Inside Ourselves That Keep the Image Alive

Susan Lytle (1990) finds "there is considerable dissatisfaction among both practitioners and researchers about the persistence of a distorted public image and common rhetoric around adult literacy." She suggests we "question prevailing assumptions about the capabilities and lifestyles of the less-than-literate adult" (3). Lytle continues:

> In an oft-cited study, Fingeret (1983) has shown how adults operate within complex social networks in which they are interdependent, offering skills of their own in exchange for the literacy skills of others within their network. She concluded that "illiterate" adults do not necessarily fit the stereotypes of dependency, weakness and failure affixed to them by mainstream culture . . . More recently Fingeret (1989) has characterized nonreading adults as "creators of their own social lives," a diverse group of people including many who have been "consistently productive workers, family members and in some cases community leaders" . . . Current synthesis of theory and research (Fingeret 1989) thus makes a case for regarding nonreading adults as dignified, diverse, and intelligent. (5)

But why is there a need to prove such dignity and intelligence in the first place? Moreover, why do such images persist, despite "considerable dissatisfaction"? Why does a statewide literacy resource center, which has been influenced by alternative views of reading assessment, still, in the 1990s, describe students reading "at a third- or fourth-grade level"?[14] Why does the term *functionally illiterate* still creep into the language of radical educators?[15] It may be because on a deeper level, those of us who critique this image still believe in it.

Though the assumptions and methods presented in this book are based, as I've said, on a direct contradiction to the dysfunctional image of adult literacy students, I also have to painfully admit that there are moments when I've found it has seeped into my own perceptions and practice—an example of not living up to my raised consciousness. What I mean are moments when I step back and suddenly realize I haven't been giving people credit for the critical thinking they are already doing, moments when I find that a myth that people with less formal education aren't as intelligent as I am has imperceptibly guided my thoughts and actions. It was in part the gnawing realization of my own assumptions, stirred by instances like the ones that follow, that set in motion my re-thinking of a framework that had shaped my goals for several years.

At the Women's School we ended a unit on AIDS (a theme identified by the group that I detail in Chapter Six) by writing our own neighborhood pamphlet. Having consciously encouraged situations in which authority would be shared in the classroom, I found myself on at least two occasions actively resistant to letting it go. At one point, a student disagreed with how I thought we should proceed with writing the pamphlet. I wanted two or three people to collaboratively continue writing the sections we'd outlined; she thought it would be better for people to write independently. When she suddenly took exclusive control of the process away from me, others joined in and agreed with her. A few weeks later, another student volunteered to call a speaker who had visited us to clarify some remaining questions. The student ended up inviting the speaker to return to class the following week. I thought we needed the time in class to write. And I had always been the one to schedule speakers and films. In each of these situations, one of the reasons I had a hard time letting go of authority was that I didn't trust the decisions being made. The other reason is that I'm sure I became a teacher, in part, because of the very sense of control and feeling "smart" it gave me.

I think something else happened, unique to that class, that had an effect on the way the women started to take on this authority. I was going through a difficult relationship breakup that spring. More subdued than usual, I worried that women I saw nearly every day might wonder about the change in my behavior. Finally, at a friend's urging, I decided to tell them what was going on. Immediately, heads nodded and individuals murmured reassurances and sympathy. At least one said, "So *that's* what's been going on." Telling them brought such a sense of relief, and I told them that as I thanked them for their support. One woman responded, "Thank you for trusting us enough to tell us." She was right; telling them had everything to do with who they were. I wouldn't have done the same thing in every class. But I do think making myself vulnerable in that way broke down the traditional scenario in which I often expect students to reveal more of themselves than I'm willing to reveal myself, and I think it had an effect on moving total authority and control in the group away from me.

I want to pay attention to these times when authority shifts, take note of my own resistance, and talk with other teachers who are doing the same. I think we can use our observations as starting points for discussion of what's really happening and what can happen in our classes.

Something else happened during that time. I'd taped a classroom discussion we had, thinking that we could all look at the transcript together to see where we'd really started to analyze something, where we'd gotten off the track, where we were expressing contradictions. This is one of those times when I really meant "they." Yet when I listened to the tape alone, I was able to interpret myself in a way I never had before. I was taken aback by how tentative I seemed, stumbling over my words, groping for new ways to say the very thing I'd just said. That's not how I usually talk, and it forced me to think about the rationale I must have been operating under. I saw an until then unconscious thread that guided some of my talk in the classroom. I was preoccupied with my language because I was worried the women wouldn't get what I was saying. Listening to their part of the discussion, it was quite clear they understood just fine. And I was too busy thinking about what I was saying to see where they were meanwhile taking the discussion.

I say all of this to acknowledge my own need to recognize assumptions that sometimes still take hold of me and interfere with my ability to see the people in my classes, to learn, and to effectively implement a theory of teaching that rests on that very seeing and learning.

I also say this to acknowledge my need to reckon, day one, with what I think is many participants' assumption that I think I know more than they do—an assumption based on their knowledge of the attitudes often evidenced by middle-class White people. I think people will use interpretive techniques and engage with reading and writing, finally uninhibited by spelling errors or a beginning knowledge of English, only when they perceive that we as teachers are honest in our desire to join in a collaboration.

This was true for me as a student in one of my recent schooling experiences. The courses in which I stretched myself were those taught by a professor who, without disavowing her own expertise, made it clear she had as much to learn from us as we had to learn from her. During class discussions with other instructors, when I was positioned as someone who was to eventually see what the professor already knew, my mouth stayed closed. This was true even when I agreed with what one faculty member wanted me to "get," her left and feminist perspective closer to my own than the aforementioned professor's had been. But I had to believe there was an honest dialogue to enter before I would step in.

A Critique of Freire, and Dreams

I will argue in Chapter Three that, in one respect, Freirian pedagogy and the popular notion of people as dysfunctionally illiterate are flip sides of the same coin. While the political motives of each are quite opposed, both give at least the impression of assuming that without literacy, people lack the ability to think critically, to act on their own behalf, to even believe change is possible.[16] Before moving to the next chapter,

I want to say that while Freire's influence in radical education is widespread, critiques of either his writings themselves or their impact in the field are only rarely published. This may be due as much to self-censorship as to the lack of a critical gaze. To engage in such reflection is to open oneself to suspicion, if not attack. One infamous example is the reaction to Elizabeth Ellsworth's "Why Doesn't This Feel Empowering?" (1989). Peter McLaren writes of Ellsworth's piece,

> [This] woeful misreading of the tradition she so cavalierly indicts [is full of] distortions, mystifications, and despair [based on her] self-professed lack of pedagogical success [and] her inability to move beyond her own self-doubt, [thereby] hold[ing] her voice hostage [and] using theory as a scapegoat for *failed practice*. (in Lather 1992, 126, emphasis mine)

Henry Giroux adds,

> She succumbs to the familiar academic strategy of dismissing others through the use of straw man tactics and excessive simplifications which undermine not only the strengths of her own work, but also *the very nature of social criticism itself*. (in Lather 1992, 126, emphasis mine)

I have also experienced intellectual attack, as well as dismay from community activists I respect, one of whom was astonished that I would criticize Freire because "he is a revolutionary!" That Freire's revolutionary commitment can be an inspiration to all of us is undeniable. What *are* worth questioning are both Freire's words and the degree to which they have been relied on by radical educators here. Most importantly, to the extent that I was previously moved by some of the very passages in Freire's work of which I am now critical, this rereading is really a challenge to my earlier, and sometimes still present, self.

I am indebted to Freire and the teachers who were inspired by him for what they have taught me about such central themes as motivation, student-generated themes, and language. But there are important ways in which I've changed since my early reliance on Freirian pedagogy. Freire wrote, "Even though my tomorrow and my there are clear to me, I cannot manipulate the students to bring them with me to my dream. . . . I have to convince students of my dreams, but not conquer them for my own plans." (Shor & Freire 1987, 156–157). I'm not suggesting we abandon our dreams or hide them, adopting a neutral stance regarding the future. But if our tomorrows are so clear, why aren't we further along in realizing them? Maybe there is something for us to more deeply deconstruct about our own consciousness—with our students—in order to reconstruct dreams, and ways of achieving them, that will come true. It's toward this end that I turn to Chapter Three.

Notes

1. I purposefully avoid the use of the terms *minimal* and *not fully developed* to describe literacy skills because to use them is to suggest we can quantify literacy, which feeds the notion that one either has or does not have it.

2. From "Class Notes, Folder Two." (Folders here refer to notes I took and work I collected during classes and workshops.)

3. From an interview on National Public Radio. Date unknown.

4. From a brochure produced by Indians into Journalism Initiative, University of North Dakota School of Communication.

5. Community publishing is a practice that's taken for granted in England, which has a long tradition of publishing the writings of "worker-writers."

6. Bulk copies of *Survival News* are available for classroom use. Write to *Survival News*, 102 Anawan Avenue, West Roxbury, MA 02132.

7. Despite what I might have anticipated before beginning, my position of authority often seems less established in these settings than when I am working with my peers. And my confidence level is lower. Not only do I want the kids to like me, I sometimes catch myself wanting to *be* them, spending extra time deciding what to wear before going to the girls center.

8. Among the most established of these is United Literacy Workers in New York City.

9. See Chapter Six for more on our investigation of AIDS.

10. From "Workshop Notes, Folder One."

11. "Marines Clean Excrement, Trash from Haitian Streets." Reprinted in the *Albuquerque Journal*, 22 September 1994.

12. Susan Shachter helped me think through my nagging uneasiness with this characterization.

13. From the Boston Adult Literacy Fund March 1991 fund-raising letter.

14. Adult Literacy Resource Institute/SABES Boston Regional Center. March 1993 Announcements of Staff Development Events.

15. See Macedo (1993).

16. Thanks to Alison Jaggar for the idea of flip sides.

Three

Putting Theory into Action

To study is not to consume ideas, but to create and re-create them.
—Paulo Freire, *The Politics of Education* (1985, 4)

Words such as these gave me sustenance during my first few years of teaching literacy. They helped me articulate how what I do is different from a traditional pedagogy, and they still do. But one summer, I began some reading that brought into sharper relief my growing unease with the practice of critical pedagogy as I was applying it in my classroom and as I saw it applied in many situations around the country. With exposure to Michel Foucault's poststructuralist theory and to radical attempts to use psychoanalysis, the previously nagging thoughts exploded, igniting a rush of questions regarding critical pedagogy. I initially felt embarrassed not to have raised these questions before, yet I eventually came to realize some of the reasons I had so completely embraced Freire's ideas. Above all, his writings are inspirational. In them, he generates tremendous hope for social change. And at first reading, his theory and pedagogy provide a clear contrast to the dominant approaches that assume teachers have all the answers to the questions they ask. But it struck me that summer that the biggest reason I tenaciously hung on to Freire was that I felt compelled to defend radical critique in graduate school. I see now that from that position, I tended toward rigid stances that didn't allow me room for exploration.[1] I found the safety I needed in a classroom of seven women, taught by Valerie Walkerdine at the Ontario Institute for Studies in Education. Assumptions about the need for dramatic change in the world were taken for granted, which opened in me a deeper look at what had been missing in my own theory and practice.

But Freire *had* inspired me to believe that change was possible. And it was in Ira Shor's *Critical Teaching and Everyday Life* (1980), with Freire as its theoretical reference point, that I first remember reading a description of *what* one could do in a classroom. Shor's cafeteria hamburger, which his class examined "critically . . . extraordinarily re-experiencing the ordinary . . . recreat[ing] the largely invisible commodity relations which deliver a fried piece of dead beef to our palates" (106), stayed in my mind for years.[2] It is, in large part, the very way the writings of Freire, Shor, and others who identify with critical pedagogy excited me in the past, demonstrating how theory and practice come together, that have made it possible for me to offer critique. It's not, certainly, that I reject the ideas of critical pedagogy in whole. And I don't want to suggest that poststructural or psychoanalytic ideas are in every way superior to or able to supplant them. In fact, I worry that there is not enough room within psychoanalytic ideas to theorize resistance, the cornerstone of Freirian pedagogy. But in radical education communities, where *problem posing, colearner,* and *culture of silence* have become household terms, there is a need to reexamine their effect on our work.

In this chapter, I will focus on the practical assumptions critical pedagogy makes about the student and the teacher, particularly through its notions of consciousness and liberation, and will then look at the ways feminist and radical uses of psychoanalysis and poststructural ideas may take us in some new directions.

What's Missing from Critical Pedagogy

The liberating classroom . . . challenges the student to unveil the actual manipulation and myths in society. In that unveiling, we change our understanding of reality, our perceptions.

—Ira Shor, *A Pedagogy for Liberation*
(Shor & Freire 1987, 172)

In their coauthored *Pedagogy for Liberation*, Freire and Shor very often make theoretical statements and suggest pedagogical practices that assume that the oppressed don't see reality for what it is, that critical pedagogy can illuminate that reality for them, and that having seen this light, people will join in a struggle for change. Yet many of my students just don't match Freire's and Shor's descriptions of them as naive. In fact, I am much more able to see them reflected in the starkly different words of Shirley Ann Williams in her forward to Zora Neale Hurston's *Their Eyes Were Watching God* (1978):

> And when we (to use Alice Walker's lovely phrase) go in search of our mothers' gardens, it's not really to learn who trampled on them or how or even why—we usually know that already. Rather, it's to learn what our mothers planted there, what they thought as they sowed, and how they survived the blighting of so many fruits. (vii–viii)

I'm not suggesting there are no myths we still hold on to. But ignored in Freire and Shor's view is why the myths that do persist are so difficult to transcend. For example, Shor (Shor & Freire 1987) suggests that the liberating classroom "can take racism and sexism as themes for critical study, showing how they divide and conquer people and help the dominant class" (166). But having an understanding of the effects of racism doesn't mean we automatically eject it from ourselves. Shor further suggests that the classroom develop a "critical consciousness, a conceptual habit of mind" (166). But having assumed it's only the "other" who lacks this habit of conceptualizing ideas, which "we" are presumed to practice regularly, how do we explain the moments of sexism and racism to which everyone is prone, including Shor and me? How do I understand the times I act against my own best interests, in ways that contradict my otherwise feminist consciousness?[3] In Shor and Freire's work, these moments remain unacknowledged.

I was beginning to see that the framework that had so strongly shaped my goals as a teacher wasn't enough. Beyond perceiving the myths that cloud our vision and understanding "who constructs them and for what reason" (Shor in Martin 1986, 6), I realized we all need to perceive how they become a very part of us and why it is they're so hard to eject, even when our consciousness is raised. In other words, understanding that something is not in our interest is not always enough to make us stop believing it. Since the people in my class do think critically much of the time, the question for me has become, what keeps them, and me, from always acting on that critical knowledge? How could students know that the Philadelphia school system was racist, for example, yet almost to a person blame themselves for "failure"? What accounts for the contradictions between their consciousness and their actions—and my own?

For Freire, the teacher's conscientization is a process of realigning her allegiance from the middle to the working class, of committing "class suicide." In the words of one labor educator, "In the process of dialogue, the conscientization of the oppressed takes place and the coordinators of the cultural circle 'fuse' with the oppressed and transcend the attitudes of domination and exploitation to which they've become accustomed" (Martin 1975, 48–49). But what forms these attitudes in the first place, and how are they "transcended"? Furthermore, there is an assumption that the leadership, the teachers, will not come from the "dominated" group; "we," the teachers, perceive our reality and "they," the students, don't. It is as though there is nothing in a middle-class teacher's own life about which to rethink, nothing in her own experience to bring to new consciousness, except her class allegiance.[4] Even if we were to accept this as true, what *accounts* for a teacher's decision to either maintain or reject her allegiance?

In *Pedagogy of Hope* (1996), Freire discusses "the fear that fills the oppressed, as individuals and as a class, and prevents them from struggling." He further writes, "The leadership, which, for any number of reasons, enjoys a different, higher level of 'immunization' to the fear that affects the masses, must adopt a special way of leading where that fear is concerned" (124). How does Freire account for this immunization? Also in *Pedagogy of Hope*, he remembers:

> My rebellion against every kind of discrimination, from the most explicit and crying to the most covert and hypocritical, which is no less offensive and immoral, has been with me from my childhood. Since as far back as I can remember, I have reacted almost instinctively against any word, deed, or sign of racial discrimination, or, for that matter, discrimination against the poor, which, quite a bit later, I came to define as class discrimination. (144)

If Freire's rebellion was instinctual, what is the origin of this instinct? How would he explain why he has it and others don't?

I should say here that I haven't abandoned a focus on critical thought—I think we all need prompting to do it at times. But the foundation of my teaching is expanding. I'm aiming toward a pedagogy that will include me in the process of figuring out what it is that keeps all of us from resisting our domination more. I know that in the past I frequently used the collective "we" when talking about myself and the participants in my classroom, when I really meant "they." I'm hoping that the more I open myself up to the possibilities of what I need to and might learn, the more collective the "we" will become.

Why "Getting the Real Scoop" is Not Enough

Many teachers I know have said that what people—our students—need is information. They need to know history and how to see underneath the propaganda in the media. Yet I can pick apart the ways propaganda works through the media and uncover previously hidden historical events—including stories of the movements of people who worked for social change—and still there are actions I take that are complicit with my own domination. Perceiving propaganda, learning about the people who've taken a stand against domination—these are the things we try to help people do in our classrooms, and they're necessary. They're just not enough.

I think about the activities I was involved in as a Central America solidarity activist in the 1980s. Like many others, the group I belonged to based much of its efforts on educational campaigns, or consciousness raising. Our work was based on the idea that if people only knew, for example, that the government-sanctioned death squads in El Salvador were responsible for the murder and disappearance of tens of thousands of people, they would be moved to take action against U.S. support of that government. But this didn't happen. More recently, even official revelations of U.S. complicity in El Salvador's campaign of torture generated little response.

In the 1990s, political activists mobilized to fight California's Proposition 187, as well as the possibility of its spread to other states. Proposition 187 denies health care, education, and other social services to undocumented immigrants. Just after its passage in November 1994, the Albuquerque Border City Project (1994) mailed a fund-raising letter with the following appeal:

Race, Prejudice and the Fear of "Foreigners"

The menacing storm clouds of immigrant scapegoating continue to gather force. California's proposition 187—which requires medical personnel and school teachers to report people they suspect are undocumented immigrants—represents an unfortunate, yet predictable swing of the pendulum. It repeats the unfounded, cyclical hysteria of prior eras. It is discouraging to have to relive such an ignominious, embarrassing chapter in U.S. history, yet some New Mexico politicians advocate that New Mexico follow California's suit. How can we counteract the irrational fear and racism fueling this "debate" and bring logic and facts to bear on the public's perceptions? We need to refute emotional rhetoric and demagoguery through discussion and dissemination of accurate information. We need to protest U.S. citizens and lawful residents whose rights are trampled by the unthinking mob.[5]

The question is why does such hysteria keep returning? More centrally, does accurate information have an effect on "irrational fear and racism"? How do "logic and facts" bear on emotion? Proposition 187 will cost the state of California more money than did the benefits voters didn't want to finance. But logic didn't appear to make a difference in how people voted. Why is the mob unthinking? Underneath, what constitutes this deep-seated "fear of the foreigner"?

Simultaneous to politicians' attacks on immigrants is an equally vicious attack on women who receive welfare. Over and over, acquaintences and colleagues cite the "fact" that welfare recipients are having large numbers of children in order to increase the size of their monthly checks, while the typical family on welfare has two children (Amott 1993, 14). Over and over, I hear that generations of families remain on welfare. Yet one study found that four out of five daughters of families receiving welfare do not go on to receive welfare themselves as adults (Amott 1993, 15). Perhaps most prevailing is the idea that women on welfare are lazy and don't want to work outside the home, which led to a federal policy placing a five-year lifetime limit on receiving welfare benefits, with states free to impose shorter limits. Yet the average length of time spent on AFDC is now only two years (Amidei 1992, 21). It's true that women who do find work often later return to welfare, but without the Medicaid and day care benefits welfare provides, families end up suffering even more living on the wages of a low-paying job than when they were on welfare. Most significantly, all of these myths rest on believing a woman would *want* to rely on a monthly check that would make her income one-quarter below the federal poverty line (Amidei 1992, 21). What nourishes these myths and refuses to let them die? Perhaps we get close to the answer when we look at another myth—that the majority of women on welfare are African American. Just as *crime* is a racial code word to demean African Americans and Latinos, so is *welfare mom*. But then the question becomes what keeps these racist notions alive?

Kathleen Hall Jamieson, commenting for public television on the 1992 U.S. presidential campaign, pointed to another example in which people held in the grips of a deep-seated fear will not easily relinquish a belief. The Republicans claimed that Hillary Clinton was a radical feminist who, as an advocate of children's rights, would have children suing their parents over their allowances. Jamison pointed out that it was futile for the Democrats to attempt to dispute this claim. She suggested that the only thing they might have done is replace it with an even more heinous image, such as George Bush having twelve-year-olds chained to radiators by their parents with no means of recourse. In her book *Dirty Politics* (1992), she points to the Willie Horton ads of the 1988 presidential campaign. The campaign used an image of an African American man who had raped a White woman while on a prison furlough to stir fears of *all* furloughs and of Democratic candidate Michael Dukakis, who approved them. As a reviewer of "The Theater of Refusal" writes, "The fear of the Black body can push "reasonable" White people to the edge of hysteria" (Armitage 1994, G6). Just think of the twelve jurors who watched while Rodney King received fifty-six blows against his body by Los Angeles police officers and decided the force was not excessive.

In none of the situations described here do accounts of "false consciousness" sufficiently explain the intensity and tenacity of such beliefs. I will turn shortly to the ways in which poststructuralism and psychoanalytic theory may help us understand them differently. But first I want to point further to the failure of critical pedagogy to adequately deal with them. In "Literacy for Stupidification," Donaldo Macedo (1993) supports Freire's idea that people need to learn to "read the world," or think critically. Again, the question is, what prevents this from happening? Macedo offers Noam Chomsky's notion of "social amnesia" as the reason people believe unbelievable things (185, 195). In the case of the war in the Persian Gulf, Macedo suggests it was "the high-tech management of the Gulf War [which] celebrated technical wizardry while it dehumanized the tens of thousands of people who were [its] victims" that kept people from protesting (194). But why don't people see through the wizardry? How is it television viewers wouldn't think of the death caused by war's technology? According to Chomsky, we fall victim to "doublespeak." But *why* does doublespeak work? What else is it interacting with to produce passivity, if not outright support in response to such violence? According to Chomsky, those who read the *New York Times* and watch *Nightline* are indoctrinated by slanted coverage and lies. For the rest, the media provides distractions like sports. There has to be something more to it than the idea that people are easily distracted or duped.

Teachers' Knowledge and the "Truth"

I began this chapter by saying that, at first glance, Freire provides an alternative to seeing oneself as having all the answers. A second look reveals how much he believes he already has the answers to the questions he poses.[6] Throughout his writings, Freire stresses the need to respect the students' "now," but respecting it is tricky within this framework that always assumes it's the educator's "then." In the 1993 edition of *Pedagogy of the Oppressed*, translator Myra Bergman Ramos notes in the Preface, "The term conscientização refers to learning to perceive social, political and economic contradictions and to take action against the oppressive elements of reality" (17). For Freire (1978), the object is a given. He knows what it is. "The educator must constantly discover and rediscover these paths that make it easier for the learner to see the object to be revealed, and finally learned, as a problem" (10). Here is where we understand that the teacher *can't* be a colearner, because within this framework, she already sees what there is to see.

There can be no doubt we have much to learn from Freire's political commitment. His involvement in the literacy campaigns of Africa—Mozambique, Angola, Cape Verde, São Tomé and Príncipe, and Guinea-Bissau—for example, were a means of supporting the liberation movements from Portuguese rule. Though I use examples from Freire's curriculum in São Tomé and Príncipe in the passage that follows, my point is not to argue about what was or is valid in another country's revolutionary context.[7] My main purpose is to think about the problems to which an almost wholesale reliance on Freire's theory has led us as radical educators in the United States.

Freire (1993) states, "To consider oneself the proprietor of revolutionary wisdom—which must then be given to (or imposed on) the people—is to retain the old ways" (42–43). The following excerpts are from the *Popular Cultural Notebooks* (which Freire describes as the generic name given to a series of books and primers) and the *Exercise Workbook*, used as basic texts in the literacy campaign of São Tomé and Príncipe:

> Let's think about some qualities that characterize the new man and the new woman.

Instead of asking what these might be, the lesson provides the answer:

> One of these qualities is agreement with the People's cause and the defense of the People's interest. Fulfilling our duty, no matter what task falls to us, is a sign of the new man and the new woman. The correct sense of political militancy, in which we are learning to overcome individualism and egoism, is also a sign. (Freire & Macedo 1987, 92)

Another lesson asks:

> Can the education of children and adults, after the Independence of our country, be equal to the education that we had before Independence? If you think that it can be the same, say why. If you think that it cannot be, say why. If, for you, the present education should be different from the education that we had before Independence, point out some aspects of this difference. (88)

Not only is there a clearly "right " answer to this question, the curriculum later goes on to suggest how it should be answered:

> [There has to be] a completely different education from that of colonial days . . . It has to be an education that does not favor lies, false ideas, or lack of discipline. (93)

In emphasizing the need to "think correctly" (76), the goal of the lessons seems to be to get *them* to understand what *we* know.

Even if the topics were identified through an investigation of the readers' lives, in these and other excerpts from the São Tomé and Príncipe texts, readers don't appear to be given credit for what they already know.

Freire has said of his curricula, "The text is designed to meet the objective of the literacy campaign, namely, for the people to participate effectively as subjects in the reconstruction of their nation" (Freire & Macedo 1987, 65). And yet they appear to be positioned as objects. Macedo speaks of the "development of a critical attitude on the part of learners" in literacy campaigns. "For example," he writes, "to what extent do learners acquire an analytical attitude toward authority in their own daily existence?" (113). What remains unexamined is the authority of the curriculum.

I want to be clear that it's not that Freire never acknowledges the interrelationship between subjectivity and objectivity. He does. But how does he reconcile these passing references with his emphasis on unveiling reality, which we still see in *Pedagogy of Hope* (1996, 30)? Freire (1996) also makes reference to what he calls "the introjection of the dominator by the dominated" (140) and acknowledges "the ambivalent feeling the colonized have for the colonizers, one of repulsion and attraction at once" (179), major concerns of psychoanalytic thought, to which I will return later in this chapter. Yet his primary focus and pedagogical response don't take these essential concepts into consideration.

Other progressive educators read Freire differently. William Stanley (1992) cites Peter McLaren's point that Freire "understand[s] truth as 'conversation' as opposed to 'reflection of essence.'" Thus, according to Stanley, "Freire claims no final answers." (127) He adds:

> Freire's use of the term "correct thinking" is unfortunate to the extent that it obscures the complexity of his pedagogical theory and his grasp of the dialogical and contingent nature of truth. Indeed, as McLaren explains, Freire's approach to critical literacy provides a direct critique of the authoritarian and precriptivist approach to literacy taken by Bloom and Hirsch . . . His critical approach to literacy assumes literacy is both multivocal and characterized by its own surplus of meaning. (127)

Yet Freire's own curricula appear to be models of the "authoritarian and precriptivist approach" of which he is critical.[8] And there seems as little room in them for multiple voices as there is in *Pedagogy of Hope*, in which Freire's response to nearly all critique is to dismiss it as "incompetent reading" of his work.[9]

There are many times when the things Freire says are motivating. Comments such as the following are often quoted in U.S. Freirian-inspired curricula:

> How can I enter into a dialogue if I always imagine that others are ignorant, and never become conscious of my own ignorance? How can I enter into a dialogue if I see myself as a person apart from others? How can I enter into a dialogue if I consider myself a member of an 'in group,' the owners of truth and knowledge, the 'pure people?' (Association for Community-Based Education 1988, 39)

> A cultural circle is a live and creative dialogue in which everyone knows some things and does not know others, in which all seek together to know more. This is why you, as the coordinator of a cultural

circle, must be humble, so that you can grow with the group, instead of losing your humility and claiming to direct the group, once it is animated. (67)

It's just that in Freire's own practice, there is little evidence of his following his own advice. What is it that he doesn't know?

The Underlying Consistency Between Freirian Theory and Practice

I want to examine Freire's seeming inconsistencies not for the sake of pointing them out, but because they are actually pieces of what I read as an underlying coherent rationale. The following excerpts come from the primer of the Cuban literacy campaign, which Jonothan Kozol (1978) says provides "a case study of the application of Paulo Freire's educational principles" (341).

The Land

The campesinos now at last are owners of the land.
The campesinos cultivate their land.
The Cuban land is rich.

The Cuban Fisherman

The fishing cooperative assists the fisherman.
The fisherman is not cheated anymore.
The fishermen now live a better life. (352)

The Cuban literacy campaign began during a time of bombings by Cuban exiles—one hit the Havana area on the same day the literacy campaign began—and the U.S.-supported attack at the Bay of Pigs. Kozol (1978) says, "In a state of revolution, as Freire himself has said many times throughout the last ten years, certain things cannot be left to chance" (354). In the words of Raúl Ferrer, vice coordinator of the 1960s Cuban literacy program, "Our time was short. We felt that we could not await forever that 'spontaneous moment' of organic curiosity so often elevated to romantic adulation in the literature that we receive from North American and British friends" (in Kozol 1978, 350). As in São Tomé and Príncipe, the need to have as many people as possible support the Cuban revolution as quickly as possible might well be a reason to point out changes those revolutions had already brought about. But can it justify a text in which the author would *always* appear to know what he wants the reader to see? Freire (1993) himself writes, "A real humanist can be identified more by his trust in the people, which engages him in their struggle, than by a thousand actions in their favor without that trust" (42). I can't fault Freire for not living up to his ideals. It's something on which I wouldn't want to be judged myself. We can, however, scrutinize the practices we develop, having used

Freire as our philosophical base, and it is to this that I will turn shortly, after a look at Freire's underlying philosophy.

> To substitute monologue, slogans, and communiqués for dialogue is to attempt to liberate the oppressed with the instruments of domestication. Attempting to liberate the oppressed without their reflective participation in the act of liberation is to treat them as objects which must be saved from a burning building; it is to lead them into the populist pitfall and transform them into masses which can be manipulated. (Freire 1993, 47)

Given the nature of his own practice, which seems to emerge out of the very framework he is criticizing, I was initially perplexed by comments such as this one. On further reflection, I see how Freire's beliefs, rather than his rhetoric, justify his top-down approach. In fact, his curricula are completely consistent with his ideology. For Freire (1985), it's the economic structure that *creates* the consciousness of both the oppressed and the oppressor, the "semi-intransitive consciousness" typical of economically and politically dependent societies, and the next "phase of popular consciousness, that of 'naive transitivity,'" emerging only with structural transformations in society (75–77). With such transformation as his goal, it makes complete sense to design an educational curriculum that attempts to get people to see what he sees and motivate their involvement in a movement to change the economic structure.[10]

I have often been told, when I suggest we question Freire-inspired practices in the United States, that these practices are based on a misunderstanding of Freire's theory or that out of their revolutionary context and distanced from their original intent, Freire's ideas are being misused. Besides wanting to challenge what, in the first case, often feel like condescending assumptions that teachers don't understand theory, my main argument is that the practices in question are, in fact, consistent with Freire's ideological framework.

The "Culture of Silence"

Freire speaks often of a "culture of silence," of oppressed people as passive, silent recipients of false information. While he does offer passing acknowledgment of resistance on the part of colonized people in *Literacy* (Freire & Macedo 1987) and *Pedagogy of Hope* (1996)—cultural resistance through language, art, and music—this seems at odds with almost everything else he says.

> The semi-intransitive consciousness . . . [is immersed] in concrete reality . . . The only data the dominated consciousness grasps are the data that lie within the orbit of its lived experience . . . [it] cannot objectify the facts and problematic situations of daily life . . . lacking

structural perception, men attribute sources of such facts and situations in their lives either to some superreality or to something within themselves. . . . (1985, 75)

He writes of Guinea-Bissau,

In certain ways, the subordinate role of the oppressed was perceived as a result of climatic difficulties (for example, there is no rain; therefore we don't have work or anything to eat) and not as calculated exploitation by the dominant class. (Freire & Macedo 1987, 100)

It is possible that some people did not, in fact, perceive that their subordinate roles were the result of exploitation and believed them rather to be the fate of rain. As I've said earlier, the point is not to evaluate Freire's work in revolutionary contexts, but to see how a reliance on Freire has led many radical educators in this country to view students here. The following are two such examples of his influence, as seen in the work of often-quoted progressive U.S. educators:

Freire's central premise is that education . . . either reinforces or challenges the existing social forces that keep [people] passive. (Auerbach and Wallerstein 1987b, 1)

Working among urban poor and the peasants of northeastern Brazil, he was quickly struck by their fatalism . . . And he insisted that education either functions to liberate learners so that they can understand and struggle against whatever keeps them in bondage, or it domesticates them so that they accept oppressive conditions as their inevitable lot. (Association for Community-Based Education 1988, 165)

In an ever-prevailing view, we begin to think of our students as passive, echoing the position into which mainstream literacy campaigns place students, campaigns of which many of us are critical! Blanket statements are made over and over about students' low self-esteem, so that we stop seeing evidence of self-confidence and self-advocacy. Furthermore, these either/or dichotomies—peasants and urban poor as fatalistic and passive or actively resistant, education as domesticating or liberating—obscure the complexity of subjectivity and processes of change.[11]

Freire's Either/Or and His Other

Kathleen Weiler (1991) points out that Freire's idea of conscientization is based on the idea that there is a common experience of oppression, which ignores the possibility of "simultaneously contradictory positions of oppression and dominance: the man oppressed by his boss could at the same time oppress his wife, for example, or the White woman oppressed by sexism could exploit the Black woman" (453).[12]

These "simultaneously contradictory positions" can be thought of in terms of multiple subjectivities. In failing to address them, Freire leaves untouched the struggles *among* people, using oppressor and oppressed as binary oppositions that halt forward movement.[13] In a critique similar to Weiler's, the editors of *Talking Feminist Popular Education* write, "Tackling men's violence against women throws us by necessity into the terrain of breaking with a conception—still too common in popular education literature—of popular communities having a simple common interest against the exploiting interests of bosses, landowner, or governments" (Chetwynd et al. 1992, 3).[14]

Turning to another critical aspect of Freirian thought, at his worst, Freire comes dangerously close to drawing a comparison between the intellectual activities of animals and those of oppressed people. In distinguishing between them, Freire (1985) points out that "unlike men, (*sic*) animals are simply in the world, incapable of objectifying either themselves or the world" (68). He goes on to say in the same essay that "the dominated consciousness does not have sufficient distance from reality to objectify it in order to know it in a critical way" (75). Once this positioning of Other in Freire's writings becomes clear, it also comes into view in the writings of some of the theorists who have identified themselves with him. In the book he coauthored with Freire (1987), Macedo writes of the need to realize that different dialects carry different worldviews. "The first important issue is that black American's linguistic code not only reflects their reality, but also their lived experience in a given historical moment. Terms that encapsulate the drug culture, daily alienation, the struggle to survive the subhuman and inhumane conditions of the ghettos—these constitute a discourse black Americans find no difficulty in using" (127).

Macedo's despairing portrayal of Black American language and a worldview it implies stands in sharp contrast to the life African American poet and essayist June Jordan (1985) ascribes to it:

> Our culture has been constantly threatened by annihilation or, at least, the swallowed blurring of assimilation. Therefore, our language is a system constructed by people constantly needing to insist that we exist, that we are present. Our language devolves from a culture that abhors all abstraction, or anything tending to obscure or delete the fact of the human being who is here and now/the truth of the person who is speaking or listening. Consequently "there is no passive voice construction possible in Black English." For example, you cannot say, "Black English is being eliminated." You must say, "White people eliminating Black English." The assumption of the presence of life governs all of Black English. (129)

It was through this same lens that I was struck by how much Claudia Tate's (1984) belief in the sharpened vision of people without

gender and/or race privilege contrasts with Freire's assertion that the
vision of oppressed people is necessarily limited:

> Their [Black women writers'] angle of vision allows them to see
> what white people, especially males, seldom see. With one penetrat-
> ing glance, they cut through layers of institutionalized racism and sex-
> ism and uncover a core of social contradictions and internal dilemmas
> which plague all of us . . . Through their art they share their vision of
> possible resolution with those who cannot see. (xvi)[15]

The Usefulness of Poststructuralism

Poststructuralism helps us see our complicity with oppressive ideas and
actions differently by seeing power as a web of relations rather than one
deterministic force, such as propaganda, that we must overcome. At
first glance, the idea that power is produced in every moment of our
lives could lead to despair. But if power is ubiquitous, then so is resistance. The notion of a web of relations implies agency. It means we can
no longer look at what domination does to us, but rather how we are
implicated in its creation and maintenance and where there is room for
subversion. I cheered when I heard Daniel Ellsberg say at the time of
the Gulf War, "The cultural hegemony of militarism is everywhere.
That gives us something to do wherever we are!"[16]

The Role of Discourse

There are several concepts key to understanding this web of relations. Probably most important, and most relevant to this book, is discourse. Discourses are the *ways of talking*, what Foucault called the
"regimes of truth," that construct what we come to see as given and
internalize into views of ourselves. In other words, discourses don't
merely describe the world, they invent it, all the while hiding their role
in this creation.

Above all, poststructuralism helps us see the *constructedness* of
things. This gets us out of the impossible task of proving that commonly
held beliefs are wrong—that not all homeless people are alcoholics,
that not all Jews are rich, that the beating of Rodney King was brutality—by instead deconstructing the regimes of truth that constitute
them as true. What the King jurors saw with their eyes was simultaneously embedded in discourses, such as police procedures and, above all,
the numerous discourses that construct racist fear, such as the equation
of an African American man with drug user; in the case of Rodney
King, a man turned into "an animal" on PCP.

All of this makes me think about the times in my teaching when I
have been confronted with misconceptions about Jews, if not explicit

anti-Semitism. One Sunday, at a *Survival News* backyard barbecue, a few of us sat inside the kitchen waiting for dessert to come out of the oven. Seemingly out of nowhere, a woman I didn't know asked, "Is it true all Jews are smart?" At the Women's School, it came up a few times in discussion that either all the students' worst bosses were Jewish, or Jews "are the best people you'd ever want to meet, smart." And I once taught at a Latina women's educational collective where I and another Jewish woman, both Anglo, were members of a mostly Latina staff. Because questions had come up in each of our classes about Jewish holidays, and some women had indicated curiosity about Jews, we decided to get the two groups together so our students could ask us further questions. We jokingly referred to it between ourselves as "Meet the Jews." Then the questions began, and "Why are Jews rich and greedy?" was the first. I have never responded adequately in these situations. It's never worked when I've said, "No, not all Jews are smart," or "How could *only* the Jews have been terrible bosses?"

Discussing racism or sexism has become particularly difficult in the current climate in which terms such as *race card* serve to obscure racial prejudice, and allegations of political correctness attempt to diminish the significance of offensive remarks and silence challenges to them. In the classroom, students will often dismiss statistics regarding discrimination as inaccurate or outdated and personal accounts as too subjective. When we try to prove the existence of bigotry, we can feel like we're banging our heads against a wall.

A different approach is to disentangle how it is we come to think what we think and see what we see, making it possible to think and see differently. It's questions such as the following that have led me to a greater feeling of efficacy, helping us to step back and see the normally unacknowledged discourses:

> Who benefits from presenting this idea as fact?
>
> How is it in your (our) self-interest to believe (women on welfare are lazy, all Jews are rich, etc.)?
>
> How does it work against you (us) to believe this?
>
> Who has something to gain from asking these very questions?
>
> Who has something to lose?[17]

Who "Sees" What?

An emphasis on representation is another key feature of poststructuralism. One of the most tenacious images of immigrants to the United States is of people who come here because of the "easy" availability of public assistance. But the problem with opposing this stereotype is that it would imply there is something wrong with the immigrant who does receive welfare benefits. It's important to have multiple images of people who are immigrants, but it's also necessary to demonstrate that *all* images, or representations, are *made*. Rather than reflecting a fundamental truth, they are shaped by the person who is doing the describing and the interests she or he has in mind.

Whenever I use media bias as a classroom theme, there are students who dismiss any analysis because they think they'll never get the whole story from the media anyway. I've wanted to move away from the whole story idea to instead looking at multiple stories of the same event, depending on who's telling it and with what interests in mind. In one class, after we read "The Way Things Aren't: Rush Limbaugh Debates Reality," I asked students to choose three facts as presented by Limbaugh. Their task was to write about whose interests were served by each and what beliefs each played into. No one completed the assignment, and though I didn't think to ask them at the time, I wonder if it was because I was asking the students to examine something in a way to which *most* of us are unaccustomed.

I returned to this idea via a different route when two students mentioned in a subsequent class that the homeless people they see are all drunks. In the past, I would have responded with something like, "You mean, you *know* that every single person you see who's homeless is drunk?" trying to encourage them to rationally reexamine their ideas, but often achieving nothing more than a butting of heads. This time, I said, "I believe that's what you see. But why do I see something different?" I talked about how what we see has everything to do with what's at stake in the perception, and having worked and been friends with homeless and formerly homeless women in Boston, my allegiances were to them, so I saw something different. This same idea also helps tremendously when students challenge the statistics I give for debunking immigration myths—indicating that immigrants *create* jobs for U.S.-born workers, very few immigrants end up on welfare, the most likely person to be abused by the Border Patrol is a U.S. citizen of Mexican descent, and so on (see "Agree/Disagree/Not Sure" in Chapter Six). "Of course," I acknowledged, "[Governor of California] Pete Wilson is going to use different statistics to back up different claims. The question is, what's at stake in believing one set of facts over another?" The underlying issue is not whose view is more objective, but where the view is situated, whose aim it serves, and what fears might motivate it.

The Artifice of Categories

Discourses are often based on categories that are assumed to be fixed, existing in nature. But we create classifications and then define people and phenomena by them, all the while maintaining they are natural groupings. For example, consider the category "race" which does not exist as an objective classification. Henry Louis Gates (1986) asks, "Who has seen a black or red person, a white, yellow or brown? These terms are arbitrary constructions, not reports of reality" (6). The life of Gregory Williams (1995) illustrates this point. Raised as a White child in Virginia under Jim Crow laws, he believed his father was Italian American. When Williams was ten, his mother died and his father took him to live with his paternal grandparents and extended family in Indiana. Before they arrived, his father revealed that his family was Black, and from the age of ten, so was Williams. Stories such as these are numerous, and more and more, they are being told. (See Chapter Five for the poem "On the Question of Race," along with suggestions for its use in classrooms to expand notions of identity.)

You might respond to this by asserting, "But what about the crucial role of identity in giving impetus to political activity? In challenging discrimination? What about the necessity of Chicano students organizing on a predominantly White college campus, of making sure there is Vietnamese representation on the Albuquerque school board? What about the need to assert Blackness when Whiteness is assumed?" Race may not exist, but racism does. Here, I want to make it clear that I believe who we are at a given moment is important. It's not that identities don't matter. And sometimes we need a united front. But we have multiple identities, shaped by context. Rather than resulting in a denial of what it means to be Chicana, African American, Vietnamese American, or White, this notion of identity suggests an expansion of it, and it shows us where alliances can be made. As a Jewish woman in *Embattled Selves*, a collection of stories from survivors of the Nazi Holocaust, says, "If people don't know that I was in Auschwitz, they can't know me. But once I tell them, they are no longer able to see me for who I am" (Jacobson 1994, 13). A single identity is never the sum total of who we are.

Zora Neale Hurston (1979) wrote about the fluidity of difference in her essay "How It Feels to Be Colored Me." Her answer, she says, depends on many variables. Barbara Johnson (1985) describes them as the following: "Compared to what? As of when? Who is asking? In what context? For what purpose? With what interests and presuppositions?" (323–324). How it feels to be who Hurston is, is more dependent on situations and positions than on an essential truth.

The Poststructural Notion of "the Subject"

The idea of discourse leads us to the poststructural notion of "the subject." Mimi Orner (1992) writes:

> Unlike the term "individual," the term "subject" encourages us to think of ourselves and our realities as constructions . . . As Chris Weedon observes, ... "Humanist discourses presuppose an essence at the heart of the individual which is unique, fixed and coherent and which

makes her what she is . . . postructuralism proposes a subjectivity which is precarious, contradictory and in process, constantly being reconstituted in discourse each time we think or speak." (79)

It was in considering Michel Foucault's ideas of how our subjectivities come to be produced that I saw Freire's underlying goal—the move from "false" to "critical" consciousness—as much more complex than Freirian pedagogy would have it seem. Mahoney and Yngvesson (1992) define subjectivity as "the experience of the self as a subject who acts, who has wants, and who sometimes must act 'against the grain' in the face of contradictory desires" (45). Foucault emphasizes the need to look at *how* subjectivity, power, and knowledge itself are constructed and how they might be constructed differently. For many who create Freirian curricula, consciousness would appear to be unified, as though it can be moved from point A to point B. But within Foucault's framework, we can no longer see ourselves as simply shedding a false consciousness in favor of a true one, because consciousness is always shaped by the discourses and the practices in which it lives. To gain a critical perspective on our beliefs, we need to deconstruct and transform those discourses and practices that are working at any given moment to position us. Michel Foucault's description of regimes of truth and poststructuralism's notion of a web of power relations that keeps the regimes alive offer more to work with than the idea of peeling away layers of deception until the truth is unveiled.

James Clifford (1991) offers a succinctly useful way of grasping the relationship between discourse and subjectivity:

> Literary studies, history and educational management all have their own discursive rules and values, as do specific religions, parenthood, advertising, television news, specific newspapers, and so on . . . When we read these discourses in the ways in which we have been taught, we are not only assimilating values; we are also being called upon to take up the limited and predetermined roles or subject positions that these discourses make available. (104)

As part of a political project that refuses to see women as merely victims of domination, and thus helpless, members of a German feminist collective are writing "memory" pieces of daily life on topics such as posture or clothes to look at the ways their own subjectivities are constructed, and they are publishing what they find.[18]

> Our collective empirical work sets itself the high-flown task of identifying the ways in which individuals construct themselves into existing structures . . . the way in which they reconstruct social structures, the points at which change is possible, the point where our chains chafe most, the point where accommodations have been made. (Weiler 1991, 466)

Like many who talk and think through the language of poststructuralism, the German feminist collective Frauenformen uses categories such as *gender* as a verb, rather than a finite noun.

The Contradictions in Ourselves

Valuing paradox, poststructuralism is about the impossibility of totalization. Judith Butler (1993b) tells a story of swimming at the Jewish Community Center in Baltimore, where she lives. She is Jewish, yet initially has the feeling that "here, I would never really belong" (236). Because of her androgynous appearance, other women see her as distinctly different and redirect her to the men's locker room. Later, "because the perception is that we are all in some way related, various individuals who have never before addressed me, stop me in the shower and ask whether I am married yet, why I don't shave my legs, whether I am observant." (236). This experience reminds Butler of accompanying her father to Cleveland's Jewish Community Center as a child, a place of "promised kinship and community, and inevitable estrangement" (236).

I read her story as one in which "exile" resides within "home." The women betray heterosexist assumptions, while at the same time, their questions are based on a foundation of assumed familiarity and an insider's conversational style. Living in New Mexico as I write this, I attend Rosh Ha Shana services at a synagogue in Albuquerque, one of only a handful in town. I go knowing I will feel alienated on several levels. When I say prayers in Hebrew, in which I can recite words I don't understand, I find comfort in listening to my voice chanting along with hundreds of others who share this insider's language. But when they are spoken in English, I am turned off by the actual meaning of the prayers. And I fidget during sermons, resenting the hierarchy it implies and the fact that we are compelled to listen without debate.

I go to synagogue most of all to meet older Jews like Herb and Sylvia, who I end up talking with at the "nosh" afterward. When I asked where they are from, Herb replied, in a loud voice and obvious Long Island accent, "Something the matter with your hearing?" This is just what I was looking for. While a friend who is not used to this kind of repartee thinks Herb might have meant offense, I felt at home. We went on to talk about missing a really good piece of ruggeleh now and then. My guess is that, had we talked at some length, we would have reached the things that separate us in terms of how we live our lives, our politics. I can't say that doesn't matter. It's a tension I and many others live with, but one I seek out nonetheless, because in home has always been exile for me. Maybe that's why I'm comfortable having the "foreign" enter into the "familiar" in my theory and practice, without needing to erase either.

Our multiple subjectivities grip us, of course, as much as they grip our students. One winter, I traveled to Vermont to house-sit for a friend, so that I could have a week to work on this book without interruption. With nothing to do but write, I of course spent the first three days not writing. I called another friend back in Boston, with the hope that talking about it would help break the freeze. At her first words, "What do you think is getting in the way?" I began to sob. An image of my father, who died nearly twenty years ago and whom I seldom think about, came into my head. It was much like the image of Woody Allen's character's mother in the film *New York Stories*: a large head and shoulders in the sky. My father was revered in his family of origin as a scholar. His family are survivors of the Holocaust, either having left Czechoslovakia in time, as did his parents, who lost parents, grandparents, brothers, and sisters; or having survived a labor camp, as did my father's uncle, whose wife and children died in Auschwitz. Rejecting his family's Orthodox Judaism, in which my grandfather was a rabbi, my father became a rabbi of Reform Judaism, and our home was not kosher. Maybe it was through his status as a scholar that he redeemed himself.

As far as I could tell, his congregants revered my father, while I knew him to be an emotional tyrant, at least at dinnertime. Except for dinnertime, he was away in his attic study or writing at a card table in the backyard. His manila folders—always filled with whatever he was working on at the moment—came to my high school graduation and choir concerts, held together with oversized two-prong paper clips and accompanied by black felt-tip pens. He wrote about Jewish history and philosophy and translated the work of others. Given his neglectful and disdainful treatment of us, I resented the books' dedications to my mother, my brother, and me, and I have never read any of them. Yet a friend who has tells me that, eerily, there is something in my father's ideas that matches my own interests. And today I find myself working on a manuscript.

It's been difficult to complete this book. There was not a lot expected of me intellectually by my family. They considered me scatterbrained, and I probably played out that role. On the other hand, I saw someone writing every day, filling shelves with his work, and it may have made me believe such a thing was possible of me. I approach my own project with both desire and resistance. Working on it means becoming like my father and defying him at the same time, writing out of an unhappy legacy that may have led me to believe I could write.[19]

At the end of her story, Butler stumbles onto a water aerobics class at the center, where older women happily lift their large thighs in and out of the water. She notices blue concentration camp numbers on some of their wrists, and she understands theirs are "compensatory thighs" (236). Butler dives into the pool, and I dig into my writing. This is where poststructuralism moves us forward. It helps to understand how my father's legacy is working to position me in contradictory ways. I don't have to completely reject it, or totally embrace it. Perhaps my next project is to imagine who my father was defining himself against and with, in the frenzy of his work and the decisions he made.[20]

Psychoanalysis and the Unconscious: One Way to Look at the Contradictions We Sustain and the Investments We Make

> Given the need for political action, it is understandable that we commit ourselves to the ideal of an autonomous and coherent female self. However, the unconscious, the most subversive element in psychic life, seems to be catching up with us.
>
> —Jane Gallop and Carolyn Burke,
> "Psychoanalysis and Feminism
> in France" (1984, 109)

While poststructuralism lets us see our multiple and shifting subjectivities, through a look at the various and changing discourses under which we live, it has never sufficiently explained to me how the discourses get inside us. While I'm not ready to embrace a particular psychoanalytic theory, the focus each shares on fantasy, fear, and desire seems vital.

To add to a theory of discourse, we need a theory of the unconscious. Why, on the one hand, *don't* we so unproblematically fit into the positions the dominant ideologies would create for us; why do we resist? And why sometimes *do* we conform, even when we come to perceive that these are positions within which we are oppressed—in other words, even when we have had our consciousness raised? Radical and feminist adaptations of psychoanalysis can be seen as attempts to understand why people do or don't get involved in the discourses in the first place. Since an understanding of regimes of truth isn't enough, what we need is a theory describing how discourses interact with unconscious fears and, what Mahoney and Yngvesson (1992) refer to as "the psychoanalytic bedrock of motivation," unconscious desires.[21] This section is a brief introduction to psychoanalytic thought and its uses by cultural critics and others attempting to apply theory directly to social change. It is, of course, only a beginning, especially in terms of how these ideas might come into play in pedagogical situations. In offering a psychoanalytic lens on issues such as racism, sexism, and internalized oppression, I hope to contribute toward its direct application to teaching.

The Desire to Be Free and the Desire Not to Be

Psychoanalytic efforts to understand the construction of our desires inevitably turn to an inspection of the infant's relationship with his or her primary caregiver. Most theories rest on the belief that an infant is born into a state of undifferentiation from the caregiver, from whom she must eventually struggle to separate. The resulting anxiety leads to "a longing for return to an earlier time of passive fusion" (Mahoney & Yngvesson 1992, 50). Thus, there's a constant tension between dependence and autonomy from which, according to this analysis, we can never escape. Psychoanalysis is used to understand the tension between what Jessica Benjamin (1987) calls "the desire to be free and the desire not to be."

Relying on Nancy Chodorow's ideas on mothering, Benjamin writes:

> Initially, all infants not only love their mothers but identify with and wish to emulate them. But boys discover that they cannot be, or become, her; they can only have her. When they grow up, they will be independent and unlike the mother, while girls achieve independence with the expectation that they will continue to be like her. This repudiation of the mother by men has also meant that she is not recognized as an independent person, another subject, but something Other: as nature, as an instrument or object, as less-than-human. (44)

According to Benjamin, this leads to an "overemphasis on boundaries between me and not-me" (45). She continues:

> This world view emphasizes difference over sameness, boundaries over fluidity. It conceives of polarity and opposition rather than mutuality and interdependence as the vehicles of growth. That is, it does not tolerate the simultaneous experience of contradictory impulses: ambivalence. Finally, it does not grant the other person the status of another subject, but only that of an object. By extension, this object status is granted to *the entire world*, which, from early on, was infused with the mother's presence. (45, emphasis mine)

The central problem, according to this idea, lies in achieving autonomy while satisfying the need for recognition. At the same time we struggle for autonomy from the Other, we need the Other to recognize us, to validate that we exist; and we need the Other to desire.

For Benjamin,

> [it's when] the psyche fails to hold in tension the polarity but rather splits them, in favor of either dependence or independence that the stage [is set] for domination. Opposites can no longer be integrated;

one side is devalued, the other idealized . . . [The] inability to sustain the tension of paradox manifests itself in all forms of domination. (50)

Benjamin claims that men who can't tolerate the paradox may resolve the tension between autonomy and connection through violence. This is a useful handle for me in understanding domination.

In "Towards a New Consciousness," Gloria Anzaldúa (1981) addresses anti-immigrant fever when she says to Anglos,

Your dual consciousness splits off parts of yourself, transferring the 'negative' parts onto us. (Where there is persecution of minorities, there is shadow projection. Where there is violence and war, there is repression of shadow.) To say that you are afraid of us, that to put distance between us, you wear the mask of contempt. Admit that Mexico is your double, that she exists in the shadow of this country, that we are irrevocably tied to her. Gringo, accept the doppelganger in your psyche. By taking back your collective shadow the intracultural split will heal. (86)

Stereotypes: As Anxious as They Are Assertive

Attempts to use psychoanalytic theory to explain domination, viewing the oppressor's Other as an object of simultaneous desire and fear, also help explain the contradictory nature of stereotypes. As Homi Bhabha points out, "It is recognizably true that the chain of stereotypical signification is . . . an articulation of multiple belief. The black is both savage (cannibal) and yet the most obedient and dignified of servants (the bearer of food); he is the embodiment of rampant sexuality and yet innocent as a child; he is mystical, primitive, simple-minded and yet the most worldly and accomplished liar" (1983, 34).

Writing also on the notion of contradictory impulses, Douglas Crimp (1992) suggests there is more to the obsessive portrayal of people with AIDS (PWAs), especially gay male PWAs, as "either grotesquely disfigured or as having wasted to fleshless, ethereal bodies," than the defensive claim that they are intended "to overcome our fears of disease and death" or AIDS activists' claim that they aim to "reinforce the status of the PWA as victim or pariah." For Crimp, these are "phobic images, images of the terror at imagining the person with AIDS as still sexual" (130). In the evocation of a desire denied by the majority of the population, yet so strong it must be vigilantly guarded against, he relies on a psychoanalytic understanding of unconscious desire.

Here, again, we can see that "showing the truth . . . to be a production in which there are no simple matters of fact" needs to be central to our teaching strategy (Walkerdine 1994, 60). Valerie Walkerdine takes the prevailing ideology on girls and math and uses psychoanalytic theory to show us an alternative to the limited options of either (1) proving girls are good at it, or (2) arguing that equal opportunity is all they need. She begins with the following teacher's notes, which she found to be typical of the British classrooms she observed:

> Very, very hard worker. Not a particularly bright girl . . . her hard work gets her to her standards.
>
> . . . can just about write his own name . . . not because he's not clever, because he's not capable, but because he can't sit still, he's got no concentration . . . very disruptive . . . but quite bright. (58)

Walkerdine's explanation for such beliefs, which have no empirical basis, is that girls' "bid for the 'understanding' [is] the greatest threat of all to a universal power or a truth that is invested in a fantasy of control of 'women'" (65). Combining poststructural and psychoanalytic notions, she argues that the need to assert the mathematical inferiority of girls is motivated by anxiety, a "terror of loss," rather than certainty (63).

Walkerdine would agree with Bhabha (1983) that the stereotype is "as anxious as it is assertive" (22). Because categories are not fixed, it's the role of stereotypes to attempt to maintain them. Border crossing of any kind is a threat to established roles. The mutability of sexuality, for example, is a threat to heterosexuality's place of domination. If "we" are also "them," where are the grounds for domination? In *Neighbors Talk*, Francisca Nuñez (Matrin 1993) writes:

> In Santo Domingo, racism is not racism. It is fear. Since you are a child in Santo Domingo, the parents say to you, "The Haitians will eat you." Whenever we saw a Black person, we would think they were going to do witchcraft. Since I was a child, I would hear these words. Well, maybe there is something of racism. But it is fear, not hatred. (Martin 1993, 58)

Writing on the discourse of colonialism, Bhabha says that in order to erase, not merely dismiss, a stereotype, we have to understand how it becomes a part of the psyche of both the colonizer and the colonized. He says, "My reading of colonial discourse suggests that the point of intervention should shift from the identification of images as positive or negative, to an understanding of the processes of subjectivity made possible (and plausible) through the stereotypical discourse" (18). This is where psychoanalytic ideas may be most useful to our classroom teaching, urging us to discover practices that not only show how all images are created but also demonstrate to students and ourselves the way unconscious issues contribute to stereotyping and the walls we place between ourselves and others.

Splitting

Adding another layer to our understanding of violence against women, racial stereotypes and hatred, and dominant images of people with AIDS, psychoanalytic theory also provides a way of seeing the ambivalence with which oppressed people regard the oppressors. Marcos Sanchez-Tranquilino and John Tagg (1992) suggest:

> nationalist discourses remain prisoner to the very terms and structures they seek to reverse, mirroring their fixities and exclusions. But the attachment is also deeper and its effects more pervasive and unconscious, as nationalisms are fractured by the drive of a desire for the very Other they constitute, denigrate, and expel, yet to which they continue to attribute enormous powers. (562)

Psychoanalytic theory views both the oppressed's and the oppressor's Others as objects of simultaneous desire and fear in order to explain domination. Returning to Benjamin, Judith Beth Cohen (1989) points out that in her analysis, "Since the desperate but thwarted desire of the infant is for recognition, a recognition impossible from a mother who is herself defined as an object, this desire gets translated into a wish to become (in the case of boys) or merge with (in the case of girls) the powerful 'other'" (76).

In "Separation and Intimacy," Susie Orbach and Luise Eichenbaum (1987) write of women's fear of "annihilating difference": "Women talk of how they stay in unsatisfactory relationships fearing a loss of self if they were to withdraw from the relationship. They seek new relationships, driven by the need not simply for connection but for identity" (55). Orbach and Eichenbaum's argument would account for the outwardly inexplicable situations women find themselves in, such as remaining with a man who is HIV-positive yet refuses to wear a condom—inexplicable, if we assume there are no material constraints that force her to remain.

> I . . . have been constantly aware that the Valerie Walkerdine that people speak well of seems to be someone else, someone whom I do not recognize as me. How come, for many women, the powerful part of themselves has been so split off as to feel that it belongs to someone else? (Walkerdine 1994, 57)

Here, too, for Walkerdine, the psychoanalytic notion of splitting becomes the explanation for such seemingly irrational feelings to which many readers of this book will relate as much as I do.

In another example addressing the dominated part of consciousness, Walkerdine (1994) relates Joan Riviere's story of the academic who feels compelled to flirt with men after delivering a paper:

The struggle both to perform academically and to perform as feminine must seem at times almost impossible. No wonder that some of us split them apart in various ways or have different conscious and unconscious methods for dealing with the unbearable contradiction. (67)

Another Look at Freirian Pedagogy

To return to Freirian pedagogy, there are what Ira Shor calls "myths" that my students have internalized and deeply hold on to—myths about personal failure or immigrant workers, for example. There are myths that I've internalized and still hold on to—about the complete fulfillment of a heterosexual relationship, about how my body should look—despite more than twenty years of consciousness raising. Poststructuralism and an eye turned to our unconscious desires and fears, our moments of complicity and those of resistance, provide more of a role for me as a colearner with my students by reminding me that I live with my own contradictions—that I haven't so completely rejected a "false" consciousness in favor of a "liberated" one.

The existence of such internal contradictions points to a further problem in Freirian pedagogy. Shor, for example, while acknowledging them in passing, does so without theorizing their source, and thus can't offer a pedagogical response. "About class-relations, I find clarity and confusion in students at the same time . . . Consciousness is often inconsistent within the same student . . . A teacher in my college can hear all these contradictory statements from students and must design a pedagogy that inserts itself into the tangle" (Shor & Freire 1987, 112). Shor never comes back to address the tangle or how we are to insert ourselves into it. Further, the complexities of consciousness seem to be situated only in students, not in the teacher. The important thing for me is that they live within me as much as within my students.

In summary, for those who use poststructuralism and psychoanalysis as a way to grasp the relationship between structural and subjective change, we need to see how knowledge both creates and is created by our fears and fantasies. We need to recognize that we are, in fact, "active subjects who participate in the construction of the wants and needs that culture enjoins [us] to desire or to resist" (Mahoney & Yngvesson 1992, 45). Once again, it's because Freire doesn't engage with this complexity that he's able to uphold the binary opposition of "worker" and "intellectual," advocating for the notion of a vanguard of teachers who can transform the consciousness of their students.

In Constance Penley's essay on Star Trek fans (1992), she argues, "I don't see why we can't provide, simultaneously and giving equal weight to each, an account of what the fans say and do (the ethnographic emphasis on everyday activity and popular logic) and what fans don't say and do (the psychoanalytic emphasis on the repressed and the taboo)" (499). Rather than combining the ethnographic with the psychoanalytic in order to study my students, I want to find ways we as a group can use these skills to study ourselves. This won't be easy. Walkerdine cautions, "Working on fiction, fantasy and contradiction is to work in dangerous and threatening territory" (1968). But while Freirian pedagogy offers us a way to show our students how their personal experiences are socially shaped so that they can see them as open to resistance and change, we need to go further. We need to look at the *investments* we make in our roles as oppressor and oppressed. Anzaldúa's words on Anglos' splitting and projection onto immigrants, for example, relieve some of the frustration with which I respond to White students' rage at antiracist curricula, even if it remains to future work to begin a pedagogical practice that takes the psychic split into account.

I realize now it is not so much that we need to add a psychoanalytic lens to that of poststructuralism, but that the two are compatible in that each wants us to hold contradictions in tension, whether regarding identities or desires. What Teresa Ebert (1991) writes of feminist poststructuralisms can as easily be said of feminist uses of psychoanalysis: "They are concerned not with the *difference between* but with the *difference within*" (892).

I now see that we neither unproblematically absorb nor completely resist sexism, racism, or other dominant ideologies. What I want is for myself and my students to better understand, even if we can never completely resolve, this tension between "the desire to be free and the desire not to be," to understand ourselves as shaped by discourses, yet not without agency. I think this look at what poststructuralism calls our multiple subjectivities has so far been missing in an attempt to fashion a pedagogy that takes us, whether educators or political activists, a step closer to making significant change.

Poststructural and Psychoanalytic Thought: A Need for Caution?

Foucault wants to privilege neither the subjective nor the structural in determining what is real. For Foucault, there is no last instance that constructs a meaning. All meaning can be deconstructed. In other words, there is a constant tension between the material real and the discourse that describes it. So within Foucault's framework, in which he shows how all meaning is constructed, how do we ever determine that one meaning is better than others? At what point do we say we know something and act on it? There is the danger of reading poststructuralism as relativistic, leaving us so unsure of where to fight, and what to fight with, that we could easily become immobilized and apolitical. I'm reminded here of film students who learned to deconstruct images so well they became too self-conscious to construct any! (See Williamson 1981/1982, 86.) But we engage in struggle by knowing exactly what Foucault knew. He was interested not in relative meanings, but in what come to be thought of as scientific truths, which control us through their translation into social practices. As Lori Dorfman (1992) says, poststructuralism "does not mean that we cannot make judgments, only that we cannot make unbiased judgments" (25).

Still, sometimes when I'm steeped in poststructuralist readings, I find myself needing to keep a vigilance against relativity. In fact, even given all I've said about the influence of Freire, it worries me that my own former graduate school of education, having only glanced passingly at Freire's writings, has turned full attention to poststructuralism, which can be read as lacking the agency Freire foregrounds. It's too tempting for educational institutions to skip the political and go to the postpolitical.

As long as I remind myself to guard against the dangers, I am willing to live with Foucault's poststructuralism inside my head. As Isabelle de Courtivron (1993) says of Foucault's rejection of fixed categories and identities, "whether we agree or not with all of his theories, we can never think again quite in the same way about our lives and our society" (29).

Regarding psychoanalysis, what remains worrisome is the feeling that one can never see the oppressed as subjects. According to Walkerdine (1994), "Lacan argued 'woman' exists only as a symptom of male fantasy. What he meant was that the fantasies created under patriarchy . . . create as their object not women as they really are but fantasies of what men both desire and fear in the Other. Women, then, become the repositories of such fantasies, and the effect for psychic development of women themselves is extremely damaging and complex" (67). Women, in Benjamin's and Walkerdine's work, and colonized people in Bhabha's, seem always to be the objects of the fantasies of men and White people, the former's fantasies being shaped only in response. Does the very notion of internalized oppression rely on seeing the oppressed only as objects? What about resistance? How do we avoid the internalized oppression to which we would seem to be destined, according to psychoanalytic ideas? How do we escape psychological determinism? What is a feminist theory that allows the psyche to be seen as mutable and points us toward a political practice based on resistance and creativity?[22] Those who criticize the essentialism of many psycho-analytic frameworks raise further issues. As Judith Butler (1990) points out, "We hear time and time again about *the* boy and *the* girl, a tactical distancing from spatial and temporal locations" (329). Elizabeth Spel-man's view of the ways in which race and class "mediate" mothering is especially helpful here. In her book *Inessential Woman* (1988), the following women make it clear that gender identity is not separable from race identity:

> To [my mother], on a basic economic level, being Chicana meant be-ing "less." It was through my mother's desire to protect her children from poverty and illiteracy that we became 'anglocized'; the more ef-fectively we could pass in the white world, the better guaranteed our future. (Cherríe Moraga, 98)

> The Black mother has a more ominous message for her child and feels more urgently the need to get the message across. The child must know that the white world is dangerous and that if he does not un-derstand its rules it may kill him. (Daryl Dance, 98)

> [We were taught that] though your body is a thing of shame and mys-tery, and curiosity about it is not good, your skin is your glory and the source of your strength and pride. It is white, [which] proves that you are better than all other people on this earth. (Lillian Smith, 100)

Spelman says of her own growing up, "In the society in which my mother and then I grew up, the differences between white and Black, middle and working class, Christian and Jew, were no less differences than the one between girl and boy" (97).

As I've said earlier, psychoanalysis has helped me look at why we come to desire something we know to dominate us or fear that which poses no actual threat, pointing toward a location for the source of these contradictions. My main concern is that the question be seen as vital, even if the psychoanalytic answers I have read so far seem prob-lematic or the pedagogical response just out of reach. Most importantly, if my still-halting grasp of psychoanalysis leaves me with much work still to do, at bottom, it provides me an escape from positioning my stu-dents as fatalistic, naive, or duped.

A Freire-Inspired Curriculum

I want to apply the lens through which I've come to view critical peda-gogy to *ESL for Action* (1987a), an influential curriculum by Elsa Auer-bach and Nina Wallerstein, where we can see Freire's ideas being taken up directly.

The goal of *ESL for Action* is to help create an atmosphere in which real change can occur in the lives of immigrant workers. It acts to retrieve what I once heard someone call "dangerous memory," the history of the social and political changes won by working people. The book provides a clear contrast to traditional ESL work curricula that train immigrants to be good workers, according to management's definition: workers who are punctual and able to follow the instructions they are given. As Andrea Nash (1993) points out, when such curricula or teacher guidebooks do take on employees' concerns, "employers expect class-generated solutions to lie within the bounds of acceptable company practices," putting indirect pressure on teachers to "avoid areas of conflict in favor of 'common goals'" (4). The concerns of *ESL for Action*, which include "The Deportation Scare," "Acting for Health and Safety," "Identifying Discrimination," and "Participating in the Union," are completely absent in the majority of commercially produced ESL curricula.

Like me, Auerbach and Wallerstein are different people than they were in 1987, and they might write *ESL for Action* differently today. The book, however, is representative of a still-current genre in progressive education. Its five-step problem-posing approach remains ubiquitous, used in innumerable Freirian curricula more recently produced around the country. Indeed, the problem-posing approach is so pervasive it has come to nearly define progressive pedagogy in adult education. I want to address that approach here and have chosen *ESL for Action* because it is among the best at uniting language skills with social action, and that's the part of Freirian pedagogy I need to hold on to. I want to look at how the curriculum reflects Freire's notions of the Other, a culture of silence, and false consciousness versus truth—and how we might expand it.

What follows is a typical "code" from *ESL for Action*:

Lesson 1: A Safe Workplace

Supervisor: What happened?

Alex: Mario burned his arm.

Supervisor: Again? You people have to work more carefully. You're not paying attention to your jobs.

Alex: It's the fumes. They make us dizzy.

Supervisor: That's no excuse. Mario was probably careless. There are too many accidents in this department.

Alex: It's not Mario's fault. We can't breathe in here. There's no air. (Auerbach and Wallerstein 1987b, 18)

Following the reading of this dialogue—or any dialogue, story, or picture that forms the base of each lesson—instructors lead students through a sequence of five questions, a strategy that provides the framework for *ESL for Action*. The questions ask the reader to describe what's going on in the code, identify the problem it represents, make a personal connection to it, situate the problem in a broader context, and strategize actions to take.

In the specific questions following the dialogue between Alex and the supervisor, the premise seems to be that people don't perceive the social causes of their problems—in this case, a policy of profits before health that leads to poor ventilation—and that once they do, they will collectively take action against them:

1. What happened to Mario? Is this his first accident? Who is Alex?

2. Has anyone else had an accident in this department? Why did Mario burn his arm? What does Alex think? What does his supervisor think? What problems do the workers have?

3. Have you ever had an accident at work? Why did it happen? Were you careless? Whose fault was it? What did you do? What did your employer do?

4. Do you think Mario was careless? Do you think the supervisor or the company was careless? Who was responsible? Do you think most accidents are caused by careless workers? Why? Do you think most accidents are caused by careless employers? Why?

5. What should the workers in this story do? What do they need to know to do this? What are the safety responsibilities of workers? What are the safety responsibilities of employers? (Auerbach and Wallerstein 1987a, 18)

What this premise ignores is the fact that people very often do perceive the social cause of their problems and don't take action for a whole host of reasons left unexamined by this approach. For example, the notion of subject positioning—that we sometimes internalize the role into which we're positioned—helps me see that Mario could well perceive that the lack of air conditioning is making him dizzy, yet still have self-doubts about his carelessness. Just as the participants at the Women's School could see that the Philadelphia schools they attended were racist, yet still blame themselves for failure. Just as I knew as an undergraduate alone with a professor in his office that he had put his hand on my knee in a suggestive way, yet wondered afterward if I had misinterpreted his meaning. Foucault's concept of power knowledge would suggest that in order to tackle Mario's self-doubts, we would need not to prove that he was careful, but to deconstruct the discourses we internalize that constitute as true that workers are not smart enough to be concerned about their own safety and take precautions.

Of course, it may not be self-doubt that has kept Mario from acting on his own knowledge. But the curriculum also pays too little attention to the material conditions that may keep Mario immobilized: fear of losing his job or a promotion, a belief that his White coworkers would fail to back him up, his location in a small shop where the prevailing ideology is that management and labor are "family." Auerbach and Wallerstein are themselves well aware of these conditions and mention them. But I think these issues need a greater emphasis in the curriculum than does the assumption that inaction stems primarily from a lack of critical thinking.

Auerbach and Wallerstein say in their introduction that "a five-step inductive questioning strategy gives students skills to identify common concerns, analyze causes of problems and strategize alternatives" (vi). If it were really so simple, why do we, as teachers who are assumed to use this strategy, live with our own contradictions? Like Freire and Shor, the authors of *ESL for Action* seem to imply that we don't. Our function is to ask questions and provide necessary background information, not to "impose [our] own answers and solutions to the questions" (Auerbach and Wallerstein 1987b, 6). If we really believe that students will come up with their own viable strategies—that we don't already have all the answers—why wouldn't we put our own solutions on the table to be considered with others?

Auerbach and Wallerstein's suggestion that the problem posed "should not be overwhelming, but should offer possibilities for group affirmation and small actions toward change" is another indication that they view the teacher as someone who poses questions to which she or he already has answers (Auerbach and Wallerstein 1987b, 4). And perhaps it's out of raising purposefully simplistic questions that a simplistic pedagogy emerges. What if the problems *are* overwhelming? What about the times when right and wrong are not so clear as they are in a typical example from *ESL for Action* in which workers develop skin rashes despite a company report that the environment is safe?

It's the influence of poststructuralism that leads me to suggest an addition to *ESL for Action*'s step four, which is meant to place the problem in its social context. The book's questions regarding the skin rash problem are:

Why do you think the report says there is no problem?

Who do you think is right—the workers or the health inspector? Who is the *expert* about health problems at work?

Who benefits from this report? (Auerbach and Wallerstein 1987b, 20)

To these we might add:

Why is the report so hard to fight?

How does what's viewed as "expert" come to be so?

To *ESL for Action*'s question of "Who benefits?" we might add:

How is this situation maintained?

How do we participate in its maintenance?

What is it that we've come to believe about ourselves that makes it so hard to fight for what we know to be right?

We can see the importance of this last question again in *ESL for Action*'s section on sexual harassment. Here readers are asked to check "agree" or "disagree" next to common attitudes, share their answers, and talk about what they would say to someone holding these views. The first reads, "Most women who are harassed ask for it by the way they dress, walk or act. It's their own fault; they deserve what they get" (Auerbach and Wallerstein 1987a, 143). What I wonder is how many of us would check "disagree," yet have some amount of self-doubt when we ourselves become the targets of harassment. Our consciousness can be raised, yet something still remains to be struggled with.

We need a paradigm that focuses not only on problems and solutions but on the discourses and classifications that maintain the problems and suppress the solutions. Among the issues included in *ESL for Action* are health and safety, hierarchy, and low pay. Again, the authors use the five-step questioning strategy to encourage students to "think critically" about their conditions. A focus broadened to address power knowledge and classifications suggests that we might view these issues from another angle, perhaps looking at what gets defined as important, or "skilled," work. We might then see that once something is classified as *unimportant*, it becomes possible to say that the people who do it aren't very bright—thus it's their fault they get injured; they need a hierarchical structure; they don't deserve higher pay. There's a regime of truth that keeps what Foucault calls "apparatuses of power" alive.

Snyder (1984) reminds us that "classifications structure our discourse and order our institutions . . . [They] determine the production and application of knowledge itself" (210). In an article intended for teachers of "advanced writing," referred to earlier in Chapter Two, she suggests a plan of inquiry that expands Auerbach and Wallerstein's and might be used to analyze the classification of phenomena such as "safe" chemicals. I adapt them here:

1. Identify the object of the classification, both overt and covert.
2. Identify what the classification excludes. Does it privilege or disadvantage any particular group of people, things, or ideas?
3. Who devised the classification?
4. When did the classification arise?
5. Where did the classification arise? (212–14)

The premise of *ESL for Action* is that "people don't have to accept the limits imposed by others on their lives" (Auerbach & Wallerstein 1987b, 11). This idea of human agency is what has always been so important to me in Freirian pedagogy. It's what has given me hope, and it still does. But I need additional tools to help us see why the struggle to shed the limits is as hard as it is. We need something more to show us how our lives have been created and sustained, so that we can re-create something very different.

Notes

1. I say this with hesitation, realizing the danger of admitting rigidity in the current climate in which seemingly everything that provides an alternative critique is dismissed as "political correctness"—a term whose use has become an effective strategy for cutting off debate.

2. Michelle Gibbs Russell's less widely read "Black-Eyed Blues Connection" (1983) also advised teachers to use everything:

> The size and design of the desks, for example. They are wooden, with one-sided, stationary writing arms attached. The embodiment of a poor school. Small, unyielding . . . Class members are prompted to recall the mental state such seats encouraged. They cite awkwardness, restlessness, and furtive embarrassment. When they took away our full-top desks with interior compartments, we remember how exposed we felt, unable to hide anything; not spitballs, notes, nor scarred knees, prominent between too short, hand-me-down dresses and scuffed shoes. They remember the belligerence which was all the protection we were allowed. (280)

3. Roger Simon's (1984) "Being Ethnic/Doing Ethnicity" was influential in raising these questions for me.

4. Henry Giroux does address the need to view colearning as learning about the self, not just the cultures and lives of the students:

> A radical theory of literacy and voice must remain attentive to Freire's claim that all critical educators are also learners. *This is not merely a matter of learning about what students might know*; it is more importantly a matter of learning how to renew a form of self-knowledge through an understanding of the community and culture that actively constitute the lives of one's students. (Freire & Macedo 1987, 22, emphasis mine)

But where is this increased *self*-knowledge in Freire's work or the work of Freirian educators?

5. In May of 1995, New Mexico became the first state to condemn Proposition 187–type measures, thanks to the organizing and lobbying efforts of such groups as the Albuquerque Border City Project.

6. "The educator needs to know that his or her 'here' and 'now' are nearly always the educands' 'there' and 'then.' Even though the educator's dream is not only to render his or her here-and-now accessible to educands, but to get beyond their own 'here-and-now' with them . . . she or he must begin with the educands' 'here,' and not with her or his own" (Freire 1996, 58).

7. And there may well be connections I didn't see. Hooks (1994) has said she felt herself "to be deeply identified with the marginalized peasants [Freire] speaks about, or with my black brothers and sisters, my comrades in Guinea-Bissau" (46).

8. Mira-Lisa Katz (2000) makes a good point when she says of the teachers using the curriculum, "We can't know, of course, how these chunks were taken up in classes and how they were discussed and dialogued—what sorts of conversations they inspired."

9. The question left unanswered is why Stanley's and McLaren's readings differ so much from mine. What is at stake for each of us in our readings? Janice Radway writes, "I must recognize that there are unconscious determinants of my thoughts, determinants I simply can't uncover myself. I have to rely on my collaborators, my interlocutors, to uncover them for me" (in Wallace 1992, 666). I welcome the opportunities for future dialogues, to which I hope the ideas here will lead.

10. In *Pedagogy of Hope*, Freire (1996) asserts, "I have never said that the class struggle, in the modern world, has been or is 'the mover of history.' . . . [It] is not *the* mover of history, but is certainly *one* of them" (90). But in the absence of further reexamination of his earlier claims, it is difficult to know what to make of this statement.

11. Mira-Lisa Katz (2000) adds, "People are anything but passive. If they appear passive, they probably have good reason, and it doesn't mean that they're not doing things on more invisible levels right under the nose of the dominant order."

12. Freire would seem to respond directly to Weiler's criticism in *A Dialogue with Paulo Freire* (1993), written with Macedo. In restating a criticism of his work to which he asks the latter to respond, Macedo says, "There exists a hierarchical structure of oppression that ranges from being a white middle-class woman to an underclass black woman who may also be a peasant" (173). Freire answers that "this position" does not "alter [his] analysis of oppression" (173). But this is not Weiler's position. She is arguing *against* such a hierarchy and *for* simultaneously multiple positions of power. Such an argument does, fundamentally, alter the analysis.

Jeanne Brady (1994) writes,

> A critical theory of literacy must come to understand how identities are constructed within multiple and often contradictory subject positions, how such identities shift, and how the struggle over identity takes place on many fronts, involving many different types of battle. As Peter McLaren notes, Freire's theory of literacy and identity formation must be extended and deepened by acknowledging how the specificities of different historical and social conditions configure to

produce, within a changing matrix of agency and determination, a range of diverse identities and subjectivities. (146)

What I don't see is how we can add this perspective on top of Freire's, when they seem to emerge from incongruent paradigms.

13. Schutte (1993) makes a similar point.

14. For other critiques of Freire's work, see Kathleen Rockhill (1988). Like Weiler and Chetwynd et al., she criticizes critical pedagogy's underlying assumption of unity and adds, "Along with the emphasis upon unity comes a penchant for orthodoxy and the assumed authority of the 'proper' political perspective. Thus, the work stagnates; it cannot handle critique" (114). See also Jay and Graff (1993), who ask, "How real can the Freirean dialogue be, when Freire clearly presumes he knows in advance what the authentic 'will of the people' is or should be?" (15). Blanca Facundo's critique "Freire-Inspired Programs in the United States and Puerto Rico" (1984) has recently been re-released as part of a Web site on suppression of dissent: *www.uow.edu.au/arts/ sts/bmartin/dissent/documents/Facundo.*

Bell hooks (1994) addresses critiques of Freire:

> In talking with academic feminists (usually white women) who feel they must either dismiss or devalue the work of Freire because of sexism, I see clearly how our different responses are shaped by the standpoint that we bring to the work. I came to Freire thirsty, dying of thirst (in that way that the colonized, marginalized subject who is still unsure of how to break the hold of the status quo, who longs for change, is needy, is thirsty), and I found in his work (and the work of Malcolm X, Fanon, etc.) a way to quench that thirst. To have work that promotes one's liberation is such a powerful gift that it does not matter if the gift is flawed. (48–50)

But the only flaw with which she deals is Freire's use of sexist language. It's not just hooks; there's a tendency to sum up critiques of Freire as "the feminist problem with his language," when there is something more with which to grapple.

15. Tate is arguing here from what has come to be called "standpoint theory," which is criticized by poststructuralists for essentializing categories such as African American women or White men. "Standpoint theories require one to believe a position that is highly contingent and constructed (e.g., race, gender, or feminist consciousness) results in or can be the basis of a not just different but objectively better, less biased, and more inclusive grasp of 'reality'". Of course, the "angles of vision" of African American women writers are no less biased than that of White men and are not singular. Yet it's clear that a particular African American woman is likely to come up with strategies and solutions inaccessible to many White men or women. Poststructuralism encourages this polyvocality. Freire assumes only some voices are correct and thus politically useful.

16. From a talk given at the Riverside Church, New York City, 7 February 1991.

17. The latter three questions are adapted from Edelsky (1991, 166).

18. The Frauenformen narratives are not autobiographies as we commonly think of them, but are rather about "'a stranger, a past 'remembered' self.'" (in Haraway 1991, 242)

19. Many thanks to Arleen Schenke for a conversation that helped me clarify these ideas.

20. A place to start may be to consider the suggestion of a friend who saw my father dedicating his books to us as perhaps reaching out in the only way he felt capable of, and to wonder if on any level I knew that.

21. Henriques et al. (1984) first raised these questions for me.

22. My hesitance to embrace what Orbach and Eichenbaum (1987) and Benjamin (1987) say comes from an inability to see such behavior as anything but inevitable within their framework. Feminists using psychoanalytic ideas would argue otherwise. Orbach and Eichenbaum believe that it is through a new relationship with a therapist that a woman is able to change, a relationship in which the desire for intimate connection, for having *her* needs satisfied, is met. In such a setting, they believe, a woman can achieve an intimacy that still allows her to experience herself as a separate self. In searching for a location of agency, Mahoney and Yngvesson (1992) point to

> the infant's struggle with issues of power in the unequal relation of parent and child [which] shapes her experience of desire and provides the ground for resistance and change both preverbally and after the entry into language. Parent-child relations are the earliest embodiment of power for the developing child, and it is in struggles at this site of power that the capacity for accommodation and resistance to other forms of culturally shaped inequality is produced. This recalls Michel Foucault's insight that all social relations are power relations and that power is not 'imposed from above' but is 'rooted in the social nexus.' (48)

For Flax (1984), it is "through 'good enough' social relations . . . [that] separateness and mutuality (interdependence) [can] exist simultaneously" (27). She further argues that "psychoanalysis encourages us to live with rather than foreclose contradictory impulses. It shows us the benefits of treating humorously the impossibility of many of our desires" (1993, 29). Nancy Chodorow, whose work provides the grounding for many feminist psychoanalysts such as Benjamin and Flax, argues it is through different child-rearing arrangements that the potential for change is possible. She emphasizes the need for an arrangement in which a father is present in the way a mother is, offering boys a way to develop a sense of what it means to be a man *within* a personal relationship. And when Constance Penley (1992) looks beyond the ideology of Adult Children of Alcoholics programs and other twelve-step models of behavioral change, "which seem to encourage religious and highly individualistic ways of thinking that lead to social and political disempowerment," to their actual uses by lesbians, gay men, and Star Trek fandoms, she finds they "address people's everyday pleasures, pains, and needs in ways a left or feminist discourse has not been able to do" (500).

Four

Teaching Writing

Rooted in slavefolk wisdom which says: "Don't say no more with your mouth than your back can stand," our vocalizing is directly linked to a willingness to meet hostilities head-on and persevere.
—Michelle Gibbs Russell,
Black-Eyed Blues Connection (1983, 277)

While I was working at the Women's School, I began to focus more on the teaching of writing, and my first thoughts were most influenced by those of African American women writers. They helped me see that the breadth by which we might consider our role as teachers of writing is wider—and the issues involved far more complex—than I had imagined when I first began teaching. It is still a hostile world within which many people speak and write. How do students' relationships to both language and White people influence what happens when White teachers encourage students of color to write in the authentic voice so often spoken about in the fields of literacy and composition? While in a poststructural view I share, the boundaries that stand between me and my students are constantly shifting, I still need to ask the question "Are there some that remain steadfast in this moment?"

I will look further at the idea of authentic voice. But first I want to say that it was the danger that comes with speaking truths, the strategies created by angles of vision different from mine, and the possibilities those truths and strategies have for shaping a new world that made me believe I needed to engage my students with writing and then get out of the way. I believed that if I could facilitate that involvement, people could then take risks as they chose in offering interpretations, changing or sharpening truths. I've since come to recognize that I never get entirely out of the way. What matters to me now is what that means in my classrooms, and it's an issue to which I will return at various points in this chapter.

Earlier I mentioned the concept of an interpretive community. Stanley Fish (1980) says a reader clues in to a context "because it [is] part of his repertoire for organizing the world and its events" (313). In Fish's interpretive community, people share a world of purposes, goals, and values and "any words spoken are heard as referring to the features of this world" (304). I used to wonder how we could respond to our students' words when, as is often the case because of race or class or gender, we inhabit different interpretive communities. I no longer see these communities as quite so fixed. But to the extent they do exist at any given moment, I find Lucy Lippard's (1992) articulation of her position as a White art critic reminds me of mine as a White teacher of writing. Her focus here is on Native American art:

> Landscape is not a passive "view" or "vista" and there is no word for "landscape" in Native languages. As Patricia Clark Smith and Paula Gunn Allen have written: "The land is not only landscape as Anglo writers often think of it—arrangements of butte and bosque, mountain and river valley, light and cloud shadow. For American Indians the land encompasses butterfly and ant, man and woman, adobe wall and gourd vine, trout beneath the river water, rattler deep in his winter den, the North Star and the constellation, the flock of sandhill cranes flying too high to be seen against the sun. The land is Spider Woman's creation; it is the whole cosmos. . . . "

> So what "look like" landscapes to a white audience may in fact be permeated with an attitude, a way of seeing that is in fact far removed from European pictorialization. Contemporary art theorists tend to regard such ideas with some mistrust as "romanticizing" and "essentializing." (18)

> Paula Gunn Allen insists that everyone look at American Indian art "from the point of view of its people." But that's easier said than done. To do so a white critic must know more than any of us know, as well as try to submerge her/his own culture and step into the hybrid state where many Native people already live. (20)

In living with all of this for a while, I have tried and am trying still to fashion a pedagogy within which sometimes dangerous words can be spoken and heard. This chapter will offer specific strategies with this end in mind, as it problematizes some taken-for-granted ideas about process writing. Inherent in any approach to teaching writing are contradictions and risks. My intent in this chapter is to make some of these complexities visible, as I document my own work on some of the issues I see.

Process Writing

The conventional wisdom . . . is that language is a means of communication. Of course it is, but in teaching the composing process what we chiefly need is a way of thinking about the sources of and the shaping of what we communicate.

—Ann E. Berthoff, *The Making of Meaning* (1981, 85)

The process writing movement is not a monolith, contrary to the prevailing ways of presenting it. Rather, it's a category into which many actually diverse theories and practices are placed. What almost all of these approaches share, however, is a focus on the concept of discovery. The concept of discovery suggests that it is *as* a writer writes that she finds what she has to say. The process writing movement often presents discovery as primarily an individual, cognitive activity that results in the expression of "authentic" voice. What Henry Louis Gates (1991a) has said of traditional ways of reading texts can also be said of process writing: "[There is an] assumption that the works [authors] create transparently convey the authentic unmediated experience of their identities" (26). For many process writing advocates, discovery means *self*-discovery, as though the meaning a writer finds comes from within the individual alone. Critics point out that we are often led to ignore the fact that the meaning we find is socially constructed. In reality, we don't discover a voice that's there, fully formed, waiting to be uncovered. We are multivoiced, and the voices are continuously changing with our shifting identities. As Gates says, "[It's] not that our social identities don't matter. They do matter. And our histories, individual and collective, do affect what we wish to write and what we are able to write. But that relation is never one of fixed determinism" (30). Mikhail Bakhtin shows us that every act of speech is a dialogue with at least one other voice, never self-sufficient. Language is always playing with the borders between one utterance and another. "Every word gives off the scent of a profession, a genre, a current, a party, a particular work, a particular man (*sic*), a generation, an era, a day, and an hour. Every word smells of the context and contexts in which it has lived its intense social life" (in Todorov 1984, 56). It's in this sense that freewriting is never free. Voices are always mediated, by where the writer sits as she writes, who she sits with, who she's writing for, and the very conventions of expression. It is these notions of multivoiced-ness and mediation that writing teachers need to take into account, as much as do educational researchers who rely on interviews to gather data and then label the respondent's words "true." An incident that took place in *United Youth of Boston* will help illustrate this point.

Boston is a city in which media portrayals of urban crime and violence in communities of color are ubiquitous. A headline in *United Youth*, created with the supervision of an adult workshop facilitator, read, "Inner-City Shadows." In the same issue is an illustration of a young guy in an eight-ball jacket holding a smoking gun. When I raised an objection to both images, the adult facilitator responded, "Talk to the teens. It's their headline; it's their illustration."

The thing is, it wasn't entirely theirs. The writings that were pro-duced in the sessions he and I each facilitate are very different. In the workshops I offered for the paper, young people wrote about colorism, interracial dating, White fear of Black youth, and advice from South-ern grandparents. These topics emerged as I jotted down notes while listening to conversations going on as the teens walked in the door or sat around the table waiting for others to arrive. But I know I key in to what I *want* to hear. And I also know that who I am encourages people to write some things and inhibits them from ever saying others. My stu-dents speak from a variety of subject positions, each created in a pro-cess of dialogue.

While I do admit to believing that the stereotypes conveyed in the headline and illustration are damaging, my point here is not to com-pare myself to the other facilitator. On the contrary, it is to suggest that there is something each of us was looking for, even if we couldn't state exactly what that was, and that this had an influence over what partic-ipants wrote. Of course, sometimes my influence is obvious, as in my choice of materials to use in a workshop or class. Following the first Rodney King verdict and protests, for example, I brought the following quote, to which I asked my community college class to react: "Protests are the language of the unheard." While students could react against the quote, there was also a possibility that those who hadn't thought of the idea before might respond positively. And certainly, I brought it in because I hoped they would.

The question is not whether the writings were reflective of the youth's beliefs or mine; they were created in a dialogue between the two.

I have wrestled with this idea. I worry that the revision strategies I teach students, discussed later in this chapter, are in fact based on an assumption of individual discovery. I have come to see, however, that what actually happens in my classrooms and workshops acknowl-edges that what writers discover for themselves is shaped by who they are in relationship to the rest of the world. In addition, I sometimes ask them to turn back to their own writings after hearing or reading others', to see if they want to make changes. Sometimes a writer's meaning changes; sometimes it just becomes more highly charged, and the author takes a stronger stance. After listening to the writings of people with relatives fighting in the Persian Gulf, one woman said she would make her own piece on the war "more explosive." Perhaps most important, the publication of community writings—often joining personal narratives together—places individual stories in a broader social context, giving them a political impact.

There is a tradition that holds that "basic writers" seldom concern themselves with their readers and a way to express their ideas to others, missing the synthesis between working out one's ideas and beliefs and finding a way to express them, because they are too egocentric to see the social implications of writing. I would argue that rather than egocentricism, what stands in the way of students' perception of the social implications of their writing is that the social implications are often meaningless to them. At best, they are contrived. The content about which the students write and the context in which they write are often equally irrelevant to them. I once heard someone suggest that it is the teacher or theorist who is truly egocentric in failing to perceive the student's alienation from a discourse community when she writes. Student-generated topics and student-posed questions on those themes (suggestions for which are found in Chapter Six), a collaborative community, and the publication of student pieces are critical components of a pedagogy which is ever to convince a student of the possibilities composing can offer.

Giving Voice or Hearing It?

On July 11, when five hundred Sûreté du Québec launched an attack on a Mohawk barricade on the First Nation of Kahnesatake, a seventy-eight day armed stand-off developed between Mohawk warriors and the Sûreté du Québec and the Canadian army. Across the country aboriginal people reacted and the local populations heard it. There was an aboriginal presence, but it was not voice. The depiction of the Oka crisis relied on the political slant of the various journalists and media outlets that recorded, interpreted, and relayed the events. The aboriginal voice was heard shouting threats of violence because it made good "info-tainment." Eloquent calls for peace and reason went unrecorded . . . The aboriginal voice is out there, it just isn't getting heard.

—Jordan Wheeler, "Voice" (1992, 37)

An attempt to rectify students' "lack of voice" often underlies progressive efforts to teach writing. Others argue that the voices are already speaking, and the fault lies with those who can't hear them. Lisa Delpit (1988) suggests that White middle-class educators fixate on developing fluency in the writings of students of color because we don't hear the fluency that already exists. I believe she's right and look to Michelle Wallace (1992) to take this idea a step further. Wallace thinks that the very notion of lack of voice is socially constructed and rests not on the numbers of people speaking from marginalized communities or even on the faulty listening of those who might hear, but rather on the prevailing assumptions about what counts as knowledge. As such, it is deconstruction that makes room for seriously considering other voices.

The Product in the Process

The shift in paradigm from product to process has been so successful in the field of writing pedagogy that product seems to have become virtually ignored. I've learned a tremendous amount from the writers and writing teachers whose work is listed in the "References" section at the end of this book, and much of what I offer here is either an adaptation of their work or was stimulated by it. But I want to emphasize that while process is key, *what* we make it possible for people to say is equally important. I begin the first day of class by asking people to think about what writing is, as well as what they might write about.

> There are memories stored away in our heads we never suspected were materials for literature. These stories made me call up some almost forgotten fragments from my own black and female past: memories of women who "did hair" in their basements, girls holding their ears so the hot comb wouldn't burn them; women in their forties and fifties who had "boyfriends"; dayworkers waiting for the Rapid Transit in Shaker Heights . . . carrying their uniforms in paper bags; churchwomen who kept the South alive in the middle of an urban ghetto, growing roses, canning peaches, baking biscuits, singing in churches on Sunday in crisp white nurse's outfits; women preachers who had their own storefront churches . . .
>
> We didn't suspect then that these experiences, these memories, were important enough to write books about, and yet these were our lives, the black women unspoken truths, kept silent in our hearts and minds.
>
> —Mary Helen Washington, *Midnight Birds* (1980, xxii)

We are important and our lives are important, magnificent really, and their details are worthy to be recorded. This is how writers must think, this is how we must sit down with pen in hand . . . Our details are important. Otherwise, if they are not, we can drop a bomb and it doesn't matter.

. . . In Washington, D.C., there is the Vietnam memorial. There are fifty thousand names listed—middle names, too—of American soldiers killed in Vietnam. Real human beings with names were killed and their breaths moved out of this world. There was the name of Donald

Miller, my second-grade friend who drew tanks, soldiers, and ships in the margins of all his math papers. Seeing names makes us remember. A name is what we carry all our life, and we respond to its call in a classroom, to its pronunciation at a graduation, or to our name whispered in the night.

It is important to say the names of who we are, the names of the places we have lived, and to write the details of our lives. "I lived on Coal Street in Albuquerque next to a garage and carried paper bags of groceries down Lead Avenue. One person had planted beets early that spring, and I watched their red/green leaves grow."

. . . This is what it is to be a writer, to be the carriers of details that make up history . . . Recording the details of our lives is a stance against bombs with their mass ability to kill.

—Natalie Goldberg, *Writing Down the Bones* (1986, 43)

Just prior to introducing writing in a class, I've sometimes read aloud or passed out one of these quotes. Other times I share the words of Meridel Le Sueur (1982), who taught working people to write their own stories during the Depression:

Who knows the fires, emotions, love, the deep glow and courage of our people? The rich spiced talk of men at night riding over the dark prairie to look for a job, the talk of steelworkers and of women knitting socks for another war? More and more we need words to write the true history of the past so that we may create a true history in the future . . . It is up to you to make this new literature, to use this tool that is in your hands. (2)

What Is Writing?

What is writing? That's the first question I ask when I teach writing, and the answers, from students as well as the teachers whom I've asked in workshops, reveal the pain writing has brought to some, the pleasures it has brought others, and some misconceptions:[1]

getting what's on your mind on paper	spelling
communication	poetry
expressing your thoughts	art
grammar	editing
a nightmare	a message
an outlet	a list
preserving history	sweating bullets
a reminder	imagination
love letters	bringing out what's in you

entertainment for someone else   reenactment of
                                                       a slap

a way to see your own changes (a diary)

Almost always students leave something off the list that I then point out—a reason to write mentioned most often by writers themselves. Once discovered, it often becomes the most exhilarating reason for students, as well: writing as a tool to create something, not merely to record what we already carry fully formed in our heads.

In class I talk about how ideas don't just move from mind to page, but from mind to page and back, new ideas being perceived as they're written. A new thought comes more clearly into view, familiar ones take unexpected turns, connections develop between experiences or notions we never connected before. Often we start out to write one thing, and something else entirely ends up on the page. One student remembered her mother shooing the children inside the house when the Ku Klux Klan had its regular marches down the middle of the main street. She found herself writing that she never saw her mother get nervous or seem afraid in front of her, and she wondered for the first time what her mother was really feeling.

Donald Murray (1985) has called composing a "constant revolt against intent," and I often mention his phrase. In writing about a past experience, for example, we don't simply document it, but very often learn something new about it that we didn't know we knew before. When I once heard bell hooks say, "Storytelling makes us live our lives more consciously," I read her as saying that we live them differently.[2]

Given all of this, it becomes possible to think of a first draft as a loosening up, a chance to see what's on our mind. Explaining this in a class or workshop, I put one or more of the following quotes on the board:

Everyone has something to say. Writing can point you to it.
                              —Member of the Jefferson Park Writing Group[3]

I write entirely to find out what I'm thinking, what I'm looking at, what I see, and what it means.
                              —Joan Didion, "Why I Write" (1980, 20)

Inside this pencil
crouch words that have never been written
never been spoken
never been thought . . .
                              —W. S. Merwin

Poetry is the way we help give name to the nameless so it can be
thought . . . As they become known to and accepted by us, our feelings and the honest exploration of them become sanctuaries and
spawning grounds for the most radical and daring of ideas.

—Audre Lorde, *Sister Outsider* (1984, 37)

when my imagination takes me by the mind
it leads me off so far, so fast
my body is left behind
yet that's why I'm most myself,
lost on a wish and a dream
and coming back
I smile
I think
we are more than we might know

—Vondee Ifill, untitled (1987, 20)

In an essay in the *National Writing Project Newsletter* (Wolfe 1986), a
writing teacher describes a student who has come to love writing as a
result of their work together. Doreen is creating a novel and though she
has previously written narratives, or "memory pieces" of her own life,
her novel "happens outside [her] experiences . . . a story of the rich and
privileged—people who own private planes and huge engagement
rings" (2). The teacher writes that *My First Novel* is "Doreen's deliberate
departure from her own life story, the result of her desire to write what
she doesn't know, to try unfamiliar territory. 'Write about a man who
does the deed and leaves the woman to have her baby on her own? I
know how to do that. This is just what Danny's family did to me. I want
to try something else.' She knows how her memory pieces will end as
she writes them. But this—a novel—provides her with the wonder of
watching something take on a life of its own" (2).

If we take seriously the notion of discovery and writers' ability to
resee our own experiences through writing, narratives can become
more than memory pieces. They become opportunities to "try unfamiliar territory," to deconstruct those very memories, as the members
of Frigga Haug's German writing collective, mentioned in the previous
chapter, are attempting to do. Writers never know the endings of such
pieces at the outset. I'm not suggesting Doreen can't write a fantasy life
if she wants to. In fact, fantasy lives can lead us to new ways of viewing our own. But I am suggesting that what we call memory pieces can
be thought of as much more.

After suggesting a notion of writing as discovery in my class, I propose a process I use most often when I begin a first draft. I want to take
care to point out here that writing is, of course, incredibly idiosyncratic.
Once people get going, they ease into their own ways of interweaving

each task, and this may vary from project to project, paragraph to paragraph. It is not as linear a process as it appears in description. In fact, it is inevitably recursive and often something beyond recursive, in which it seems that the writer engages in some tasks simultaneously. But to get students going, I suggest that the initial key to a first draft is to produce words without judging them at the same time, since it's in large part the constant evaluation of what we're saying as we're saying it that immobilizes my students and me from getting past a few sentences, if we can even start. Right here we can see the role of content in process, because it's only in beginning from content that's *compelling* that I find people letting themselves suspend judgment and write.

I talk about how stopping to look up a word in the dictionary or even asking someone else how to spell it interrupts the process of finding out what's on your mind. I suggest they instead try drawing a line in place of the word, knowing that they can go to the dictionary or ask someone for the spelling later. I explain that they can use a line to signify a word they can't spell, or they can put the first letter of the word before the line if they don't want to stop to guess at a spelling, (for example, b_____ for beautiful). Before they try it, people often think they'll forget the words they skipped when they've finished the draft. Yet even writers with a line in every sentence have been able to remember each word.

I write "Revision" on the board and ask people to identify the root word and then the entire meaning, using the prefix, defining revision as the point at which you step back and resee your own ideas. In doing so, maybe you realize that what you really want to say comes out only at the very end of the first draft or isn't on the page at all but pops into your mind when you finish reading what is there. Adding, crossing out, rearranging, and starting over all become possibilities for a next move. It becomes clear that revision is really the heart of composing, allowing us to resee thoughts sometimes only barely perceived before we put pen to paper. Those students who believed good writing comes out fully formed when a writer first sits down have told me it's this idea of revision that, though seeming crazy in the beginning, turned out to be the most freeing.

I know that grammar, punctuation, and, above all, spelling are still many students' primary concerns. I reassure them that we will turn serious attention to these, but I suggest they view them as ways to further shape and mold what they have to *say*. I explain, for example, that since that is punctuation's sole purpose in life, the words to mold—the words they care about enough to *want* to mold—need to be on the page first. Over and over I've seen people internalize the uses of punctuation so much more easily when it becomes a tool to give final shape to ideas they are trying to convey, rather than when they're trying to learn it from a worksheet. I use the word *editing* to describe grammar, punctuation, and spelling and suggest we will return to each later. However, once students get going, none of these parts of the process need be done in any inherent order, and in fact they are often intertwined as meaning influences grammer, for example, and grammer influences meaning. (For more on this, see the section on editing later in this chapter.)

From the teacher's perspective, too, it makes most sense to look at grammar, punctuation, and spelling only after several revisions. So often, some of the mistakes made in a first draft disappear in later ones. It's important to initially read past the mistakes, to what the piece is saying.

I know many teachers who prefer to begin teaching writing by asking students to write, not by talking about writing. But I believe knowing ahead of time that what they write isn't frozen on the page, that the mechanics skills they seek will come from an involvement with words, and that lives such as our own are the basis for literature has helped people in my classes pick up the pen the first day and let it move.

Strategies for Getting Writing Started

Key Words and Phrases and a Guided Imagery

Like many teachers, I'll often begin a semester with a discussion of education itself. I might ask if anyone found it hard to walk through the door that morning—almost everyone has—and what it was that made it so hard. Answers range from having to first get children out the door with your sanity intact, to getting yourself to face a school situation again, to overcoming a husband's objections. I might ask what people remember about the last time they were in school, whether they had to stop in second grade or finished high school. Sometimes just asking the question is enough to start people talking. Other times I've used a form of guided imagery to get the conversation going. Guided imageries are usually used to help people take on someone else's skin. I've seen them used in social service agencies to help workers develop empathy with clients, imagining their own response to a rape or an act of child sexual abuse. The facilitator creates a history and a scene and places people in the middle of it. I've adapted it for classroom use. I ask the students to close their eyes—not everyone will, and that's okay—and imagine themselves in school. Maybe they're in a classroom, the cafeteria, or a courtyard. Maybe they're seven, maybe fourteen. What does the place look like—the buildings and the landscape? What else do they see? Who comes into the picture? Is anyone talking? If so, what's being said? What do they hear? What do they smell? I've found it's important to ask these questions slowly, giving people plenty of time to think.

I used this technique in *Neighbors Talk,* where people came together to write about their neighborhoods. The guided imagery often went something like this:

> You're at home. It's August, and it's hot—so hot that you can't imagine using the stove, or the dryers at the laundromat, or hardly moving at all. Hoping to catch some air, you put your fan outside on the stoop or porch or sidewalk or fire escape. Get a picture of yourself. It's 7:00 in the evening.
>
> What do you see? Are there other houses or apartment buildings? What do they look like?
> Are there other buildings?
> Are there trees? What does the landscape look like?
> Who do you see? Adults? Children? Who is near your home?
> Do you hear these people talking? If you do, what are they saying? If you can't hear them, what do you imagine they're saying?
> What are the other sounds at 7:00 in the evening?
> What are the smells?

Sometimes I ask people to open their eyes and immediately write and other times I ask for verbal responses. During the discussion that follows in the latter case, I sit next to the board, listen, participate myself, and lean back to write what I hear as key words or phrases, whatever seems to have something more behind it—anger, bitterness, humor, fear, resolve, joy. After everyone has spoken and whenever it seems right, I ask that each person take a word or phrase on the board that is his or hers and write the story behind it, keeping the pen moving and letting words come out. I also tell them if something else pops into their heads, they can always write about that instead. Nancie Atwell (1987) writes, "I always feared I'd encounter the beast that lurked: The Class with No Ideas for Writing. It never happened . . . all my eighth graders wrote every first day" (76). I also get nervous each first day, yet like Atwell's students, people have always written.

Eliciting key phrases does not depend on using a guided imagery. During a four-day teachers institute I facilitated, I asked the group members to participate in another writing activity using key phrases. I wanted to do something unifying at that moment—something that could be lighthearted at times and serious at others—and asked everyone to remember her or his first job as I jotted notes on the board. The conversation and the writing took us away temporarily from the Gulf War, news of which we'd listened to during lunch and discussion of which we'd been having for days, away from the intensity of the self-critique we'd engaged in, and it helped us reveal other sides of ourselves to each other. I pointed out that it wasn't important to precisely remember experiences that were as many as forty years old; recollecting them meant reinventing them as well. As Stuart Hall points out,

"The past is not waiting for us back there to recoup our identities against. It is always retold, rediscovered, reinvented . . . We go to our own pasts through history, through memory, through desire, not as a literal fact" (In Sanchez-Tranquilino and Tagg 1992, 564).

Among the phrases were:[4]

gefilte fish	watermelons
wigs	home by home
I went down on the ships	Mrs. Milby
I took an oath	4:00 A.M.
a *lot* of money	Ma Bell
I just wrote checks	

I believe two things happen in the process I just described. I realize as I write this that I'm only guessing. Sometime, I want to ask students what makes them able to pick up the pen and write, so I and they really know. But one thing I think happens is that people who claim they have nothing to say do say something. Also, I and other people in class have *responded* to it, by writing it on the board and discussing it.

Often I walk into a class, hear something that sounds like it has a story behind it, and want to turn to writing. These are also good times to use key phrases. For example, a conversation at the Women's School about why so many students had been absent the week before turned into writing about the health, housing, and welfare systems that had tied students up in endless appointments and waiting lines. Another time, during a discussion about our fears regarding AIDS, I asked everyone to whip out a piece of paper and just write whatever was on her mind at the moment. Not only did these writings help us move our discussion beyond what scared us, they later became important to our neighborhood AIDS pamphlet (see Chapter Six).

The second day of a workshop for family literacy teachers in Williamsburg, Kentucky, I walked in ready to facilitate a critique of traditional parenting materials written for adult literacy students. But as I was organizing the materials for display, I overheard first one and then another and then another of the women talking about a man in her family, or in the life of someone she knew, moving south to find work. I joined the conversation and asked if a lot of men were leaving. As I talked and listened, I wrote the following on the board and then asked for the stories that lay behind their words and phrases:[5]

strangling to death	druthers
potatoes in the ground	50 mines
"Them people stink."	wild greens

"This isn't a depression."	lost our car
I don't know where we're going to run to next	shanties
soup bean pie	belt line
bean salmon patties	work gangs
$21 to get through the month	cabbage in the hole
bean hamburgers	

I used a variation on the key phrase idea during a *Neighbors Talk* workshop. While talking about Roxbury and its changes with a group of women from the Freedom House Goldennaires, Mrs. Atkins got up and performed a cheer for us, one she and her girlfriends used to chant:

> Roxbury, Roxbury, who are we?
> We are the girls of Roxbury.
> Are we in it?
> You *bet* we are!
> Roxbury, Roxbury, Rah, Rah, Rah.

When we turned to writing, I suggested Mrs. Atkins put the cheer down on paper and see what happened next. This is what she wrote:

> We used to sing that on our way to school. That was more than sixty years ago. I grew up in "Lower Roxbury" (as it's called today). And Upper Roxbury was called "Sugar Hill" because of all the beautiful homes.
>   We were one of the first groups of "Blacks" to move up. The street was called Elbert Street and it led up to Franklin Park at the top of the hill.
>   I have been living on my street now for about thirty years, but I am not planning on moving or selling. This is my home. My kids want me to come live with them, but no. I'm staying. I'm a girl of Roxbury.
>   "Are we in it? You *bet* we are. Roxbury, Roxbury, Rah, Rah, Rah!" and we would hold hands and make a chain and sing along.
>
> —Mrs. Catherine Atkins, *Neighbors Talk* (Martin 1993, 7)

Obviously, in order for key phrases to generate writing, everyone needs to speak. I've never been in a group in which someone has insisted on remaining silent. I have been in groups in which the things someone says don't seem to reveal a story. But the person who asserts, "I've never had problems at work," will say later in the discussion, "Well, now that you mention bosses . . . !"

There have been times when I've looked around the room and found someone who wasn't writing. If someone says she can't get started, I ask which is the strongest image on the board for her. Recently, someone said, "I want to say Puerto Rican music, but I don't know why." I put "I hear Puerto Rican music on my street" on the top of her page and asked her to keep writing, and she did. I've done this at other times, and the writer's pen always moves.

Below are further examples of key phrases:

School Memories

When it rained, they would look for us.
The boys would do me over.
Everybody be watching you breathe.
Mr. Givens liked the light-skinned girls.
I wanted to have what they had.
You have to fight back.
"Colored children only need home economics."[6]

Memories of Work

You'd do it all, or there would be someone else waiting to take your
 job.
I always take a cab when I'm quitting.
They take it out of you.
2,000 zippers a day.
I used to press while I was asleep.
Stayed full of chill.
piecework.
"Want a drink, boy?"
They rented me out.
I *scrubbed* them steps.
I don't like to serve nobody.
You can't swear at the public.
We were living middle-class.
I should've stayed on the slow side.
If you think you're equal, get into some trouble.
I did a lot of crazy work.
The people didn't want you to touch them.[7]

Memories of the South

They tell you up-front down South. They're sneaky up here.
Devilish preacher would eat up everything at Sunday dinner.
They teach us some of their ways from down South.
Down South, you ate in the kitchen; you went in the *back* door.
My grandfather worked on somebody else's farm all his life.
Everyone has a MaDear in their life.[8]

Teenage Sex

"I wanna knock your boots."
They'll be dissin' after I say no.

Disease is nowhere in their mind.
"Are you light-skinned?"
I'm Black, hey!
You won't admit that.
"I could hit that."[9]

The Neighborhood

Good living.
"Do you want to sell?"
"This ain't your street."
Sugar Hill.
White people want it back.
You have to have your place.
I don't want my sons to be cops anymore.
I hang with White guys.
Lead paint.
I hear Patwa.
"Yo, Man, do your job!"[10]

Welfare

$30.24 to the penny.
I thought I was different.
No headstone.
Monitored.
I'm home, but I'm working!
I worked double through my pregnancy.
I do my wash in the bathtub.
The system says, "Work!"[11]

The following are some of the writings that were generated from key phrases.

The System Says, "Work!"

The system says, work, you can't stay at home and collect. You're able to get out there and work. You get a job and you can pay your rent, have plenty of food on the table, and have everything you want—if you just get a job and work. No, you'll never get ahead on the system—welfare, G.R., S.S.I., whatever . . . you need a job.

Since that's the way to get what I need and much more, I'll get a job and I'll work. I'll work as much as I can so I can have things.

Great, Parking Officer (metermaid) city job. $417 start, $432 end. Benefits, union, everyone knows I work now. I see my friends, I even see some of the workers, (social, housing) "Great, Florence," everyone says.

"Time changed, you doing so good!" I think to myself, if I am, I sure don't feel so good. Yesterday I went to the Section 8 office and I took them a pay stub. OK. My worker told me you'll now pay $314 per month for rent. I used to pay $80 per month. What am I to say besides OK? Now it's time to let the welfare go. I've been working for 2½, almost 3 months.

So welfare stops—Medicare, food stamps. So I make $417 a week and I pay for food, rent and dental and eye care. Because city has no coverage. My son's teeth are not the best. They're not the worst either. But they need care.

I pay all the bills, I get all the food, etc. I have less than enough money to get the bus to work the next week. I don't have any more than I had when I was on the system. But I was told that you get a job, and you get all these things. I'm not trying to have everything, but I feel like on welfare I got something out of not worrying about how much more I'm gonna have to pay the next time, and if I'll have enough.

—Florence Taylor, *Survival News* (1992, 20)

I was Afraid She Might Call DSS on Me

I do my wash in the bathtub most weeks. My hands hurt from the water being too hot or cold and the soap sometimes gives me a rash. The clothes take a long time to dry because I can't seem to wring them tight enough. The house looks like a sight with them hanging all over the place. There's always more to do. They never get clean enough for my liking. But worst of all is the embarrassment of having a teacher pull me aside on teacher/parent day and tell me she was concerned about my son wearing dirty undershirts and things to school. She felt some of them were "play clothes." When she told me this my knees went weak. I wished my face didn't turn red so easy. I could not hide my embarrassment, feeling like a piece of shit for her to feel it necessary to check up on my apparent neglect. She pointed out to me that her understanding of my son was that it was *very* important that he have friends and be accepted. And that his clothes were causing him problems.

I sat there like the idiot or loser she must have thought I was. I could not find the pride in myself to tell her that in fact I did wash his undershirts but did not use bleach as the clothes were mostly third generation hand me downs, and bar soap didn't always get the stains out, and I had sore hands from arthritis so squeezing the dirt out of their things wasn't always successful. I felt like anything I said was just an excuse for not doing what was only right for my son. Deep inside me I feel this is true. I sometimes choose between bus fare or laundry, food or laundry, sanitary products, toilet paper, toothpaste, deodorant or paying to do the laundry in a washer with real laundry soap, somehow getting it the three blocks to the laundromat. I was afraid she might call D.S.S. on me, and that even if I told them the truth, they would say, "You're neglecting your children's needs."

—Laura Walker, *Survival News* (1992, 17)

"She Sent the First Check!"

A lot of people in Central America made a big sacrifice to come to the U.S. Sometimes they had to borrow money to arrange the papers, another time to buy their ticket. All this with the promise that when you earn your first paycheck here, you will send it for the people who lend you the money. The people in our countries believe that when you come here you start to get the dollars easy. They don't know that many of the times, you have to suffer first before you get a job. And what kind of job, no? Cleaning, washing dishes, picking up garbage— left over work.

When some of us come here with "good luck" and after one or two months you can send the first check, this is a big thing in the neighborhood where you live in your country. They think you are rich now, probably because you send $50 or $100, that means a lot of money in my country. And if you do this every month, then you are going to receive a letter from another family member—your sister or brother, your grandmother, your father, sometimes an aunt or cousin. Everybody got a problem and they ask you for money. Even though they are not here, the people back home have their "American dream," too. My husband is going next week to Honduras to see if we can get visas for our kids. My sister wants him to bring her a typewriter; my mother wants some satin for a dress to wear in a wedding.

You are in the U.S.A., so that means so much. You can hear comments like how "so-and-so's mother lives" or how her children are, how they have their mother in the U.S.A. and how they are dressing.

But the sad thing is when the American dream is not a reality, like when you can't get a job because you are illegal or because you can't speak the language. Then some of these people start to do things less pleasant to forget the hard things of life, and to forget the people at home who need the money.

—Leslie Garo, *Survival News* (1992, 18)

"Do You Speak English?"

When people ask, "Do you speak English?," sometimes you know inside their minds they think you are stupid. The problem is you are not stupid, you are just a person who is starting to know where they are, where they are living.

Sometimes the economic, political situation is hard in your country, and that situation forces you to find some possibilities to help your family. You don't worry about speaking English, you worry about getting money to send your family at home. And always you think someday when I can get some money, maybe I can go back home. But in reality, you never go back, and the time is gone.

You don't speak English, and for that reason you can't explain, "I'm not stupid, I only don't know English."

—Angeles Merlín, *Neighbors Talk* (Martin 1993, 89)

My Ideas on Being a Cop

I was once a mother who wanted her sons to be cops. I thought it was a noble field to be in. I saw them as a force to help the neighborhood, find lost children.

Today, they are somebody that I fear. Not only for me but for my children, too. I do not want my sons to be cops anymore.

—Zelletta Mae Hunt, *Neighbors Talk* (Martin 1993, 26)

I acknowledge that I am not merely a conduit in writing down key words and phrases. Obviously, I play a role in choosing and shaping what gets said and explored. I need to begin asking other people in class to take on the role of listening and writing on the board what they hear as key. But where I used to think that this would elicit more authentic stories, based on an assumption that the students share an interpretive community, I see now that whoever does the choosing, the act is one of mediating what gets written. I realize that I could have asked students to take a turn at the board by now, especially in the *Survival News* group, where we all worked together over a relatively long period of time. And I'm forced to admit it may be because I've *wanted* to shape the writings that I haven't gotten myself to do it. During a discussion at the Women's School about why there is no cure for AIDS, I wrote on the board:

Not enough money.

Government wasn't concerned about it.

Let the Blacks get killed, let the gays get killed.

Black people won't be able to afford it.[12]

These were the women's own words, taken directly from the discussion. I asked everyone to relook at her own first draft in light of these thoughts. I'd successfully used key phrases as a way to revise in the past. But rather than the usual sustained writing, this time there was very little writing and a lot of unrelated conversation. Patricia said she'd write it at home, something totally new for her. Adela said she could only write what *she* felt. I wondered if they hadn't revised because they thought of the points on the board as mine, not theirs, or if this analysis was something they weren't yet ready to commit themselves to. There have been other times when I've written student's words on the board and they've ignored them and written about something else entirely. I always offer this as an option; often new ideas do pop into one's head. But I've wondered if people sometimes do that to avoid something too painful or too daring. It can take a while to feel ready to commit yourself to exploring something on paper or to feel enough trust to do so in a classroom.

The discussion at the Women's School came at a point when I didn't feel confident enough yet to ask what was going on. But the ideas did come up again in later discussions, and they did end up in writings. It's my hunch that they needed to sit awhile.

From Pictures to Titles to Writing

Another way to tap into a perspective or experience that gets writing started is to hand out a picture and ask people to call out titles they'd give the story that might go with it. To keep people on track if they start talking about the picture, ask them to turn those thoughts into titles. Title writing can sometimes help you cut to the core of what you're seeing.

Often, just when I've been about to stop because we've come to a lengthy silence, a slew of new ideas comes out. So I've learned to allow plenty of time for this activity. Once again, after writing these titles on the board (often several emerge from each person), I ask people to choose one and write the story that lies behind it. When the picture has come from a text, I often go on to ask people to compare their own stories to the originals, using writing as a way into reading.

The following titles were created by a class in Philadelphia in response to an illustration of two young African American women that accompanies the short story "Sisters," by BarbaraNeely (1986). One wears a business suit and carries a briefcase; the other is dressed in a cleaning uniform and holds a mop. Each is standing in a bucket of cement.

Uppity

Sisters

Two Different Worlds

You've Come a Long Way, Baby

Your Mama Was a Black Woman, Too

A Pedestal

Sometimes You Don't See the Cement[13]

The following titles came from a group of teachers in Virginia. From *Hillbilly Women*, by Kathy Kahn (1973), the photograph is of a woman in a workplace, sitting at a sewing machine and looking into the camera.

Trapped

The Electric's Off Again

I Quit

Ain't I a Woman?

Maybe I *Will* Join the Union

Go Ahead, Take My Picture

My Contribution

If I Knew Then What I Know Now

Only Until My Children Are Gone (or We Hit the Lottery)[14]

Adult literacy textbooks often present pictures, with questions underneath them to stimulate writing: "Who is this person?" "What is his name?" "Where is he from?" "Who is in her family?" Asking for titles seems a harder question, and it's often met initially with silence. But I interpret the silence as thought, and I think this question opens up more worlds of possibility.

Writing Reactions

By calling for search on sight, by abdicating control of neighborhoods to the police, supporters are painting a degraded image of themselves. They are arguing that African Americans live in a barbaric state . . . Citizens who beg for search on sight do so at their own risk. Many studies show that drugs and crime do not decrease from massive police presence alone. They decrease when citizens organize and police work with them . . . African Americans do not need any more policies that assume guilt before innocence.

—Derrick Z. Jackson, *Boston Globe*

Right now, the police have to do what they have to do. Unfortunately, there are good kids who are stopped and searched. But I've heard people say: "In these times, I don't mind. My child being searched and having nothing is better than me seeing him in a coffin . . . " Instead of yelling about the constitutional rights of the kids, we have to explain to them that times are hard right now.

—Georgette Watson, founder of Drop-a-Dime

Many African American youth have been stopped and searched by police in Boston neighborhoods. Some have been stripped before they are searched—on the sidewalk, in plain view of anyone passing by. Some youth and parents have fought back with publicity and lawsuits. I brought the two quotes above to a writing workshop of African American teenagers in a Boston public housing development and used a technique that helps people respond to a text and sometimes develop a writing out of that response. I asked each participant to jot down three reactions he had to the first quote, one on each of three small note cards. I explained that their reactions could be whole sentences but didn't need to be; just a few words would do. When I first began using this technique, I often got summaries in response. Now I explain that a reaction is something the reading makes you think—an agreement you have with it, a disagreement, a confusion about it, a memory that it provokes. Three-by-five-inch cards are good because their size makes them less ominous than an entire blank page and bolsters the idea that these are just to be quick reactions. I did the same with the second quote. The participants then had six cards each in front of them. I asked them to choose the two strongest reactions and put those on top. Then I asked them to look at their other reactions to see if they fit with the two strongest in some way or were really very different and could be set apart. If they fit, I asked them to order the reactions in importance. Then with either the one or two strongest reactions or the several that fit together, I suggest that they have the beginning of an idea to write about or ideas for a revision of an existing piece and propose they begin.

The reactions don't always come easily. I used this technique with a group of Native American youth in a nine-week workshop in Boston. It was my fourth meeting with them. Up until then, the majority of the writings had, in one way or another, compared Boston to home, the Micmac reservation in Canada. "If you hear a siren at home," one woman wrote, "you run toward it to see if you can help. Here it's either background noise, or if you do notice it, you stay away out of fear." At the same time, there had been no explicit reference made to their identity as Native people. Their writings were to be submitted to *Neighbors Talk*. They would likely be the only Native Americans in the book, a book about a city in which Native people are virtually invisible to non Natives. I suggested that the book could make their community more visible. Since so much of the writing so far had been about relocation, I put the following on the board and asked for reactions:

> There is no word for relocation in the Navajo language. To relocate is to disappear and never be heard from again.
>
> —Pauline Whitesinger, Navajo elder[15]

I read the note cards:

I don't get it.

I never heard of them.

Don't know nothing about Navajo language, or never heard anything about it. So I can't say too much about it.

To tell you the truth this is the first time I ever heard of this kind of Indian, Navajo, and you learn something new every day.

I don't know even where their location is, from all I heard is they're from the West.[16]

Feeling very stupid, I had to quickly figure out a next step. I remembered that with many activities, if I take a deep breath and just keep it going, it often moves into something useful. Out of my own ignorance, it had not occurred to me that they'd be unfamiliar with Indians from the Southwestern United States, and I told them this. "So not having heard of the Navajo reservation before, what reactions do you have when you look at her words again?" Then followed one of those seemingly interminable silences when I make myself wait for pens to move or someone to speak. Slowly they started to jot reactions. Most were about language. Some agreed with the quote. Others wrote:

> That's what we're here for, to keep our culture going.
>
> There is a location for us, and we still have our own language.
>
> As long as you take your language with you, you don't disappear, you still have a home.[17]

The group expanded many of these reactions into writings that were published in *Neighbors Talk.*

Keeping a Journal

Once people have had the experience of writing and seeing sentences or paragraphs develop on a page, I sometimes ask them to start keeping a journal. This has worked much better for me when I've waited a few weeks before introducing the journal idea, rather than suggesting it when people still believe in all the obstacles to writing. I just propose that anything that strikes them—a conversation they overhear, a scene they observe, an event they participate in, a person they notice—can be jotted in a special place in a notebook and pulled out later to mine for writing.

Sometimes I pass out the following words of Meridel Le Sueur (1982):

> You see John Jones going down the street tomorrow morning and you look at him keenly . . . you can tell whether he quarreled with his wife, or got indigestion from eating too many pancakes, or was afraid to go downtown because his loan note was coming due at the bank. You don't see a deadpan John Jones. You see a man writhing and twisting under all kinds of pressure and stimuli . . . There is a story there . . .
>
> Or suppose you go to a meeting. Can you tell your family what happened? If you try to write it down you'll find out what a poor observer you are, you'll find out that you remember only half of what is said, that you cannot describe the speaker, that your eye is very slow

and your ear slower. You'll have to practice. The next time, you'll see more and perhaps you can take down some notes while you're there.

    . . . The thing to do is to get a notebook . . . and begin. Don't pay any attention to how you write, simply write down what happened during the day. Don't scare yourself by reading it over right away, just keep on writing. Write how you had lunch with someone, try to put down the conversation, how you felt commuting to work, the characters you saw, what happened at the shop. Just let yourself go. The secret is not to get self-conscious about it, not to feel, "What does this amount to? This isn't interesting." Keep on writing it down and pretty soon you'll find out that it is interesting, that when you read it to others they are excited and interested and may add something that they saw or heard, or they may say, "That's good, that's how it happened alright, that's the spittin' image of him alright." And then you know you're getting on.

    . . . You [can't] learn writing except by doing it, and what you do is worth all the instruction in the world.

    So write! (10, 7)

I'm actually ambivalent about journals. They really work for some students, while they never become more than a chore for others.[18] But when I don't use them, I inevitably feel regret because I think one student in that class is going to miss something, like what came to Joanne. After jotting down a summary of an uneventful day with her boyfriend, she began to write about the constant presence of boyfriends in her life, since she was thirteen, and what else she might have done if she had that time back. At the end, she added about journal writing: "I did like this time out for myself. Got carried away, but I liked it."[19]

Fast Details

It's useful to ask students to write fast on occasion, rather than deliberating. Writer Donald Murray suggests writing fast for the "happy accidents" it can produce. This also contradicts students' oft-held conviction that they have to get everything right when they first put pen to paper. If words are left out in the rush of ideas, they can always be filled in later, and writing happens as students lose some of the immobilizing self-consciousness.

The idea of fast details is adapted from Murray (1985) and can stimulate initial thinking about a topic the class is about to delve into. Passing out a large note card to each, ask students to list all the details about the topic that come to mind in four minutes. Here again, note cards are useful because they reinforce the idea that these are to be quick jottings, not paragraphs filling a page. When four minutes are up (a timer is helpful here), ask participants to first circle anything that they are surprised to find on their cards. Most often, only a few will have something truly surprising, but for those that do, it's usually key. Next, ask them to draw arrows between ideas that are connected. Then have them look at what they've got and see that they have a focus for a first draft on this theme.

At the community college, we used this technique to work on "the most boring composition assignment imaginable," in preparation for the departmental exit exam. Once the class decided on "What I Would Do With a Million Dollars," I set the timer and we began. Gregory, a professional rapper and DJ, was surprised that he didn't put down his music as something he would devote money to and went on to write about his ambivalence. For Caroline, who kept coming back to funding AIDS research, the focus of her writing became her frustration over her family's view of her as materialistic.

Dialogues

I've sometimes seen a piece of writing from one student to which I think another student might resonate. The resulting dialogues have often become some of the richest pieces themselves.

Hyde Park and Grove Hall

Julia: The cage is where the "receptionist" sits. It is an enclosure of a hard see-through substance, probably bullet-proof, above waist level with a small metal grate to speak through and wood below. The cages are only at certain offices. Most of those offices are located in the cities—Brockton, Grove Hall . . . What are the cages for? What do they tell us? That the workers need to be "protected" from the recipients? What is it they need protection from? Or is it to protect the recipients from something within the office?

Different workers provide different information. At one time your verifications are fine. Switch to another worker, and they're not. In one office, it's okay if you're in school, in another office you have to quit and find a job.

Florence: In Hyde Park, they made sure you understood everything. The social workers took the time. Made sure that you fully understood. Hyde Park had the info and will call you, or send info to remind you of the starting date. But yet I go to the Grove Hall, and there are no questions asked. Just go over to the E.T. workers, then you will be finished. "No, I don't know how long it's going to be. You have to wait until it is your turn. No, you can't do it later. That needs to be done now. Mr. Smith, the E.T. worker is going out to lunch. He will be back at 1:30." I was told not to wait. I had to do it now. But now Mr. Smith has to have his lunch. I guess I don't need lunch. Mr. Smith comes back at 2:30. "I really don't have any info on Northeastern EMT program. I'll put your name down and you can call me in a few weeks. No, I'd rather you call me." That's all for E.T. at Grove Hall.

Julia: There are reasons to keep the welfare system ineffective and function-
ing this way.
　To keep people from applying and getting benefits due them.
　To keep the stigma of receiving welfare lower than having the lowest pay-
ing job.
　To force people to take the low wage job as opposed to getting welfare.
　Either way, you pay a price.

Florence: Always that feeling of trying to get something that someone else is
giving.

—Florence Taylor and Julia Wood,
Survival News (1992, 19)

Looking Underneath Technique

Where's the Assignment?

I use key phrases, titles, and journals as ways to help people start writing because in none of these am I asking people to write in response to
an assignment I've predetermined. As I've said, one of the things I
think is basic to writing is a compelling reason to write—an idea you
want to explore or an experience you want to share. For this reason, I
don't use sentence starters, story starters, or similar exercises commonly found in literacy and ESL texts and workbooks. I encourage
even truly beginning writers to start with reasons, and words, that are
theirs.

Moving Beyond the Language Experience Approach

Teachers sometimes ask how the techniques I have described so far offer something different from the language experience approach (LEA).
In LEA, people dictate an experience to the teacher, or another student
with more developed literacy skills, who transcribes it using the
speaker's exact words. In the process, people's own ideas and language
are affirmed, and the text created is then used as material for reading.
Thus, people learn to read by working with their own words. LEA has
its own invaluable place for all of these reasons. But it shouldn't be confused with writing or expected to replace it. I've often talked with
teachers who do LEA with people they think aren't ready to write. But
they're really two separate activities, and the same people who are
orally dictating stories can be encouraged to simultaneously begin
putting words on a page themselves, even if there aren't many in the
beginning and the spelling is largely invented. I've found that when
readers see they can make meaning out of what they've written, it
helps them cross a hurdle and start digging more fully into the process
of expanding their literacy skills.

"You Grab a Kleenex and Keep Writing."

People sometimes cry when they read and occasionally when they write—and I sometimes cry while listening. I usually suggest, as Kate O'Neill (1991) advises, "Grab a Kleenex and keep writing" (16).

I decided to take a risk in one teachers workshop. I'd considered using work or education as a writing theme, topics I've used before in workshops with teachers I haven't met, knowing everyone will have had an experience with each. But the war in the Persian Gulf had begun two weeks earlier. Many people grappled during that time with a feeling that ongoing activities were meaningless in the face of the war, even though we knew the slogan "Fight the war at home" was more than rhetoric. This was my way to at least acknowledge the war's impact. As it turned out, this war was present in several teachers' lives. At least two had immediate family in the Gulf; others had extended family members there. All of these were people of color, and it was they who read their writing and talked. One woman read her piece out loud until she began crying and then asked the woman sitting next to her to finish. For me, it wasn't only her words that were moving—her title was "Homecoming," and she said it was planning for her son's return that made his absence bearable—but the fact that, despite being unable to continue reading herself, she wanted them read. When I asked the writers to look back at their own pieces to see where they might take them in light of the writings they'd heard, one woman said, "I would make mine more explosive."

During a writing exercise I facilitated for teachers in East Boston, a Latino participant revealed that his uncle had been murdered in the neighborhood, the victim of a racist attack. There was silence when he finished reading. He was a new teacher, and I asked if he'd told anyone else on staff—all of whom were sitting around the table. He said he hadn't, and I encouraged him to keep writing, using the revision strategies outlined later in this chapter. I was sure that as others continued to read their work, people would begin to respond to his story and conversations would also take place outside of that evening's workshop. However, before the next person began, another teacher said he could never ask someone to just keep writing after revealing such a story. In fact, at that moment, I saw that writing is one of the most powerful things you can ask someone to do.

Initial Response and Revision

I arrived at a workshop one afternoon exhausted from the heat. The lack of ventilation in the room made me even more lethargic, and I said to Joel, "This piece needs more details." He looked at me sharply and asked, "Are you a teacher?" This was a workshop at a community center, sponsored by *United Youth of Boston*, and I'd never said I was a teacher. Up until that day, I had helped the teens use revision as a way to find answers to something *they* needed to know, which is what produces details. Suddenly I was asking him to answer *my* need for detail, and I got busted. This section looks at the strategies I've used more successfully!

Each of the methods I use in responding to a first draft rest on believing there is more complexity to a piece than is yet on the paper, even when I haven't a clue where it will go or how deep. Even when I'm *afraid* there isn't more, even when the writer isn't sure there is or isn't ready to say more, there almost always is more.

One student's first draft was about her grandparents' farm in South Carolina. She wrote about how they'd baked their own bread, canned their own fruits and vegetables, and made their own wine. If I'd had to guess, I would have said the piece was going to be about self-sufficiency or the contrast between Southern country life and living in urban West Philadelphia. However, it turned into a story about her grandparents' resistance to the KKK, her last sentence reading, "I think it would be bloodshed if it started up here, because you look on what you've come from and you know you are never going back."[20] I thought this was going to be a piece about an idyllic place; in fact, it was a place to which the writer never wanted to return. This is another reason that I want to respond to writing in a way that won't predetermine how it gets developed further, essentially giving the writer a chance to be the first respondent to her work. The following are some of the responses I've found help me avoid telling the writer what to do, while at the same time encouraging people to keep writing.

I should mention, of course, that sometimes people aren't interested enough in what they're writing about to revise their work, and in that case, leaving it and going on to something else makes sense. Revising isn't mandatory. It's offering the opportunity that's essential.

"What's the Most Important Thing You're Saying?"

To give the author an opportunity to perceive what is not yet there or to dive more deeply into what is, I often ask, "What's the most important thing you're saying?"

To the frequent "I don't know" answer, my response is, "Take some time to think about it," with a persistence that says the judgment is hers to make. As the writer makes that judgment and begins to relook at what she's written, she may go on to talk more. Suggesting that it sounds like there's more there, I ask her to just keep writing. It may turn out that the most important thing she has to say is not yet on the page. One woman said it was most important that her character "couldn't see her way out" of a bad situation. I asked her where she would go next in writing more, and she replied she thought she'd begin the story earlier in the character's life to find out why she was trapped.

The phrase "Take some time to think about it" usually helps. But one time Dan insisted that none of the things he'd written about the reservation where he's from were important. He came across first as angry and then disinterested. I pressed on: "But if you had to pick one thing, which would it be?" I remember him saying, "You're really pushing me," and I remember saying, "I am. Because I think there's something there, and I want to find out what it is." "This is the strongest," he finally said, pointing to the idea that on the reservation where he's from, the only yelling you hear is someone being called to the phone. "In the city," he explained, "people are yelling *at* each other." I asked him to put that on his paper and keep writing, which he did.

"What Came Into Your Head as You Finished Reading?"

When the look on a writer's face when he's finished reading seems to show that the draft has had an effect on him, I sometimes ask, "What came into your head as you finished reading?" The following piece is what Louise had written from her phrase "They'd cook the food from scratch."

> When I was a little girl, I went to school in Bishopville, South Carolina. The school was Dinnest High School. I can remember all of my teachers. One thing that stands out in my mind is the good food they served for lunch. Some of the food: milk, orange juice, and good, hot corn bread.

I asked her what thoughts immediately came to her as she reread what she'd written. I said she didn't need to tell me; she could just write them down:

> Thinking back over from time to time how many times I went to school without food for lunch and walked home from school about three miles, leaving home in the morning at eight o'clock and returning back about four o'clock. No wonder the orange juice and corn bread was so good to a little girl like me.[21]

Another time when I asked someone this question, she said, "I thought this story was really boring, but then when I was done reading I heard a 'tick, tick, tick,' like something else was about to happen."[22] She kept writing to discover what that was.

Silence

Sometimes just attentive silence helps the person think about her words after she's read them. Margie, who grew up in South Carolina, had only good memories of school:

> I liked to go to school because I got along with all the kids. We played well together. And after school sometimes we would visit each other sometimes to go pick flowers or take long walks in the woods.[23]

When she finished reading, I saw that her eyes were welling up with tears. After a few seconds she said the only problem was she'd had to quit school early on to go to work and she never went back. And so she wrote more.

If I had asked Louise to write more about a specific piece of her draft, it probably would have been to describe one of her teachers. With Margie, I might have asked about the other kids. Yet, they each wrote something entirely different. And for both Louise and Margie, the stories they ended up writing took a twist from their first drafts, although it is the first draft which is all too often what gets printed, in edited form, in adult literacy publications.

"Where Are You Going to Go Next?"

> I was working for a lady some years ago. She was nice, but the only thing I didn't like about her was that when I would get the pail to clean her house she use to always stand up over me while I was working. I put up with it for a month. I went in to work this day and I had to tell her I wouldn't be able to work for her any longer. She told me she was not aware of doing that. No one can give you their best when you make the person nervous by standing over them.

Sometimes my first question is "If you were going to keep writing this piece, where would you go next?" Adella's reply, which I've heard from so many people, was, "I could write a book." I suggested she start writing where she'd left off and she did:

> She's just one of the people I work for, I can write a book. About some of the people that I work for. If you do everything they ask you to do you would be a nut. This same person asked me to scrub her floor on my hands and knees. I told her I prayed before I left home. I kneel to God, only. I am sorry if I can't clean your floor with a mop, I am afraid you will have to get on your hands and knees and scrub your floor yourself.[24]

Randell began with:

My parents would question me if I went with a white girl. Probably because they feel that I was meant for a black female and not a white person. But it wouldn't be any chaos about it. I would tell my parents that it doesn't need for them to ask questions. It's my life; I'm old enough.

The same question I asked Adella prompted Ian to continue:

But I wouldn't walk around with a white girl in Mission Hill. The reason why I say that is because of what my peers would say. Maybe because they would think I would be putting my race down. But the white girls I used to like were in grade school, so it wouldn't matter now. I go to South Boston. Some of the girls are cool; we're friends and stuff. But most of them, they stay with their own kind. They would pick boyfriends who are on the hockey or swimming or softball teams, sports white people are interested in.

For me, I would still think about going with a white woman.

In Rick's first draft of "My Night Out," he sounded like a happy-go-lucky guy out nightclubbing:

The weekends is my time to myself, you know, to enjoy and have a good time. Usually on Friday nights I would come home around 5:30, 6 o'clock, have dinner, iron my clothes for the night, take a shower around 8 o'clock, call up a couple of my friends. I'm saying, you know, like one or two because clubbing with a crowd of guys sometimes can create a lot of trouble 'cause when they see a crowd, they think you're gang members. But that's not true. Me, I'm just a single guy, going out dancing and talking to, you know, a couple of girls. Maybe dance with them for a while, you know, conversate with one another. At a night club, it's a good place to meet new and interesting people. Clubbing can be really fun, if you enjoy dancing and listening to music. I love it because I enjoy them all. Also, it's staying in shape.

I asked him where he would go if he were to keep writing this piece. At first he said he didn't know, then he started to talk. I asked him to stop explaining and write.

But it's not the safest place to be because sometimes there can be some action going on, you know, like maybe some fight for a stupid reason. For instance, it could be if you step on someone's feet or accidentally bump into them and spill your drink on their shirt, that can create a fight.

Well, that's my night out, and it's better than hanging on the street corner, looking stupid, doing nothing, waiting to get shot by a bullet that wasn't meant for you.

—Rick Rigaud, *Neighbors Talk*
(Martin 1993, 18)

"Do You Hear Any Voices? Do You See a Scene?"

When I hear a first draft in which the writer has made a point, but the point is very general or vague, I might ask, "Do you have a scene in your head?" or "Do you hear anyone's voice in there?" or "Is there someone alive in there?"

I could just ask the writer to create a dialogue or write a scene. The distiction between that and the questions I ask is subtle, but I think the latter invite people more openly to see what's there that, once again, I can't know.

"Can You Place a Check Where There's More to Tell?"

Lucy Calkins (1983) suggests asking the writer to read his story over and put a mark on the page wherever there is more to tell. This can work well when there is a bare-bones sketch of a story already there. While students often place three or more checks in their writing, sometimes expanding just one detail can radically change the impact of a piece. Tawana Brooks (*United Youth of Boston*) integrated the second paragraph into the first after using this technique.

> I think that boys judge girls on how they look. ✔ I think that if a boy likes a girl he can go with her just for her. And boys sometime say if you do not have sex with me, you do not love me. But I think you can not love a person if you just met the person!
>
> Like they ask you on the phone, "Are you light-skinned?" And my line will be, "Hey, I'm Black, does that matter?" If he thinks he's too much to go with a dark-skinned girl, I hang up. It's like he doesn't want his friends saying, "Oh, you go with that dark-skinned girl?" [25]

Nicole's first draft mentioned all the people who would come to her grandmother's house for food and conversation. After placing checks where she had more to tell, Nicole wrote a second draft that said *what* people came to her grandmother's to hear: news about the political situation in Haiti, which her grandmother got from "inside sources she couldn't reveal." [26]

In Nicole's community, people gather to hear inside news of the political situation in Haiti; in Tawana's, African American teenagers talk about skin color. In both cases, it was essential that the writer find her own next move.

Of course, the "more to tell" can be as simple as moving from saying that the neighbors down South used to "chitchat over the backyard fence" to describing what they were chitchatting about—"their rheumatism or how the greens were doing." Other times, telling more leads to the heart of a whole new idea.

It's only in the first two weeks or so that I formally ask people to volunteer to read aloud to the group or talk to me about their writing and let me respond. After that, I remind them of the possible strategies for moving to a new draft and ask that they choose from among them whatever seems most helpful at the moment, whether reading the current draft to the group—or maybe to one other person, or two people, or me—or simply getting up to have a cup of coffee and stretch. At this point in a semester I give the students a list of questions they've responded to previously as revision strategies, and I ask them to begin using them themselves, where and when they're helpful. At the top of the sheet I always write, "Was there anything surprising on the page? If so, go with that!"

Another Look Underneath Technique

Underlying Beliefs

As I've said, our classroom methods can reflect our deepest, if unacknowledged, beliefs. To help bring these to the surface, I suggest evaluating a particular teaching technique through a look at its goals and the attitudes it reflects about students, teachers, and literacy. What does it assume the student is learning? What does it assume the teacher is learning? What are its underlying attitudes about students and teachers? Are they true? Does it reinforce or contradict the image of people struggling with or strengthening literacy skills as dysfunctional?

Let's look at the assumptions behind two kinds of responses to writing—one that asks the author to place a check where she has more to tell, another that asks her to elaborate on a specific point. The phrase "Tell me more about . . . " is based on a belief that the student needs the teacher to take control, that the teacher already knows what direction to take, and that literacy is an exercise done for the teacher. It conveys a view of people as dependent and nonthinking.

Asking the writer to place a check where she has more to say assumes the student can take control of the process of exploring ideas, that the teacher doesn't *know* what ideas should get developed further, and that literacy is a tool to dig into ideas. It contradicts the dysfunctional view by assuming the student can make her own well-thought-out decisions.

Open-Ended Questions and Strategies

Many times I've heard teachers express the belief that if a strategy is too open-ended, students won't know what's expected of them, and it will be too difficult for them to respond. I find that the more open-ended, yet compelling, the assignments I give, the more student's writing has something to say. I found this when I designed and implemented a writing placement for a small Native American college. I placed fourteen essays, poems, and newspaper articles in piles at the front of the room. Each dealt with a Native American theme; some were written by faculty and former students. I simply asked each student, all of whom were new to the college, to choose two and write a response to each. Other than encouraging them to work through drafts and then edit at the end, I gave them no guidelines. Faculty had protested that this would make the students so uneasy it would be difficult for them to write. They later agreed that the writings the students composed were, on the whole, a compelling reflection of their concerns as Native people.

More Than Feelings

I once asked the participants in a teachers workshop what they noticed about my responses to the writers as they read aloud. One woman said she liked that I asked people how they felt about what they wrote. In fact, I hadn't used the words *feel* or *felt*. The closest I'd come was to ask, after someone looked up from reading her piece, "What are you thinking right now?" I think the misperception is critical. I'm convinced that, as adult literacy and ESL teachers, we are so used to asking people how they *feel* about something, almost conditioned to do so automatically, that we don't ask what they *think*. This idea is so prevalent that even when I didn't ask about feelings, people perceived that I did. While the library administration still had control of the *Neighbors Talk* manuscript, it added a disclaimer that said the writings expressed the "feelings of individual writers and not those of the Boston Public Library." Feelings are something very different from ideas, strategies, and opinions.

There can also be something intrusive about asking for feelings, as in suggestions for journal writing such as "Make a list of all the joys and sorrows of your life," "Describe your favorite relative or your least favorite relative," and "Discuss a deep fear or a cherished hope." I would be uncomfortable revealing the sadnesses in my life in a classroom situation and can only imagine being asked to do so by a teacher who regarded me as less than her equal.

The Possible Traps in Active Listening

As I've said, my initial response to a work in progress is shaped by a desire to keep control in the hands of the writer and to demonstrate my respect for her authority. These goals give me something else against which to consider methods of response I hear of and might want to try.

Teachers often use Carl Rogers' counseling technique of active listening as a way to respond to student writing. In fact, one three-week seminar I attended offered it as the primary method of response. Through active listening, readers verbally feed back to the author what they understand him to be saying. While seemingly clear-cut, I believe active listening actually carries with it two problems to consider. One stems from a tendency I've noticed in myself and other teachers to repeat in our own words what our students say during discussion. While my intention is to validate what they have said, I actually may both change the student's meaning in the rephrasing and convey the message that the way she stated it wasn't good enough. I think when teachers use active listening too often, it's easy to fall into these traps. The other problem is the tendency on the part of some students to agree with the teacher, so that when we feed back what we think we've heard, some may be hesitant to correct a misunderstanding of their intended meanings. This latter issue points out, once again, that we need to look at techniques in the context in which we use them. When people are writing about ideas they care enough about to defend, within an atmosphere in which concerns are openly exchanged, such hesitation may well be lessened.

Writers' Attitudes About Reading Aloud

I always tell writers that any piece can remain private. But I've also seen people hesitate to read aloud the first day and later ask for the chance to read once they've heard others' work.

I don't think you can always know why someone doesn't want to read, and I've only just realized this. When Kelly said in class that she didn't want to read because her piece was "stupid," I thought she'd probably feel more confident once she heard other students' drafts. But she later wrote to me:

> I said out loud that I didn't want to read it because it was stupid and queer, but to me it really wasn't. I was just afraid of what people were going to think. That subject about the boys' family and being close to them is important to me, but I don't like everyone to know that so I try to cover up by making a joke of it or just blowing it off like it's nothing.[27]

Afraid to Say Anything!

One group of teachers I worked with in Vermont had been asking students to elaborate on specific points, and they were drawn to the more open approach I described. But some felt frozen after we talked, afraid to say *anything* for fear of being interventionist. I can identify with that kind of immobilization. I mentioned it earlier, when I'd suddenly begun questioning the very foundation of my teaching and was afraid to make any move at all. Fortunately, the immobility didn't last forever. The key was realizing that what's important is creating a situation in which students can resist something they see as too directive. We don't have to change overnight or be afraid of doing the wrong thing. We only need to see what Ann Berthoff (1981) has pointed out, that "the form-finding and form-creating powers of the human mind are the teacher's chief ally" (85), and keep engaging those powers in our students. That one idea has helped me out many times.

Issues Teachers Raise

The following are some issues raised by teachers in workshops I have facilitated on writing pedagogy, along with some responses.

"But you never told the writer it was good!"

I can't remember who first wrote about "the teacherly 'Very good,'" but I do remember that once I read it, I started biting my tongue. The "very good" seems teacherly because it's a reaction I could have only in a situation in which the content is irrelevant and I'm judging form. In everyday conversations outside the classroom, I don't say "Very good" in response to what others say. I've found no one needs me to say his piece is good if my response indicates real interest, if he sees that his work sparked someone else's thoughts, if the content becomes a jumping-off point for a group discussion, or if it simply helps him write more. It's these reactions that are more real, and people seem to perceive the difference, spurred on to keep writing.

"But the ESL students I teach want their writing to be perfect in terms of grammar and spelling. It doesn't matter what I ask them to write about, even something as simple as what they ate for breakfast."

Sometimes the reactions we've come to expect from people—that they won't suspend a single-minded focus on spelling, for example—have more to do with our technique and belief than they do with real immovable resistance. Besides, what else *is* there to focus on when writing about what you had for breakfast? In fact, simple topics can be more difficult to write about, taking away the complexity that makes working on an idea through writing such a satisfying experience. Othello, a participant in *United Youth of Boston*, said, "I like to express myself. Not like in school where they ask, 'What did you do today?' I came to school, and I did what I had to do. There's really nothing else to say. Or, 'List your twenty favorite foods.' 'Where would you go if you could fly?' 'What would you do if you inherited a million dollars?' I don't know anyone in my family *with* a million dollars, so I really don't know!"[28]

There are ESL teachers who ask students to write about compelling things from the very beginning, even though the students' knowledge of English is limited. I did the same with a beginning ESL class I taught in Boston. Using key phrases to start writing, students wrote about doing child labor on a New Jersey farm, getting rid of a philandering husband, seeing a ghost in a childhood home, and working in tobacco factories in Puerto Rico. Some of the spelling was difficult to decipher; some of the words were in Spanish. But much of the writing turned out to be more than people thought they were capable of writing in English, once again stretching beyond what they *thought* they knew.

"I think my students would get discouraged if I asked them to revise, as if their first attempt wasn't good enough. So often these first words are themselves a real accomplishment!"

This question comes from a genuine understanding of the difficulty with which adult literacy participants and many students in community college classrooms write. Yet I believe an invitation to look again at one's own words, to see what else may lie there, becomes a reason to write. As a woman in one of my classes said, "When I reread what I wrote, I look at it and say, 'There's more.'"

This point is key because teachers frequently ask how they can motivate students to write. Once again, if the content people are exploring through writing is compelling, the question of motivation becomes moot. I think Freire put it so well when he said that "motivation takes place in the action . . . It is a moment of the very action itself" (Shor & Freire 1987, 4). It's in this context that people eventually begin to write spontaneously, in class or at home, on the heels of an episode with the welfare department's fraud unit or after waiting in line at the housing authority.

"What do you do when someone's writing seems bland, almost like a Hallmark card?"

I haven't always been successful at encouraging people to approach something that has real meaning for them. Maybe the Hallmark-like prose is a standard some are familiar with and try to emulate. Maybe others consciously choose not to reveal something. And some may wish to avoid confronting their own long-held beliefs.

Dolores wrote an essay on child rearing in which she listed many pieces of generic Ann Landers–type advice, but none of them resonated with the complexities I knew she must have experienced. I asked her to pick one piece of advice. She chose the need to let go of children once they become adults, and I asked her how she'd achieved this herself. She said that she hadn't, and that it wasn't something she wanted to write about, so we let it go. Corie was writing about one of her first jobs, and the drafts didn't seem to be going anywhere. After class, I asked her if there was another work experience she might try writing about. "I had to work from the time I was seven, but I won't write about that."[29] While working with Gary through drafts of his piece on work, he finally said to me, "This is really boring. I have beat it to death. Besides, I got fired from this job." That's what he was avoiding in the paper, he said, because it was humiliating. Gary chose finally to write about being fired, but Corie chose another topic. Sometimes the more mundane writing comes out of an intentional decision to wait awhile until feeling, if ever, that this classroom is the place to write about certain things.

If writing produces something unexpected for writers, what happens when "in writing, the perceptions upon which they have built their understanding of the world get called into question" (Mayher 1990, 237)? For some students, retreating into vacuous prose may be as much a way to resist a confrontation with their own beliefs, as are hostile reactions to classroom discussions for others. The last meeting of a nine-week workshop I facilitated for a neighborhood educational program participating in *Neighbors Talk* became intensely emotional. The class had been writing on the theme of housing for their submissions to the book. Suddenly on my last day at the program, Nelly spoke in a voice she hadn't used since I'd been there. It was a conservative voice, challenging the prevailing classroom stance on tenants versus landlords. "It's not the fault of landlords that tenants don't keep their apartments clean so that there are rats and roaches," she said. Another student responded, "I keep my apartment spotless, and I have roaches!" This was followed by an uproar of agreement, a congenial one, but an uproar. The group appeared fairly unanimous to me. Next Nelly spoke on discrimination against people from the islands and people on welfare, which the classroom discourse had taken as a priori for the past nine weeks. "How do you know it's discrimination?" she asked. "Maybe that's not what's going on."[30] Again, there was an immediate response. Three women verbally responded, again strongly disputing what Nelly said. I looked around the room and perceived the nodding as agreement from others that they'd experienced discrimination and knew it existed. Then Nelly added, "In my job, I don't know if what I'm going through is discrimination." She had written about her work early on—she's a nurse's aid on a hospital floor—and the feeling that her supervisor was treating her unfairly. She's the only Chinese person and the only nonnative English speaker on her unit, yet she had been counseled by another staff member that the treatment she was receiving was not because she is Chinese or her English is not fluent. At the moment she spoke about it in class that last day, she started to cry. Though this is clearly my reading, I now see Nelly's hostility to the idea that discrimination exists against tenants, or West Indian people, or women on welfare, as a possible reaction to being compelled to acknowledge the racism she faced as a Chinese woman.

"My students talk about being abused and in foster homes or being fifteen and having their first kid. They kind of recite it like a history book instead of their own lives."

Several others nodded when one teacher expressed this frustration in a workshop. As I think about it now, the students she described remind me of myself going through a series of interviews at various neighborhood health clinics a few years ago, in my search for a counselor. Since the people conducting these initial interviews were intake workers and not themselves potential counselors I might see— in fact, I wouldn't even see any of them again—I responded honestly to their very probing questions, but with what must have seemed like marked detachment. In fact, one worker commented on this. I was resentful when she did, wondering why she thought I should fall apart for her during an intake. There seems something similar in an expectation that students will always choose to explore painful subjects with us. I can imagine responding mechanically or in vague terms to the request, "Tell me about your biggest frustration in life," as a way to get at a language experience story (Association for Community-Based Education 1988, 57).

Further Revision

Responding to Later Drafts

When a writer is working on later drafts, I often ask questions intended to help her hone in on her focus:

"Is there more than one piece of writing here?"

"Where does this piece really begin?"

"Is there something here that doesn't fit?"

When I asked Patrick Cedeno the last question, he decided to delete his rambling first paragraph, and the second and third became one of his submissions to *Neighbors Talk*:

Listen Up Clearly

Sometimes they search me for no reason. Listen up clearly. This is an action I have had experience with. Me being searched for nothing at all. I could've been on a drug street where someone that knew me called my name to get my attention. Sometimes the police would see me walking down the street and they will stare at me like I have done something wrong.

So their actions gave me the impression they wanted me badly. So I started not to care about what they stared at or said to us. That meant I have gained more of a street mind towards certain things in life. (Martin 1993, 47)

I like Nancie Atwell's (1987) idea of asking, "What do you want your readers to know or feel at the end of your piece?" and suggesting the writer look back to see if there is anything to take out, add, or change, so that we will know it or feel it. One young woman said she wanted us to know her grandfather was a great guy. Looking back, she realized she'd shown us that. Then she mentioned, "The Irish of his generation didn't have it easy," and realized that wasn't yet clear because she'd only just thought it. This strategy provides another way for the author to stand back and think about what she is saying.

I'll sometimes ask students to relook at their first and last sentences when they believe they're done, to see if they need rewriting. Often, they've done some revisions to the middle of a piece that change the premise or conclusion. Other times, it's simply in relooking at these that they decide to alter them.

It can be more effective to teach compare and contrast as a revision strategy than as a rhetorical mode. When Eddie asked himself if there were anything in his piece to compare or contrast, he saw ways to highlight the differences between working for someone else and being self-employed. He added details to heighten those differences: wearing a uniform versus your own clothes; working in someone else's house, as his grandmother had done, versus working on your own land, as his grandparents were eventually able to do. Juline looked at her piece on the expense of renting an apartment in her Boston neighborhood and added a paragraph on the home she owned in Haiti.

Other effective strategies for helping students work through later drafts include asking, "Can you change the order of your ideas?" and encouraging people to pick up scissors and tape and see what happens. Sometimes writers cut up sentences within a paragraph. More often, they move paragraphs around. Sometimes I encourage the writer to jot a one-word summary of her paragraphs in the left margin and then use the words as guidelines to see if the piece would benefit by moving paragraphs around. Lois' "noise, gangs, West Indies, children, higher rent" guided her scissors and tape.

Finally, there are times to ask, "Does this topic raise other issues for you?" when one concern seems like it could lead to another.

It's clear that I'm directing the writing when I use the questions suggested in this section. I ask, "Is there something here that doesn't fit?" and "Is there more than one piece of writing here?" when I think there is; "Can you change the order of your ideas?" when I think the writer could. What's important is that once we've used them in class, all of these questions are added to the students' list of revision strategies, so that they can begin to make their own decisions about when and where the strategies would be useful.

Seeing Common Themes

I once heard someone say, "When we write about ourselves, we are writing about how we see the world around us." When people wrote about their work lives, I began to see common themes emerging in different classes I was teaching at the Women's School: the different and not-so-different experiences of work in the South and in the North; the tension for mothers between their work lives and family demands; attitudes toward "personal care" work—as hospital workers, domestic workers, home health attendants—and both the similarities and differences between these and the ways in which people wrote about factory work; the knowledge for many of us that our mothers always wanted us to do something different from what they had done. I created a time in which people who'd written about the South and people who'd written about the North, or people who'd written about factory work and those who'd written about home work could go off in a corner together, read each other's work, and talk. In the reading and the talking, people find new dimensions to their own experiences as they look for similarities and differences, the relationships among their experiences, and conclusions. I like encouraging a group of people to look at their individual pieces as a possible whole—with a collaboratively written introduction, transitions, an ending, and a commentary—as yet another way to see their own experiences through a new lens and communicate what they see. This could be a way, too, for tutors who work one-to-one with individuals at the same site or teachers who have more than one class in the same place to bring together people who haven't met, creating opportunities for the new ideas that come with collaboration. I find it useful to ask, "What are these stories together saying?" making it clear I don't assume any of us know yet.

I was inspired in this effort by a passage in *Claiming Our Economic History*. It's a booklet in which participants in a sociology class in Jellico, Tennessee, relay eighteen stories—some their own life stories, some based on oral histories conducted with neighbors, relatives, and friends. In their introduction, the authors write:

> [These experiences] tell us about changing work patterns, land ownership, migrations, booms and busts, survival strategies for hard times, work in the formal and informal economies. They also tell of our ability to survive and maintain our families, of our lost and reclaimed dreams, and of the courageous and creative struggles for economic justice and development in our community. (Rural Community Education Cooperative 1987, 1)

That paragraph helped confirm a growing perception of what's been missing in my own teaching of writing, and in much of the student writing I've seen coming out of literacy programs: a move from looking at personal experience to looking at what these collections of stories *together* have to say and then writing more. Patti Lather calls it moving from asking people to articulate what they know to asking them to theorize about what they know.

Through *Neighbors Talk*, I had another chance to ask students to reflect on their writings as a body. One community group had chosen housing as the topic about which they would write for the book. When the pieces were in varying stages of final draft, I asked that everyone read the entire pile of writings and come up with a one-word summary of each. The intent of the exercise was to provide a tool to help people stay engaged as they read. This meant everyone had to read fifteen pieces by the next class. I was worried, actually, that they wouldn't make it through them; some were still a bit rough, so they were awkward to get through. But they completed the activity and returned with lists of words, which I put on the board. We then created three categories for the summaries: reactions (such as outraged and disgusted), conditions (overcrowded, discriminatory), and positive things (pride, structural changes to apartments at tenants' own expense). This provided us with an outline for an introduction that would precede the set of published pieces. We created the final introduction by creating prose orally while someone wrote it on the board, then moving sentences around and crossing some out.

We're All in This Together: It's Time for Change

There are housing problems all over. Everybody has something: Discrimination, slumlords, unsafe neighborhoods. The system stinks. We feel outraged, disgusted. Some of us feel homesick for Haiti and Antigua. We think about condos replacing low-income housing, about overcrowding, about how people from the islands and people on welfare are discriminated against because of other people's ignorance. We're tired of the fear of drugs and violence which keeps our children in the house and keeps us from taking out our garbage at night.

A lot of us are stuck while we wait until we can earn more money or get into public housing. But we still take pride in our homes and fix them ourselves when the landlord won't. We loved the story of the slumlord on Geneva Avenue who was ordered by the court to live for a month in his own cockroach and rat-infested apartment where people have to hang blankets in the windows to keep out winter drafts. Justice was served. For some of us, the dream of owning our own home has come true. We end with Catherine's story, the perfect justice, of *everyone's* dream coming true.

—participants at the Odwin Learning Center, *Neighbors Talk* (Martin 1993, 72)

When using the same strategy in a neighborhood literacy class, we decided to let the words alone become the introduction to the writings:

Home	Scared
Friends	Hustle
Bullets	Laughter
Stand Up!	Legends
Fed Up!	Extinction
Cramped	Poverty
Safe	Connection
Anchored	Wild
Belonging	Posse
Action	Wolves
Unity	Sticking Together
Pride	Change

—participants at WAITT House

It often seems, as it did at Odwin and the WAITT House, that it's particularly through writing on collective themes that people come to perceive that things important to them can be written about, and that writing about them means we can start talking about them.

There is one thing I have had to watch for in doing this, however, and that is to make sure differences in experience, as much as commonalities, are being expressed and heard. Within *Survival News*, as the White women stressed the common threads in the experiences of group members, the Latina and African American women sometimes asserted the differences.

Editing

I guess by now it's clear that my first piece of advice when it comes to editing is to keep a piece moving through revisions—as long as it *is* moving—before starting to edit. When a piece stops, I'll glance at it to spot patterns that need work. Sometimes enough people in the same class need to focus attention on the same area that a whole-group or small-group lesson makes sense. Other times I'll just work with someone individually or ask another student with a particular strength to do a mini-lesson with someone else.

If I see students writing paragraph-long sentences, I frequently do a lesson on subjects and predicates. When I first ask them to define each, students almost always struggle to talk about nouns and verbs, and some wonder if adjectives have a place in there somewhere. I suggest they forget for the moment about nouns, verbs, adjectives, and adverbs, thinking instead of the two whole units any sentence needs. A subject—the person or thing the sentence is about—and the predicate—something *about* the subject, what it is or what it's doing. After explaining the options a writer has when there are two subjects and two predicates, I ask them to make up sentences on the spot about some current topic, which we put on the board to punctuate. Following this practice, I begin to pull sentences out of students' writing to show that editing is a further way to take control over your words. One woman had written, "I hated to cook I ended up cooking all my life." After sifting through the recommendations of others as to which of her options to use, she decided to add a period after "cook," to sharpen the contradiction between the hating and the endless doing.

This woman was one of the collaborators on the Women's School AIDS brochure a number of months later. She wasn't in class the day of the deadline to edit a short piece of hers, so I called her to do it over the phone, each of us with a copy in hand. "Take out the 'but'; I don't like it there. And add a period. Capitalize 'It's' . . . '" [31] By that point she was able to quickly and confidently make changes, knowing how she wanted her piece to sound and that she could manipulate the mechanics to achieve that sound almost without thinking about it. Nothing magical helped her take that leap. Her skills developed in the process of engaging in a task that was real. In class after class, the elevation of large units of meaning over the discreet parts that make them up has helped people gain an ease with punctuation.

After a group lesson, I ask people to relook at their own pieces to see what changes they themselves may need to make. Sometimes people spot things right away, and sometimes it takes practice. In either case, I offer help if people want it but ask that they take control over the process.

As I've said, sometimes I'll suggest editing in pairs, matching two people who can benefit from each other's strength. In whatever way the editing occurs, I follow the advice of many teachers to focus on only one or two areas at a time—only on past tense, for example, even though ultimately the person will also need help with pronoun agreement, punctuation, and contractions. Thus, sometimes a piece is "finished" even though it still needs further editing. Frequently, people go back to these writings later in the term to make changes based on newly developing skills. Finally, for pieces that turn into longer essays, I suggest the writer make the text more readable by creating subheads.

"But isn't it embarrassing for someone when you use mistakes from her writing in front of the group? Aren't people reluctant to point out each other's mistakes when paired together because they are afraid to hurt the other's feelings?"

These two questions are related, enabling us to again see that any technique needs to be considered in its context. When it works for the group to critique the punctuation in one person's work is when we've started with revision first and a respect for the *meaning* she's creating. In this context, her knowledge and expertise are given; they aren't called into question because of her lack of facility with pronoun agreement. One person's hesitance to point out another's need to work on past tense slips away when her partner has had a chance to demonstrate some of her knowledge at other times in class.

"I fight with myself over teaching to the GED (or to pass the end-of-semester exit exam) and doing a more innovative kind of teaching. How do I reconcile this?"

The GED writing test—and many pre-freshman composition exit exams—want to see people organizing their ideas in a way that makes relationships between them clear. They want to see main ideas supported by details and clear conclusions. Honing your words through revision—using paragraphing as a way to resee relationships between ideas, writing till you discover implications you didn't see before, and so on—leads to these very same results.

Publication

The questions of who is to speak, who is to be listened to, and what kinds of voices and ways of writing are to be valued, are always questions of political power.

—Morley and Warpole,
The Republic of Letters (n. d., 116)

Issues of Representation

I was asked one summer to help with the creation of a text to accompany an exhibit of neighborhood photographs at a Boston art museum. The photographs from *Neighbors Talk* were among those to be exhibited. Others included images from Boston's Chinatown, a Latino public housing development, a Chasidic Jewish community, a mostly White wealthy community in Cambridge, and scenes from a lunch counter in the African American/Latino/White neighborhood of Jamaica Plain. As a part of the exhibit, the curator wanted to include the ideas of the people *in* the photographs regarding what the images said about their communities.

I prepared for a meeting with the photographers whose work would be a part of the exhibit, because the curator was going to ask them to solicit the words to go along with the images. I started by thinking about how language and visual images are different, which led me to think about the ways in which they are the same. I remembered that when Hakim Raquib took the photos for *Neighbors Talk*, the images said something about the communities, and what they said was crucial. There was no image of a sad face with hollow-looking eyes staring from behind a screen door, partly because the people in the pictures chose how they wanted to be portrayed and where.

The curator of the exhibit kept repeating that she wanted to have people's voices present. The question I wanted us to keep in mind was "What kind of voice?" As I've said, people speak with different voices in different contexts. Participants in a community college class, where they are positioned as students, can look and sound different when they are tending the barbecue at a neighborhood block party or conducting a church choir rehearsal. I wanted to encourage a process in which the words in the art exhibit—especially the words from immigrant and poor communities—would contradict the typical positioning of people in these neighborhoods as much as the photographs did.

The *kind* of voice is especially important when, as in this exhibit, some people are native language speakers and others are not, some are wealthy and some are poor or working-class. The curator said, "I want some kind of voice. If people say, 'There are different colors and different cultures in my neighborhood,' as simple as that is, it's okay." But, when poor people lack the chance to express all of what they're thinking, this expression is still seen as a reflection of who they *are*, and simple words are often interpreted to mean the speaker is "simple-minded."

A Different Discourse

As I described in the previous chapter, I've come to see that we can't just demystify consciousness without a simultaneous shift in the discourses, or ways of talking about the world, that help *shape* consciousness. Discourse doesn't merely reflect reality. It creates it.

This new understanding has strengthened my belief in the importance of community publishing. (Not that the words published represent the "true story." In the case of *Neighbors Talk*, for example, who are neighbors talking to? Each other? Me? An audience outside their communities? Narratives, or autobiographies, are always contingent.) Clearly, the ways of talking about the world that dominate now are not those of poor and working-class people, and we need competing discourses. A story told by Sharon Cox reminds me of the complexities glossed over in common portrayals:

We're going through a tenant's problem now. If I want to live in the building I live in without drugs, I have to turn my girlfriend's son in to the police. And I do want to live in a drug-free environment. But how do I turn in my girlfriend's son to the police? See, I have all these dichotomies that go on in my life and they say, 'The black community doesn't want a better environment.' But how do we put our sons and daughters in jail?[32]

The Writings of Youth

The writings of youth show why publication is important. There are a number of youth newspapers and magazines around the country. And, while youth don't speak with one voice, there are similarities in their writings. Whether talking about the police, physical or sexual abuse, interracial dating, or growing up gay, they speak to power relations. In doing so, they challenge us to broaden our notion of *political agenda* to include fighting to change the foster care system—under which some youth cynically refer to themselves as "state property"—as hard as we fight police brutality. This is information we need in order to ground our own theoretical and practical work for social change on a more complete body of knowledge. I would add here that it's not only valuable because it informs adults' work; some publishing projects are tied directly to youth who are organizing for social change. For those projects that are not, having a context in which young writers and editors are making decisions important to them, where their words are granted authority, makes it more likely they will resist being pushed around by the system ten years from now.

> When people ask me what I am I say, "Well, my mother's Vietnamese, but I don't know what my father is . . . Do I want to meet my father? I really don't know. Meeting him would mean finding out if I meant anything to him. Was I a mistake? But meeting him and knowing what had happened would also give me a clear outlook on my life and give me more of an identity.
>
> Lyn Christensen, "The Father I
> Never Knew" (1992, 18)

> I moved here about four months ago because I kept having problems with the foster homes I was living in. They would freak out about me being gay.
>
> —Tracy, "Growing Up Lesbian"
> (1991, 13)

To many of us, to be in the child welfare system means to be moved around from place to place, group home to group home, every time a problem occurs, or when a placement is not working in the eyes of the social worker or staff. Is there a solution to this or should we accept it as just another part of being in the custody of the courts?

—Douglas Lee James, "Doing the
System Shuffle" (1990, 10)

I am a single mother with one daughter living with me, trying to make it on my own. My daughter's father has been locked up since my daughter's birth; a week before she was born to be exact . . . He is supposed to be coming out between the months of May and July and most likely we will be together, but I'm not planning to jump right into it. It has been three years, and I know for a fact jail changes a man.

—Miladie Cosme, "Married with
Children" (1995, 8)

It's not that all of the writings reflect a clear political agenda. In fact, some contain things I wish they didn't, such as expressions of homophobia or sexism. Still, their very contradictions reveal the complexity of young people's lived experience no differently than the contradictions in my own writing reflect mine. And whatever else they're saying, these publications are produced by teenagers who've not done well by the system—education, child welfare, legal—and the writing has a critical edge.

I previously mentioned the tendency teachers have to ask our students for their feelings about an issue, rather than for their analysis. In a similar way, youth are positioned in a way similar to poor people, seldom asked for their analysis, encouraged only to express the feelings they have about their lives. While studies of education often cite the high dropout rate among Latino students, for example, seldom do we hear an analysis offered by youth themselves. Amarilis Chavez (1991) tells us that many Latino students see dropping out of school as an act of self-preservation. "[Latino students] quit school because . . . we are too smart to believe that we can be part of a group that tries to make us forget that we are Latinos, and so we leave, thinking that's the way to make a difference" (9). Aman Evans (1991), writing in *United Youth of Boston*, says, "Instead of making up theories about what teens need, adults should just listen when a teen speaks" (1). Analysis is often there in the writings of community residents and youth, although those of us who are middle-class or adults don't always recognize it.

Just as published descriptions of poor and working-class communities are most often written by people who live outside of them, young people's lives are written about most often by adults. And I've seen how the media images, particularly of urban youth of color, can seep into a community's own perception. There are women I know in Boston neighborhoods who are afraid of the teenagers who live on their block. And the teenagers feel it. For community organizations, it presents a barrier to creating alliances. What may be most important about youth publishing is that it defines the political as creating one's *own* image and articulating one's own situation (see Morley & Warpole, n.d., ix).

Oral History of a Different Kind

More typical than publishing the writings of young people is encouraging them to take part in oral history projects. Dating back to the popular *Foxfire* series begun in Georgia in 1972, youth have been documenting what poor people in their communities have done, with dignity, to survive. But their struggles for *change* are seldom documented. The organizers of the Central Manchester Caribbean English Project in Manchester, England, found that many of the young participants expressed the idea that their parents had "taken a lot of racist treatment and done nothing to defend themselves" (1986, 27). Begun as a project by Caribbean youth to investigate the African heritage they were never taught about in the schools and to talk about the meaning of the Rasta experience, the participants went on to interview their parents and grandparents. The result was *Triangular Minds*. They chose the title "to reflect the influence of Africa, the Caribbean and England on our lives and on our way of thinking" (3). The book documents the young people's experience of life in British society, points to their alliances with other groups who have a similar history of colonization, and presents recollections of older people who came to England in the fifties. Just as the book contradicts the image of Black youth transmitted by the media, it contradicts the young people's image of their own parents "as a docile, accepting people" (27). Transcribed in Patwa, the stories tell of people's daily acts of defiance and solidarity in their jobs in Manchester's dye and canning factories.

The stories they recorded made the youth wonder: "Were they just sitting back and accepting things? Were they in control of their own lives? Would they themselves be blamed by their own children for being docile?" (30). The experience of the Manchester youth reminds me of a comment made by a member of Free My People, a Boston youth group. She had read some of the early contributions to *Neighbors Talk* and, urging other members of the organization to participate in the project, she said, "This is not about 'look at the quaint people of Roxbury.'"

Issues of Language

I know the dominant language, and I can see underneath the dominant language. But I still like to keep my hands in the street talk. To keep hold of something that's being created daily.

—Sharon Cox, "Listen
to a New Word" (Martin 1989, 6)

If you really want to hurt me, talk badly about my language. Ethnic identity is twin skin to linguistic identity—I am my language.

—Gloria Anzaldúa,
"Speaking in Tongues" (1981, 59)

We must stop being almost hysterically convinced that students who cannot read or write the standard language cannot "make it." Students of nonstandard languages in the United States do not fail because of a language failure; they fail because they live in a society that lies about language. We in English in an information economy in a country that calls itself free make the lie palpable.

—J. Elspeth Stuckey,
The Violence of Literacy (1991, 122)

I mentioned in a previous section that I teach grammar as part of the mechanics a writer uses to edit her piece. In a certain way, that's not entirely true: grammar isn't only that. I do find that people explore ideas more freely in writing when they're absorbed in the meaning they're making and letting that meaning find its own form. At some point, though, people in my classes often need to decide the kinds of changes in form they are going to make, if any. In other words, they have to decide *whose* grammar and syntax they will use, given their intent and their audience. And they have to consider how these will change their meanings. A teacher in one workshop spoke of our role as that of "keeping people's spontaneity, but giving them a new vehicle for expressing it." But it's not that easy; the vehicle is not neutral, nor does it stand distinct from the content, as Alice Walker illustrates in her reflections on one of Zora Neale Hurston's best known works:

Reading *Their Eyes Were Watching God* for perhaps the eleventh time, I am still amazed that . . . the language of the characters, that "comical nigger 'dialect'" that has been laughed at, denied, ignored, or "improved" so that white folks and educated Black folk can understand it, is simply beautiful. There is enough self-love in that one book— love of community, culture, traditions—to restore a world. Or create a new one.

—Alice Walker, *I Love Myself When
I am Laughing . . .* (Hurston 1979, 2)

In classrooms where people come from many different countries, there will inevitably be a rich discussion of colonization and language. In one class, every student—whether from Haiti, Vietnam, Cape Verde, or Puerto Rico—connected in some way to these words of a Moroccan student:

In Morocco, my oldest brother is forty-one years old. He can speak and write French, but he's having a big problem with Arabic. I feel so bad about that, even my father can't read Arabic as well. Right now the government is trying to change over to Arabic but they are still having a major problem that when we speak, our language is all mixed, one word Arabic and the other one, French.[33]

The kind of discussions we have in these classes grounds us in the use of language as a colonizing tool, and it's a theme many classes end up returning to.

But the prevailing view of language in this country is that there is one way to use it. Many, though certainly not all, people who grew up in this country and who speak their home language have internalized the view that it's incorrect, whether they are from East Tennessee, the border region between Juarez, Mexico and El Paso, Texas, or West Philadelphia.

Students want, and need, to learn the conventions of Standard English, so that they can manipulate it easily for their own purposes. But we need to teach the conventions without deifying them. One way is to demonstrate that they are not fixed, and that their standardization fits with political goals. There is often an implicit assumption that categories such as Standard English and non-Standard English are found existing in nature. But as I've argued, we constantly create classifications and then define people and phenomena by them, all the while maintaining these are natural groupings. (See Chapter Six for suggestions for classroom activities with which to examine the theme of language.)

There was never complete agreement on the underlying issues of language at the Women's School. Some of the women held to the idea that the way they spoke and the language they used in their writing was incorrect. Others believed something else. There was a lot of discussion as we came close to publishing our neighborhood AIDS pamphlet, which the group utlimately decided would be taken more seriously in Standard English. Our being able to talk about the issue from as many angles as we did was due to the fact that some women in the room believed their language was important and took the lead in arguing it. But what if they weren't there? Poststructural ideas show me a way of moving forward, in suggesting that the point may not be to prove that languages other than Standard English are real, but to deconstruct the discursive practices that constitute as truth that they are not.

Notes

1. From "Workshop Notes, Folder One."

2. I want to say here that writing isn't *necessary* for deeper exploration of an idea but it's one tool we can use.

3. From "Workshop Notes, Folder One."

4. From "Workshop Notes, Folder One."

5. From "Workshop Notes, Folder Two."

6. From "Class Notes, Philadelphia, Folder One."

7. From "Class Notes, Philadelphia, Folder Two."

8. From "Class Notes, Philadelphia, Folder Two."

9. From "*United Youth of Boston* Workshop Notes Folder."

10. From "*Neighbors Talk* Workshop Notes Folder."

11. From "*Survival News* Workshop Notes Folder."

12. From "Class Notes, Philadelphia, Folder One."

13. From "Class Notes, Philadelphia, Folder Two."

14. From "Workshop Notes, Folder Two."

15. From a wall poster, source unknown.

16. From "*Neighbors Talk* Workshop Notes Folder."

17. From "*Neighbors Talk* Workshop Notes Folder."

18. I have recently begun assigning a learning journal in my classes, asking students to keep a notebook of responses to class discussions, readings, their own writings, visiting writers' lectures, and so on. For other ideas on using journals, see Fulwiler 1987.

19. From "Student Writing, Boston, Folder One."

20. From "Student Writing, Philadelphia, Folder Two."

21. From "Student Writing, Philadelphia, Folder One."

22. From "Class Notes, Boston, Folder Two."

23. From "Student Writing, Philadelphia, Folder One."

24. From "Student Writing, Philadelphia, Folder Two."

25. From "*United Youth of Boston* Workshop Notes Folder."

26. From "*Neighbors Talk* Workshop Notes Folder."

27. From "Class Notes, Boston, Folder Two."

28. From "*United Youth of Boston* Workshop Notes Folder."

29. From "Class Notes, Boston, Folder Two."

30. From "*Neighbors Talk* Workshop Notes Folder."

31. From "Class Notes, Philadelphia, Folder One."

32. From an interview with Rachel Martin, November 1989.

33. From "Student Writing, Boston, Folder Two."

Five

Reading Your Way into Writing, Writing Your Way into Reading

So many valuable things have been written and said about the processes of reading. In the "References" section of this book are resources on holistic theories and methods on which I've relied in developing my classroom practices. They outline techniques that help people become involved with and scrutinize what they read. This chapter begins with a look at the way a particular reading can lead to the kinds of reflections on identity discussed in Chapter Three. It goes on to demonstrate the uses of various strategies to encourage students to read things they may never have believed themselves capable of before. Along the way, I will look at choosing materials, reading "levels," and the current boom in "learning disabilities." At the end of this chapter, I will come back to reexamine some of the techniques described from poststructural and psychoanalytic perspectives and suggest some new directions for their use.

Reflections on Who We Are

At the community college in New Mexico where I worked, I chose *Mother Tongue*, by Demetria Martinez (1994), as the novel for a developmental studies reading class. As Eleanor Duckworth argues, complexity makes a text "more accessible by opening a multiplicity of paths into it" (1991, 9). *Mother Tongue* offers a chance to dig into the multiple and contradictory paths of identity and the ways they are always being renewed, and I thought that would help keep students engaged, while also helping us reflect on the ambiguity of racial and other categories.

Mother Tongue begins when Mary, a nineteen-year-old Chicana woman, meets José Luis' plane as he lands in the United States. He is a refugee from the war in El Salvador. She is grieving her mother's recent death, unsure of her own plan. Immediately upon meeting, Mary recognizes the chasm between herself and José Luis. "I asked a man who had fled his country, did the airline serve you peanuts or a meal?" (7) Her realization continues in their initial meetings, as when she helps him choose a name to use in this country:

> He said, Roberto, Juan, any name will do. I said, why not Neftalí, or Octavio? I wondered, why not pan for gold, for something weightier than the silt of ordinary names like Robert or John. He said, in my country names turn up on lists. Or in the mouths of army officers at U.S. embassy parties. A few drinks later, someone, somewhere disappears. Pick an ordinary name (9).

José Luis, too, feels the gulf:

> The problem is we're not seeing the same things. Even church bells mean something different to us. She hears them and sets her watch. I hear them and remember the endless funerals in the villages outside the capital (78).

Mary's dreams then were of "aid[ing] la revolución with computer bulletins to Central America" (31). She is able to view the war with a distance he, of course, cannot. Yet very slowly, Mary's own experiences emerge, and Martinez allows us to see the connections between a man whose "life is destined to be a statement about the time" and a woman who "suffers the times in [her] body" (23). We begin to understand that the state of limbo in which a refugee lives bears similarity to that of living with a fear that has no name, that to live as the target of death squads bears a resemblance to living as the victim of a less visible crime. After making love to José Luis, Mary makes a casual remark that suddenly turns her face into that of the man who murdered the woman he loved in El Salvador. He begins to beat Mary, and the beating just as suddenly brings back to Mary the memory of the sexual abuse she silently suffered. At that moment, she calls herself María, and "the ghost of the man with the minus sign smile fled. The demon could not bear it. He could not bear the sound of my true name" (104). In "the silk and the barbed wire" of that night, María and José Luis' son is conceived: "Earlier in the morning he made love to a Chicana. But after telling him the news of the nuns' deaths [in El Salvador], I am transfigured. For a terrible, disfigured moment, I am a yanqui, a murderess, a whore" (75). For José Luis, Mary's identity is always shifting.

To herself, she is both Mary and María, eventually coming to accept what Vévé Clark calls "Marasa," or double consciousness. Once she felt herself "lucky" as she listened to the stories of Salvadorans, "stories about torture, dismemberment, hunger, sickness . . . I had lost a mother to cancer and a father to infidelities. My losses were natural. Or so I thought then" (45). Later, the distinction between "natural" and "unnatural" causes no longer makes sense to her. Dichotomies continue to dissolve in *Mother Tongue*. "Ordinary actions . . . reverse the tides of life as in the theory of physicists who say the dance of a butterfly can cause volcanoes to erupt" (10). Remedios work because they contain both the sickness and the cure. Panic and desire coexist, as do the napalm and the bougainvillea of El Salvador. Distinctions between psychoanalysis and testimonio fade, as both become "facts assembled to change not the self but the times" (21). As Clark points out, testimony itself "implies reformation of contradictions . . . apparently incompatible codes, such as Catholicism and communism, militance and motherhood are syncretized to produce a flexible field of signification and political intervention" (1991, 55). Further embracing contradiction, Martinez allows us to acknowledge the twisted ways in which we receive liberating legacies from our cruelest oppressors, as Mary/María's abusive neighbor gives her a cigar box filled with pens and blank notebooks, with which she begins her life as a writer.

Midway through *Mother Tongue*, I began a class discussion by asking students what stood out for them in the passage they had read for that day. Several agreed it was the following, quoted also above. "Earlier in the morning he had made love to a Chicana. But after telling the news of the nuns' death, I am transfigured. For a terrible, disfigured moment, I am a yanqui, a murderess, a whore" (75).

I said that the shift between Chicana and yanqui mirrored how for many people, identities change. I mentioned what a former student, who identified as Mexican American, had said after a visit to class by my brother, who at the time was the only Anglo living in a small town off the coast of Colombia. Miguel had asked, "If I went there, what would I be, Mexicano or gringo?"[1]

Anette responded with a story of traveling by Greyhound through Louisiana in the 1960s. The bathrooms at the bus station were labeled "Black" and "White," and she didn't know which to use. She finally decided to use the latter, but very quickly, before anyone questioned her. I asked the others what they would have done, but except for Nathan and Robert joking about "whizzing outside," there was little response. While I wondered if it was a productive question to pursue, other students began to tell more stories.

Frances' son, who is half Hispanic and half White, is called coyotito by her grandmother. She told us the name of her grandfather on the other side was Louis Solomon. He was very prejudiced against Hispanics, and she thought he was White.

Anette asked me, "Is Pollack a Polish name?" It was her grandfather's. I suddenly perceived Eastern European features in Anette's face, much like my own: small eyes, a round nose. I'd never seen them before. I said this, and she and others nodded.

"I'm the lightest in my family," Kathryn said. "I was visiting my boyfriend's family in Mexico. They asked him, 'Is she a guera?' I was really insulted. I'm not American!"

Ricky continued, "My father is from Mexico, and I'm the darkest in my family. My brothers and sisters used to tease me." I asked her if the teasing hurt. "No," she said, "I'm glad I'm dark."

Jeanette said, "I'm the darkest, also. They used to tell me I was adopted."

Paul responded, "My father is adopted. He was told his parents were Dutch. Then he found them in Colorado, and they're Hispanic. [His ancestors] came from Spain in the 1600s."

"So, maybe you're part Jewish," I said and asked if anyone had heard of the conversos, or hidden Jews. No one had, so I mentioned how sometimes a single Jewish custom will survive in otherwise Catholic New Mexican households, carried over from Jewish ancestors who fled the Spanish Inquisition.[2]

I know Paul's father. He's the building supervisor on campus, and we both sing in the college choir. He's dark-skinned, with black hair. How did the belief that his parents were Dutch override the evidence of his own body? It's a question I wanted to pursue, but it seemed too personal.

Paul continued, "When I was little, we used to go to the beach in Texas. One time I said to my mother, 'Look at the Mexicans,' and she said, 'What do you think you are?' I never knew till then."

We ended this discussion for the moment with a dramatic reading of the dual poems titled "On the Question of Race" (Aviles & Banks 1992). As suggested by the poets, we intertwined the two as we read, according to the numbers placed before the stanzas. (Both stanzas 5 and stanzas 11 should be read in unison. This is a bit complicated, so if you want to do it, just have the readers in your classroom mark their passages ahead of time.)

On the Question of Race

1. They ask me to write down my race
and I think
and think
and consider
writing down the truth
and have my answer read

I have a dark man
listening to a bolero
lighting a match
inside this body

I have an old lady
showing pictures to her children
talking in a language called Spanish
inside this body

3. I have a drunk man
asking directions
he wants to go home
wants you to tell him
which highway leads to Cuzcatlán

I have a kid in the fifth grade
who says he's American
"but my father's from El Salvador
and my mother is black"

I have all these people
these guiros
all these aguacates

this prescribed latinhood
this Hispaniard name
that doesn't agree with
English only

5. They ask me to write down my race
and I think
and think
very seriously
and consider writing down the truth
and have my answer read

7. I have my tia Menche
tia Zoila
a mi abuela

A la señora con chile
a la pupusa lady
and Lorenzo's
inside my body

9. I have 18th & Columbia Rd
15th & Irving
Petworth
Shaw
Julio Iglesias
The Jackson 5

and Lilo Gonzalez
inside this body

I have a son
named John Enrique
who's black and brown
and human and tender

I have you inside this body

11. But I stop
And simply write down

13. "Hispanic."

—Enrique Aviles

On the Question of Race

2. They ask me to write down my race
and I think
and think and consider
writing down the truth
and have my answer read

I have a cargo of stolen people
crossing the Atlantic
inside this body

I have a brown man
he is painting a picture
we share a secret
it hides in the memory of a kiss

4. I have an old man
he is singing
patting juba
passing the tradition on
through the rhythms in his hands

a school girl in Bahia
and a young man cutting cane
just outside of Santo Domingo

I have all these voices
that have not learned to speak
orisha
sewas
ancestors
all these rhythms

these languages
these songs

5. They ask me to write down my race
and I think
and think
very seriously
and consider writing down the truth
and have my answer read

6. I have my Aunt Josephine
my Uncle James
and my grandfather's poetry

double-dutch
miss mary mack
and king of the mountain
inside this body

8. I have Rare Essence
that E-flat boogie
Five Blind Boys
the Shrimp Boat
and a Yaqui deer song
inside this body

10. I have a blanket of memory
woven from my grandmother's laughter
inside this body

11. But I stop
And simply write down

12. "Black."

    —Michelle A. Banks[3]

When we finished reading, we used the fast details exercise, described in Chapter Four, to list all the places and ancestors, "real"
or chosen, inside of us and talked about the people and places that
emerged.[4] But the question remains: what binds a people together *as*
Chicano, African American, Jewish, urban Appalachian? In *Black Is . . .
Black Ain't*, Marlon Riggs' (1995) camera returns throughout his film to
the image of a simmering gumbo, representing the diversity among
African Americans. The film's accompanying discussion guide points
out that he leaves unexamined the binding roux and asks what viewers think the ingredients might be. I will ask this question the next time

a discussion like the one described previously takes place. Ann Berlak (1996) captures my own goals when she writes, "I want my students to know stories of racial and cultural identities as ongoing processes of fixing and unfixing identities and of cross-pollination, *as well as of bloodlines and roots*" (98, emphasis mine). I want to find ways to keep this conversation going, which is always my aim.

The Tensions That Rise from Change

I've written about my own resistance to the very classroom changes I've worked to create. I want to say a few words here about the resistance on the part of some students, because it's an objection teachers so often raise to the kinds of activities suggested in these last three chapters. Many of us have met with requests for worksheets and spelling drills when we've just suggested freewriting and ungraded journals. To most of us school was worksheets and spelling drills and many students say they want to do school again and this time get it right.

My own strategies for easing the tension between what people may expect and what I offer include beginning a semester talking about real memories of school. What people often remember are the ways these traditional techniques served to humiliate them, not to mention the fact that they didn't work—how being asked to read aloud in front of the class led to inevitable loss of ability to speak as "everybody watched you breathe." But I think the most effective thing I've done is consistently articulate the underlying reasons for any technique I suggest that's new, leaving it open to informed, authentic challenge and making room for the possibility that everyone will get involved in the creation of what we actually do. When I can't offer a rationale that satisfies people, it forces me to see that I probably don't *have* one.

It's also been helpful to offer something to take the place of the success people hope to create by receiving an A on a test. That feeling of achievement has come as people create *ideas* as they read and write. Until that feeling is palpable, there's almost always an initial period of tension, which I usually let us live through. Though, as I once admittedly whispered in a teachers workshop, I've also chosen to ease it sometimes with a few small worksheets.

The tension hasn't always breathed out of every student. One woman at the Women's School made what was for her a difficult decision to leave and go to a more traditional public library program. On her last day, another student referred to a technique we'd used (described in Chapter Six) that she herself had initially thought was strange: "Don't forget your clusters. They open up a mind."[5]

A Close Look at Techniques and Compromise

As I demonstrated in Chapter Four, we can evaluate techniques used in teaching writing based on their relationship to the dysfunctional view of people with minimal literacy skills and the further assumptions each makes about the student, the teacher, and literacy itself. And, of course, we need to see what they really accomplish. Here is an example, based on reading pedagogy.

It's common in literacy curricula to see a story or poem followed by a set of questions for the reader. Often, these questions are looking for literal answers, for example, "In what year did Mattie Helen die?" Their goals are to help the teacher check the student's comprehension and to provide the reader with a sense of accomplishment that comes from responding with a correct answer.

This strategy carries with it two assumptions about reading. The first is that the ability to remember individual facts demonstrates comprehension and, conversely, that the inability to do so indicates a lack of comprehension. The second is that reciting these facts is easier for students than forming a reaction to the text. In fact, neither assumption is true. We know for ourselves that we can read something with great satisfaction and not remember the date on which some event occurred. In reality, this strategy accomplishes neither of its goals. Also, it's a question asked by a teacher who's not looking to learn something from the answer. Rather, there's the understanding that the teacher already knows the answer and wants to see if the student does.

Such questions can be discarded completely in favor of asking for a reaction to the text, something that emerges from the reader's involvement with it. Asking for a reaction avoids viewing literature as though it "belonged to nobody and is addressed to nobody" (Bakhtin 1986, 99). It implies that the teacher may gain a new way of looking at the text. Such a strategy gives the message that there is not an unambiguous meaning to "get." It allows us to "check comprehension," as we see if the reader can do something with what he read, and it provides the students with a "sense of accomplishment" that comes from the act of reading itself.

A teacher in a workshop I facilitated responded to these ideas with a request for a middle ground. My guess is that the request came out of a desire for some feeling of safety or control. Someone else objected to my "polarization" of methods. But I maintain that some methods do stand in opposition to one another. They give opposing views of reading, writing, the text, and students, with opposing implications for outreach, classroom dynamics, and testing. We can't take our pick out of a grab bag of techniques, as though there aren't important outcomes at stake. We may decide consciously to compromise sometimes, out of fatigue, lack of paid preparation time, or feeling rushed or under pressure from an administration. But it's important to see the dissonance and acknowledge what it is we're compromising.

We'd been talking about the Persian Gulf War in the same teacher workshop. A woman from Trinidad mentioned how shocked she was the first time she heard the U.S. national anthem, a celebration of "bombs bursting in air." I think that's one of the things we try to do in our classroom as radical educators—to remember to be shocked at what we've come to accept as commonplace. I once heard someone say, "I drank my first cup of coffee this morning; I made my first compromise." There are compromises we may need to forget we're making in order to just make it through our day. And then sometimes, we need to remember, realizing when we're doing it in our teaching and when we and our students are doing it in our lives.

Choosing Materials

Often called "life skills" or "survival skills," there are an enormous number of curricula typified by, first, their assumption that students don't know how to do such things as balance a household budget and, second, an acontextual view of what it means to live or to survive. They tell a reader to call 911 in an emergency, when there are communities of color in which the way to survive a life-threatening situation is to find a solution *other* than 911. The Boston-based drug prevention curriculum mentioned in an earlier chapter suggests that "it may be very useful to ask a member of your local police force to come to a class to show drugs and drug paraphernalia. A visit by a police officer may also help the students and the police to better understand one another." (J. F. Martin 1991, 45). But the police themselves, through harassment and brutality, have been a threat to the survival of many people of color in Boston. Furthermore, many students in neighborhood education programs suspect the police have a role in bringing drugs *into* their communities.

This is the same curriculum that suggests teachers remind students that "it is best not to drink and drive." (21) Carol Edelsky (1991) writes of the "trivial Disneyfied themes" she's seen in K–12 classrooms (162). In adult education, the themes are nontrivial, but they are just as Disneyfied. Underlying their approach is an effort, as I once heard someone say, to "change the behavior of the poor to conform to the needs of a society which created poverty in the first place."

None of the texts I use in my classes are evaluated for reading" levels" because none are written for "beginning" readers. My own criterion for evaluating a text's usefulness is whether it will help us think about an issue we've decided to delve into.

Simplified Texts and Complexity

If every teacher in the world were to read only one thing about teaching reading, I would recommend it be Eleanor Duckworth's "Twenty-four, Forty-two, and I Love You" (1991). Duckworth inverts the typical adult education discourse on accessibility by arguing that complexity is its key. She argues, "present[ing] a subject matter in all its complexity makes it more accessible by opening a multiplicity of paths into it" (9) and quotes Lisa Schneier on the dangers of rewriting texts to simplify them: "'We sand away at the interesting edges of subject matter until it is so free from its natural complexities, so neat, that there is not a crevice left as an opening'" (7).

The dominant belief in the adult literacy field is that what we, as proficient readers, read and what our students read are necessarily different, exemplified by the numerous texts rewritten for "simplification." It's been my experience that virtually any text can be used with students—excerpted, but unaltered—as long as three things are true: first, that I provide strategies that offer paths into the text; second, that there is a context for the reading; and third, that I believe I will learn something from our collective thoughts on what we read.

Until I became convinced that complexity was a resource to be used, I was proven wrong many times when I assumed a reading would be too difficult. Mildred, a participant in The Woman's School, was especially taken with Frederick Douglass when I mentioned the subversive means he used to learn to read and write, and she wanted to know more. I knew of two sources of information. One was a chapter from a book titled *Famous Black Americans*, published by Steck-Vaughn, which I'd seen on the Women's School shelf; the other was a selection from Douglass' autobiography, *Narrative of the Life of Frederick Douglass: An American Slave* (1968). Written in the style of the nineteenth century, Douglass' own work seemed difficult, while the Steck-Vaughn chapter was purposefully written to be "easy to understand." In Douglass' words, however, were ideas the other text couldn't convey. And specifically left out of the Steck-Vaughn selection were references to the powers of reading and writing, so feared by slave owners and coveted by slaves. In quoting his own slave master, Douglass writes,

> He said, "If you give a nigger an inch, he will take an ell. A nigger should know nothing but to obey his master—to do as he is told to

do. Learning would spoil the best nigger in the world. Now," said he, "if you teach that nigger (speaking of myself) how to read, there would be no keeping him. It would forever unfit him to be a slave. He would at once become unmanageable, and of no value to his master. As to himself, it could do him no good, but a great deal of harm. It would make him discontented and unhappy." (49)

Also left out were the ingenious strategies a young Douglass used to trick White children into teaching him to write.

I gave Mildred a three-page excerpt of the autobiography. She went off to a couch and read with few interruptions to find out the meaning of "difficult" words, though there were what I considered many. She learned what she had wanted to know, and I began to learn not to underestimate what people can take on.

I relearned the same lesson a few weeks later. Along with talking about the outlawing of literacy for slaves, I had mentioned the assassination of literacy workers by forces opposed to the Nicaraguan revolution. In response, some of the students raised questions about Nicaragua and asked to do some reading. This time, there wasn't the option of considering a text produced for "new readers." I chose an excerpt from *And Also Teach Them to Read*, by Sheryl Hirshon (1983). The book concerns itself with the central role of education in the Sandanista revolution in Nicaragua. Many of the strategies I describe in this chapter helped the students and me dig into the book and begin to sort out some of Central America's complexities. When we finished, a number of people said they wanted more information about Central America than Hirshon's book could provide. I brought in a map of the region and brief summaries of the political and economic situations in each country. Each woman chose a country to read about and then reported back to the group on what she had learned. In some instances, two or more women read about the same country, and I asked them to go through their selections together. (See "Chunking" in the section that follows.) The reading was far more challenging than anything we'd done before, with statistics on per capita income and U.S. military aid and unfamiliar political and economic language. But students dug in, coming out with yet more questions, including: "Why are these countries so poor?" "Why is Reagan giving so much military aid to Honduras, El Salvador, Costa Rica, and Guatemala?" "Who's right and who's wrong?" "Why are we in everybody's business?"

From there we went on to read materials from the Central American Organizing Project, an organization housed in the same church as the Women's School, which worked with some of the African American churches in Philadelphia and sponsored trips to Central America.

One teacher with whom I worked noted, "I always felt like, I hope this reading, this difficulty here or there, doesn't make them feel uncomfortable, doesn't make them want to leave class. I really need to let that resistance go a little and provide techniques and strategies more than ease."

Reading Strategies: Taking Time to Linger

> You can't depend on your eyes when your imagination is out of focus.
>
> —Mark Twain

Much of the curricula used in teaching reading in adult literacy programs and developmental studies courses assume the notion of a fixed meaning in text. The Association for Community-Based Education (1988) handbook defines its approach to reading as follows: "Language learning should focus on receiving and transmitting meaning, rather than on the mechanical techniques for doing so" (54). I would agree that an emphasis on meaning over mechanics is what we're after, but we need to further urge students to see that there is no unambiguous meaning to either transmit or receive, and this is what is most exciting about reading. As Mikhail Bakhtin has helped us see, the border between transmitter and receiver is always eroding.

Students often say their difficulty with reading stems from an inability to concentrate or the lack of a good memory. They complain that not much stays in their heads. Sometimes I'll put Twain's words on the board. They introduce the idea that you need to bring yourself along when you read. When you do, you no longer struggle to stay awake or shut out the noise your kids are making, because you're too busy loving, disagreeing with, or getting mad at what you're reading to be distracted by fatigue or what's happening in the next room. I tell people I'll be suggesting tools that will help them jump in and become a part of what they read. Even something as simple as summarizing what you have read becomes a constructive act as, in the words of Mikhail Bakhtin, you automatically "enter into dialogue with it" as you retell it.

The ambiguity of meaning becomes clear to students the moment we begin a collective reading. I used James Baldwin and Yoran Cazac's *Little Man, Little Man* (1976) to stimulate the writing of live people into the essays of the women in *Survival News*. The following is Baldwin's description of Miss Beanpole:

> The inside is dark and Miss Beanpole ain't never dressed. She always in her bath-robe, with her hair tied up. She always tie it up in the same old rag. The rag older than TJ and TJ almost five. TJ know a color when he sees one, he knows green from purple and yellow and green and red from blue, he already learned that, but he don't know what color the rag is. He don't really know what color Miss Beanpole is. She

look like she a little bit white and a little bit colored, kind of more white on top than she is around the mouth, but she probably more white than colored. TJ more colored than she is. But he don't know about her hair, he never see it. Miss Beanpole is very old. She smells like peanuts.

She never in the street. That why she always send you to the store for what she want. (42)

To some of the women, it was self-evident that Miss Beanpole didn't bathe often; others disagreed, sure the smell came from the oil Miss Beanpole used to rub her sore muscles. To some, it was clear that she didn't leave her apartment out of fear. To the same women who "knew" about her oil, it was entirely possible that she was in too much pain to leave. And while Miss Beanpole's head scarf suggested she was bald to many, at least one woman saw it as "covering the prettiest hair."[6]

A teacher once described how she always overprepares for class. "I walk in, sit down, and boom, the race is on," she said. There are reading strategies that save us from having to overprepare and encourage us to *linger* over texts. Each of the following has encouraged my students, and me, to slow down, dig deep, and mine even a short reading for all it's worth.

Chunking

I often use this strategy, which I learned from Susan Lytle. The teacher breaks a text down into small parts by simply putting a number in the left-hand margin next to each "chunk." She asks the reader to stop after the first chunk, and before going on to the second, ask herself what questions she has that she hopes the rest of the piece will answer. After reading the second chunk, the reader again jots down new questions, as well as any answers she may have found. For people who complain that the minute they finish reading something they forget what they've read, this process has shown them that they can remember it and use it.

The reading can be done individually or in pairs. If done in pairs, I ask partners to talk to each other after each section about the answers they are finding and their new questions. Alternatively, I've asked students to check with themselves after each chunk, "Do I understand what I just read?" If the answer is no, I ask them to write about their confusion and then read on. Other times I might ask students to write a one-sentence summary after each chunk instead of a question, and then three reactions to the whole piece at the end. One thing I like about these activities is that none rely on my participation. Self-generated questions encourage both engagement with the text and autonomy in reading. Jotting down confusions helps students let go of their frustrations over not understanding every detail, knowing they can come back to confusions later, unless, as is often the case, these clear up by the time they finish reading. It's also a way of talking back to the text, which I want to encourage.

Textbooks designed to encourage critical thinking as students read ask them, "Does the premise match the conclusion? Is the conclusion supported by the evidence? Are facts supported? Are there fallacies?" These are important questions, ones many of us answer without consciously thinking about it as we read. But I think they're very difficult for someone who hasn't felt confidence as a reader or hasn't found a way to enter into the text in the first place. The strategies outlined here, however, end up leading to answers to these very questions.

Talking Back

Another way to engage with the text is to literally talk back to it, with your pen, as confident readers often do. I encourage students to put exclamation points or scribble "Gross!" next to things that appall them, to write an emphatic "Yes!" or "Cool!" next to things they like, and then to begin to write fuller reactions. I've shown them examples first, such as the following one. The essay is "Voice," by Jordan Wheeler (1992). The student is Native American.

Essay: The dominant society doesn't know how to listen.

Student: Or doesn't want to.

Essay: There is much spiritual knowledge that will not be shared for fear that it too will be stolen. As a group, aboriginal people have learned not to trust.

Student: Unless the price is right.[7]

Reacting to a Text

Early on in a class I suggest that one way into a reading is to talk back to it, fight with it, love it, question it, *react* to it. Along with one of the initial in-class readings we do, I pass out the small note cards I mentioned in Chapter Four and, once again, ask for three reactions to the material.

After students write their reactions, I ask each to turn to the person next to him and, through discussion, decide which is the strongest reaction he has. After students have talked in pairs awhile, I ask everyone to come together and contribute his most compelling reaction in a group discussion. More people participate when I use this technique. Jotting ideas down on a card gives someone a chance to gather his own thoughts. Talking to one other person then provides an opportunity to give voice to those ideas, making it seem more possible to contribute them in a larger group discussion.[8]

I should note that some people are reluctant to offer reactions to a reading early in the semester. My hunch is that this is at least in part due to seldom having been asked to contribute their ideas in a school context before, and a belief that the teacher—and, in the case of many of my students and me, someone White—thinks she already knows the answer to any questions she asks. Once again, I think demonstrating that my desire for their ideas is real is key to encouraging students to contribute them.

Predicting, Questioning, Writing the End

Each of the activities described here has made the act of reading come alive for me and the people in my classes.

I gave one class (as well as a group of teachers) only the last paragraph of a book's conclusion:

> I did not write this book to be read and then set up on the shelf to gather dust. I wrote it with the hope that it will generate some action from the people who read it. Read it, put it up on the shelf and then begin, like these proud women, to resist. (141)

I asked them what they thought the book was going to be about. Among the guesses:

> Wife abuse . . . Women in South Africa . . . Women like Rosa Parks . . . Women like Norma Rae . . . Women unionizing in the South . . . Women in the Underground Railroad . . . Lesbian women . . . Women dealing with no/lousy/expensive health care . . . Women whose sons are being sent to war . . . Women in bad marriages . . . I don't know yet, but this author expects me to do something. Maybe every author does, but she needs more help . . . I don't know, but there's a fight there.

As each person made a prediction, she both revealed her own interests to the group and began to give a purpose to her subsequent reading, comparing the women in the text with what she knows of Rosa Parks or the women in the Underground Railroad. Listening to each other's ideas allows everyone in the group to gain a broader perspective as together we build a bridge from the familiar to the unfamiliar.

Next I asked people what they hoped to learn from the book. The questions they raised gave further structure to guide us as we read: "Who are 'these women'?" "Who is 'I'?" "Are they the same?" "Do these women meet each other?" "What are they proud of?" "What did they resist? What makes them want to resist?" "What kind of action did they take? Did they act together or separately?" "What did they accomplish?" "What is there still left to do?" "Who did the author write this book for?"

One teacher responded, "I can tell I'm not going to like this book. It sounds too depressing. Our students need something to move ahead." So the question—and her purpose for reading—became "Where is the hope in these stories?" [9]

Finally, I passed out earlier excerpts of the brief conclusion to the book, which is *Hillbilly Women*, by Kathy Kahn (1973). I asked people to pick up their pens when they reached the end and keep writing where the author left off. Here's the excerpt from Kahn's conclusion:

> I'll never forget the day Myra Watson got indoor plumbing in her house and the pride she felt because she had finally saved up enough money to have it installed. Why did she have to wait sixty-four years for indoor plumbing? Why did Granny Hager have to walk mile after mile in the rain and snow from her house to the Social Security office before she was granted the benefits she was due? Why do the women in Goose Creek, Kentucky, have to pick over clothes rejected by the Salvation Army when they and their families need something to wear? And why is it that Shirley Dalton, her husband and seven children are forced to live on thirty-two dollars a week when they can't find work and have to draw welfare? Who is responsible for Artie Chandler's nervous breakdown? Why does Jack Smith have to spend the rest of his life in a wheelchair?
>
> . . . I remember a family of nine who lived for a week on a loaf of bread and a jar of mayonnaise. And a working-class family whose house was burned to the ground by company-hired nightriders because the woman and her husband were organizing a union in a local factory.
>
> I remember the faces of the Hyden widows shortly after their men had been murdered in the Hurricane Creek Massacre, faces filled with pain, anger in their eyes. And the smug composure of the coal operators and county officials who pretended to be sorry. (139)

As people wrote from there, they began to take the story on themselves. In one class, comparing the final page of Kahn's conclusion to what we had each created led to a discussion about the different ways to view resistance, anger, and pride. The three activities together—predicting, questioning, and writing the end—created individual and group contexts within which to then begin reading *Hillbilly Women* and learn from the women of Appalachia.

> "I'm home, Ma."
> Myrna pressed down hard on the doorknob and stared blankly up into Kenny's large brown eyes and freckled face so much like her own he was nearly her twin. But he was taller than she remembered. Denser.

> He'd written to say he was getting out. She hadn't answered
> his letter, hoping her lack of response would keep him away. (Neely
> 1986, 56)

These are the first words of "Spilled Salt," a short story by Barbara-Neely about a woman whose son has returned from prison after serving four years for rape. After a time, Myrna had stopped visiting Kenny in prison and stopped answering his letters. She moved to a different neighborhood following his trial, never mentioning she had a son to her new neighbors. After he returns, we see Myrna grapple with her feelings of guilt, her love for Kenny, her rage at him, and her fear of him.

I passed out a copy of the story up to, but not including, its conclusion. The handout stopped at the point at which Myrna, sick over Kenny's presence in her house, lies on her bed considering what to do next. I asked the participants in the group to write the conclusion.

Pages turned and pens moved. It's a gripping story. Twelve people out of twenty read aloud what they'd written—I'd planned to stop after four or five, but the activity took on its own momentum. Some of the conclusions: Kenny leaves; Myrna and Kenny have a moment of reconciliation; Myrna gives Kenny a hug in one last gesture of affection; she has no answer yet; she asks Kenny to leave her home. Our differing visions of what Myrna would do demonstrated how each of our readings is shaped by the angle from which we view it.

As we read and discussed our endings, we referred to different pieces of the text, attempting to back up our conclusions or refute someone else's. The standardized reading exams many students must pass often ask for inference and a demonstration of the ability to distinguish between the main ideas and the supporting details, exactly what discussions such as this one lead us to. Then we read Barbara-Neely's conclusion, in which Myrna slips out of the house while Kenny sleeps, leaving this note:

> Dear Kenny,
> I'm sorry. I just can't be your mother right now. I will be back in one
> week. Please be gone. Much love, Myrna. (64)

We talked more about the issues the story raised, looking back for evidence that would lead Myrna to this conclusion. Afterward, I asked for reflections on the reading and writing processes. Many people agreed with the woman who said, "The story became mine."

Connecting Readers Theater and Writing

There's a scene in *The Women of Brewster Place*, by Gloria Naylor (1982), in which a young woman refuses to tell her father the identity of the man with whom she had sex and by whom she became pregnant. Filled with rage, he beats her with the jagged edge of a broken broom handle. Her mother climbs on his back to try to stop him, then grabs a shotgun and fires it past him:

> "So help me, Jesus, Sam," she screamed. "Hit my child again, and I'll meet your soul in hell!" She cocked the gun again and this time aimed for the center of his chest. "Look! Just look a' what you done!" . . .
>
> A slow moan came from the pile of torn clothes and bruised flesh on the floor. Sam Michael saw that it was his daughter, and he dropped the stick and wept. (24)

We read *The Women of Brewster Place* at the Women's School. For this scene, someone in class read aloud each role, plus that of the narrator. At first the readings were monotone. Gradually they became theater, though nobody moved from her chair, as each reader began to build more and more emotion into the voice of her character. The scene came chillingly alive. When we were through, I asked that, holding on to the silence, everyone take out a pen and write what might happen next. The writings revealed hopes that Mattie and Sam would reconcile, that Mattie and her mother would leave Sam, that Mattie would leave and move in with her baby's father. As we read the rest of the book (Mattie leaves and raises her son on her own), we kept returning to our own perceptions of what each character would do, and how they differed from the author's, investing ourselves in the story and its characters.

Beginning with the Picture

Just as creating titles from an illustration can be used as a way into writing, it can also be used as a way into reading. I brought to one ESL class a photograph in which middle-aged Asian women face helmeted figures wearing large goggles and masks. The latter are holding body-length metal shields between themselves and the women. One woman, with a grimace on her face and her arm muscles taut, is swinging her purse at one of the figures, who has a shield in front of him. In the background, young men watch the women, one pointing his camera at the woman swinging her purse. Looking at the image, one group came up with the following titles for the accompanying newspaper article, which they had not yet read:

Limits	Leader	Division
Onslaught	Irony	Huelga
Confrontation	Grimace	Power
Aggression	Strength	Protest
Strike	Masks	Frontline
Immovable	Standing Up	Barrier
Pain		

They then raised the following questions and made the following predictions:

"What is the cause of the conflict?"
     shooting students; reproductive rights; brutal force; travel
     restrictions

"Who is on either side?"
     police; the Army;
     mothers; students; workers

"Where is this happening?"
     Taiwan; Korea; China; Philippines; Cambodia; Washington,
     D.C.

"What happens next?"
     tear gas; arrests; beatings; injuries[10]

In fact, the picture is from Korea, and the women are protesting the shooting of students. As with the predictions of *Hillbilly Women*, the discussion of the ideas above revealed students' histories, political concerns, and knowledge. And when we finally read the article, as with most readings preceded by exercises such as this, everyone in the room immediately dug in.

About Vocabulary

I used to prepare prereading vocabulary lists, but found I very often wrongly predicted the words people would find difficult. Then I read Christine Nuttal's *Teaching Reading Skills in a Foreign Language* (1982) and I abandoned lists forever, replacing them with vocabulary strategies determined by the reader as she reads. Nuttal argues that most words are not learned by being taught but by meeting them in context and assimilating their meaning. She points out the use of probabilities instead of certainties. "The more we read . . . [the more] probabilities gradually turn into certainties without our being aware of it." (72) Making use of context . . . give[s] us a rough idea of its meaning; and with every subsequent occurrence the meaning becomes a little more precise" (70). She gave me the confidence to show students it's possible to understand new words without being told what they mean. Now I ask students what happens when they interrupt their reading to look up a word in the dictionary, eliciting the inevitable response that they lose their train of thought. I offer strategies they can use to deal with specific words they find difficult and ask that they bring back to class any burning questions they still have about a particular word after using them. Then I ask everyone to guess at what the word means. I find that when I ask them to reach beyond what they think they know, people very often come up with a definition that makes sense. When they do, I want that experience of success to give them encouragement to trust their instincts the next time around, instincts being based on knowledge we don't always realize we have.

Reconsidering Learning Disabilities

During a workshop at an adult literacy program located within a two-year college, each teacher present voiced the assumption that the majority of his or her students were learning disabled. This conclusion was based on such evidence as the fact that a student had been in the program a long time with little progress, was unable to remember what she'd learned in an earlier class, or had a "case history of mental illness or participation in special education classes."[11] Once the preliminary "diagnosis" was made, the student was sent to the Special Needs Center at the college for a battery of exams, including the IQ test.[12]

Included among other criteria commonly used to identify learning disabled students are: exhibiting loose thought patterns; being disoriented in time, often arriving at class late; being unable to retain new information without excessive rehearsal and practice; being unable to recall familiar facts on command, but able to recall them at other times; seeming restless, shifting position often during reading tasks; and having a halting and jerky reading style.

My own reading of the discourse of learning disabilities owes much to the works of Peter Johnston (1985) and Gerald Coles (1987). It was Johnston's "Understanding Reading Disability" that first allowed me to consider that reading ability might have more to do with factors such as attitude, motivation, strategies, and situations than neurological dysfunction. I have seen teachers in programs in which I have worked apply the term learning disabled to nearly every student they teach, with no more rationale than that used by the program mentioned at the beginning of this section. That may be because this is easier than seeing our own strategies and classroom structures as ineffective. I believe this situation results from a literacy field that assumes anyone who can read and "cares" can teach reading, and it places underprepared tutors and teachers in untenable circumstances, in which learning disability seems the only explanation for lack of progress. I have heard the argument that the learning disabled label reframes a view of students who once would have been thought of as "slow." But at least in the context of the adult literacy or basic writing classes in which I have taught, students very often assume the new label means they will always be "low-achievers." As Johnston points out, the category learning disabled implies that the students are "constitutionally less able" (171).

Lev Vygotsky's and Mikhail Bakhtin's arguments against a metaphor of "possession" regarding intellectual and linguistic abilities further supports an expanded focus on social, as well as neurological, bases for learning disabilities. The argument has equal implications, of course, for viewing children as gifted. Vygotsky's and Bakhtin's work would also support a look at the ways attitude, motivation, situations, and strategies influence such things as memory, attention, and literacy activities.

Gerald Coles (1987) suggests that to find out why the diagnosis of learning disability has become so pervasive, we need to look at the learning disability industry boom and its impact on the way schools are organized and reading is taught. There is no impact, and this is his point. Placing learning disability within the context of biological dysfunction means that "new classrooms might be opened to help 'disabled' students get around their biological flaw, but the school—and the school system—remain unchanged" (xvi). While we're looking at the reasons for the classification's overwhelming presence, remarks like the following can't help but be compared to the discourse of "the illiterate":

> Our prisons and juvenile treatment centers are filled with inmates who manifest major learning disability patterns. Seventy-five percent of those serving time tend to be learning disabled.
>
> —Jordan Diagnostic Center

It's easy to see how Foucault's emphasis on the role of classifications can help us think about why "learning disabled" labels are so pervasive.

A Second Look at Reading Pedagogy

I end this chapter with a look at reader-response theory—on which I based much of my teaching in the past—and recent challenges to it raised by cultural critics using poststructural and psychoanalytic thought. Reader-response theory emphasizes the reader's subjective response to the text. It's not that the words by themselves are unimportant, but neither are they autonomous from the person reading them. Reader-response theory views reading as a transactional process; both reader and text are changed when they come into contact. James Gee (1988) problematizes this interaction between reader and text as it occurs in a classroom:

> Whatever our politics, any literacy (any practice of interpretation) comes with built in perspectives and assumptions that serve as a test of whether one is correctly practicing that literacy . . . The phrase "think for oneself" is the culprit here. It obscures the *social* nature of interpretation . . . One doesn't think for oneself; rather, one always thinks for (really *with* and *through*) a group—the group which social-

ized one into that practice of thinking. And, of course, one 'thinks for' different groups in different contexts. (209)

In my own classrooms, I have always emphasized that the interpretations of the texts we read will be varied. I want especially to counter students' long-held beliefs about right and wrong answers, since theirs have inevitably been "wrong" in previous classrooms. Yet more recently I realize that, of course, I have a fairly consistent way of interpreting the texts we read—in particular, through a specific political perspective. That this is apparent to my students came home to me when a young woman last fall asked me about the final grades for the semester. She pointed out that she and I "always disagreed" in class, and asked how this would affect my evaluation of her work. Covertly, I *was* looking to see if students were "correctly practicing" a particular literacy, and some of them, maybe all, knew it.

The point is not only to encourage various interpretations, but to collaborate in *questioning* the meanings we make. As John Clifford (1991) argues, "Although a reader-response pedagogy encourages students to react in this spontaneous way, to openly give their opinions on textual events, this can only be an initial critical move. What students say is and should be valued as significant, but why they are responding in this way seems more significant, more critically and culturally relevant" (109). I would add only the idea that the teacher's meanings need be examined as much as the students'.

This focus on how we make the meanings we do and why—what is at stake in our interpretations—speaks to issues I raised in Chapter Three, as well as the concerns of cultural critics. Elizabeth Ellsworth (1992) asks how we might view a dance performance or a theater piece "without trying to make difference less strange, less threatening, less out of control by reading it through one's own cultural positions and interests" (7). She suggests we explore the social constructedness and historical roots of unfamiliarity, "to turn the othering look back on itself" (8). Judith Butler (1993a) similarly cautions that identification with a text is not "a simple matter of 'sympathy' with another's position, since sympathy involves a substitution of oneself that may well be a colonization of the other's position *as* one's own" (118). It seems that this notion of identifying with, yet not possessing, might be similar to the psychoanalytic goal of living with our multiple tendencies without splitting them. Is this always the challenge in terms of race, as well as gender and sexuality?

Clearly, I want to encourage students to read for personal empathy *and* text-based analysis, to engage feelings and critique. But I also want to make the reader conscious of herself as a reader. This is a difficult task for a reader alone in her living room, one much more easily facilitated by a group in which various readings become evident and its members can collectively foreground and scrutinize their assumptions. As simple a process as writing and sharing our summaries of a particular passage becomes a chance to compare our readings and examine the histories, values, and knowledge that shape them, to show, as David Bleich (1991) puts it, how a particular piece of literature "'lives' in us" (22).

But *how* to "turn the othering back on itself" as Ellsworth suggests? Gloria Anzaldúa (1981) writes, "White eyes do not want to know us" (165). When I read Anzaldúa's essays, what are my motives? What is at stake in my interpretations? When I say my students in Boston and I "created individual and group contexts within which to begin reading *Hillbilly Women* and learn from the women of Appalachia," how did the contexts we created then structure what we learned? What was excluded? When many people agreed with the woman who said, "'Spilled Salt' . . . became mine," what did this ownership mean? When the readers theater helped us invest ourselves in the story (of *Brewster Place*) and its characters, what were we invested in?

Among the questions that will help me and my students think about these issues are the following: Do our responses to this text demonstrate a stake in the Otherness of the people represented? On the other hand, are there times we've *over*identified with someone, overlooking what's unique in his experience? In other words, have we made the strange become familiar rather than the familiar strange? How can we consider the ways in which this reading might make our own worlds seem, as James Clifford might put it, 'newly incomprehensible'?

Notes

1. This quote and each of the following from this classroom discussion come from "Class Notes, New Mexico Folder."

2. Families may, for example, place a mezuzah at the front door, light candles at sundown on Friday, or prepare unleavened bread at Easter. These customs are seldom acknowledged as Jewish. In fact, many family members may not know that they are.

3. Quique Aviles is a Salvadoran actor, poet, and performer whose aim is to encourage dialogue on social issues that affect everyone who lives in America. Michelle Banks is an artist/educator living and working in Washington, D.C. Previously published in *Redescubriendo América*. 1992. A. Ramos, D. Menkart, G. Belli, and L Holmes-Bonilla (eds). Washington, D.C.: Network of Educators on the Americas.

4. This idea was adapted from a suggestion in *Redescubriendo América*, published by the Network of Educators on the Americas, Washington, D.C. in 1992.

5. From "Class Notes, Philadelphia, Folder One."

6. From "*Neighbors Talk* Workshop Notes Folder."

7. From "Class Notes, New Mexico Folder."

8. I learned this technique in a workshop given by Ira Shor.

9. The accusation of using too many negative or depressing materials is a familiar one to progressive teachers. Interestingly, while teachers often raise this objection to particular readings, students rarely do, and it seems like a somewhat patronizing, if well-meaning, determination of "what students need." A dialogue found in *Unmasking Face to Face*, by Belliveau, Marchant, and Yankwitt (1995), turns this notion around. "'Sometimes it's depressing to learn the truth about things,' said Denise. Iris looked at her with a big grin and said, 'Yeah, but this is information we can tell other people, especially when they're putting us down for being on welfare. These are fighting words!'" (35)

10. Titles, questions, and predictions from "Class Notes, Boston, Folder Two."

11. In the ten years I have been teaching literacy and basic writing, the majority of each and every class has been made up of students who were placed in some variation of "special" classes, by whatever name they were known in their setting and period in time. If it's criteria such as those listed here that were used to place the students there, it's very easy to see how bias operates in this tracking.

12. It seems as though many teachers have little problem acknowledging that the IQ test is biased as far as culture, class, and gender. Yet that knowledge does not keep the same people from continuing to refer to its results as a foundation for classification.

Six

Creating Theme-Based Curricula
More Strategies for Reading and Writing

Where else to begin a class on reading and writing than to find out what people want to read and write about? Some of the questions teachers often raise—"How do we help people become less afraid to write?" or "How do we motivate people to read and write?"—really do become moot once people are engaged with reading and writing, using literacy to root out answers to questions they have identified, in an investigation they have structured, believing there are people who will collaborate with them in the study and listen while they think out loud.

The focus of this chapter is on classroom themes for collective investigation—both those a teacher brings to class, such as the themes of education, work, or language, and those the group identifies, from date rape to colonization. Here again, I offer specific techniques as tools for digging in once the class has chosen an issue.

But I want to point out here that, of course, talking and writing aren't always enough. One day I noticed a student who had previously written easily wasn't picking up her pen. "Why is it hard today?" I asked. "This is only talk," she said. "Things never change." I remembered two *Neighbors Talk* participants who came from an adult literacy program asking me why I always asked them to write "negative things." I looked at my exercises and asked myself and them if I was really doing that. We weren't sure, but it didn't look like it. When I asked one of the young men about the positive things he would like to write, he an-

154

swered, "I don't have a foundation for knowing what they are." Both
examples point to the need for a relationship between adult literacy
programs, where people write, and community organizations, where
people work for change.

First Themes[1]

I've learned that rather than encouraging participation, I have to begin
with it. Yet I don't usually start a semester by asking that we identify a
theme together because we're not a group yet, and because I haven't yet
proven that a real exploration of something people really care about is
possible in the class. In the past when I tried to have students generate a
theme in the beginning of a term, the frequent responses were variations
of "I don't know. You decide; you're the teacher." I've come to think this
response is not just about traditional expectations of teachers' and students' roles; I believe the "I don't know" is really, "I don't have anything
to say that I think you want to hear." That I do want to hear students'
ideas and questions, that there's a community of people in the room
that wants to hear them and can help explore them, are things I have
yet to prove at that time. So I come in the first day with a theme to start
us off, usually work or education, followed by language. Though the
first two are much broader than the themes we usually come up with
later, they are subjects about which everyone has a story to tell, which
helps us begin to demonstrate what we know and who we are.

I start on the first day of class introducing a few of my ideas as a
teacher, the most important being that the reading and writing skills
people are there to work on—which they very often identify at that
point as reading comprehension or spelling—are best honed through
the acts of reading and writing themselves. I explain that *what* we read
and write about matters.

Teachers have often come up with regional concerns when I've
asked what themes they might use to begin a class. In Jellico, Tennessee,
some suggested "What will we do when the coal is gone?"; tobacco
prices emerged in Dungannon, Virginia, as did sewage and community-
owned businesses. Many teachers picked summer tourists as a prob-
lematic issue in Maine. And in Vermont, a number of people thought
they might take a historic look at the changes brought to local towns as
developers and "flatlanders" moved in.

While I have ideas in my head before we begin, in practice, the topics of work, education, and language are always led in new directions
by the concerns that come up in students' initial writings. And whatever comes up—our family backgrounds, the places where we grew
up—become reference points we use in later themes. The following are

some of the ideas I've used to get us started. All involve discussion, writing, and reading.

Education

School Memories As I mentioned earlier, many people have written about feelings of personal failure in school on the one hand and the racism of the schools they attended on the other. Once students have articulated some experiences, try asking everyone to jot a quick reaction to the following student, quoted by Herbert Kohl (1991) in *I Won't Learn From You!*:

> To agree to learn from a stranger who does not respect your integrity causes a major loss of self. The only alternative is to not learn and reject the stranger's world. (16)

Education as Forbidden There have been many situations in which education has been seen as a threat to those who want to maintain power. Readings and discussions on the assassination of literacy workers by the Tontons Macoutes in Haiti and by the contras in Nicaragua provide two powerful examples. An examination of Haitian and Nicaraguan literacy curricula that are tied to social change, and the oral histories of slaves who learned to read and write despite laws against it, provides further opportunities for a class to explore the connections between education and freedom.

Alternative Ways to Organize Schooling Readings on the Citizenship Schools of Appalachia, where literacy was tied to voter registration and civil rights in the 1950s, and on such alternative college programs as that created by the National Congress of Neighborhood Women in Brooklyn introduce the ideas that school can look very different from what we've known. These ideas can lead to a more fruitful discussion of the question "What would your ideal school look like?" Following this, create a collective set of guidelines to use in making your class look more like the ideal ones. Important questions to consider while doing so include "What are the concrete conditions that will make it hard?" "What is it we've come to *believe* that may make it difficult?"

Work

First Jobs Ask everyone to say a little bit about his first job. Among students, first jobs have included going to work in a cigar factory at thirteen and swatting flies on a neighbor's stoop for a penny a piece at age five. Even women who've never been paid for their work have held jobs. Ask students not to say too much, so you have time for everyone to speak, but enough so that you hear the beginning of a story and can jot down one or two key words or phrases. After initial writings, listen for the common themes and build on them. As mentioned in Chapter Four, these have included the different and not-so-different experiences of work in the South and in the North; the tension for women between their work lives and demands at home; common attitudes toward personal care work—as hospital workers, domestic workers, home health attendants—and both the similarities and differences in the ways people wrote about these and factory work.

A further way to explore underlying themes in work experiences is to read published work narratives before looking at the differences and similarities among our own.

Grandparents' or Parents' Work As I mentioned earlier, the majority of students at the community college where I taught came from segregated Boston neighborhoods. Many were sitting for the first time with people from other communities, with whom they assumed they had little in common. Yet in writings about their parents' or grandparents' jobs, similarities emerged in the work experiences of Irish and Portuguese immigrants to Boston and African American grandparents. The lesson I learned in *Survival News* made me realize that breaking into small, multicultural groups for discussion and revision of their pieces furthered the writings' ability to expand students' perceptions of one another.

The Ideal Job: Alternative Ways to Organize Work Readings on worker cooperatives and worker-owned businesses from day care centers to print shops—in the United States and around the world—help open up discussion and new thoughts on ways to organize work.

Investigating Work Using the What Do You Know?/What Do You Want to Know? exercise found later in this chapter, a class at a school of office technology generated the following list of questions, based on their own past experience in office work, restaurants, trucking, and the postal service:

What kind of equipment do I need to be trained on?

Is it the same as what I'm training on here?

Is there room for advancement in my career?

What if the boss doesn't like my personality?

Can I take initiative or am I just supposed to take orders?

What if the boss expects me to sleep with him?

Can *I get* the job?

A discussion of these questions revealed that the equipment many of the students were learning to use was out-of-date and that the jobs for which they were preparing had little room for advancement. To address other questions, we read literature from organizations such as the Workers' Rights Law Project and the 9 to 5 Working Women's Organization and interviewed representatives from each.

Language

Home Language Using the reactions exercise described in Chapter Four, ask students to respond to the following quote by novelist Amy Tan:

> When I was growing up, my mother's "limited" English limited *my* perception of her. I was ashamed of her English. I believed that her English reflected the quality of what she had to say. That is, because she expressed them imperfectly, her thoughts were imperfect. And I had plenty of empirical evidence to support me: the fact that people in department stores, at banks, and at restaurants did not take her seriously, did not give her good service, pretended not to understand her, or even acted as if they did not hear her. (1991, 198)

Or ask students to respond to the following:

> Who is to say that robbing a people of its language is less violent than war?
>
> —Ray Gwyn Smith
> (in Anzaldúa 1981, 53)

Standard English Use the idea of taking apart categories, discussed in Chapter Three, as a way to look at how one language viewed as proper and one viewed as incorrect came to be seen as such. Once again, writing teacher Carol Snyder (1984) suggests the following tasks and questions:

> Identify what the classification excludes.
>
> Does it privilege or disadvantage particular groups of people, things, or ideas?
>
> Who devised the classification?
>
> When did the classification arise?
>
> Where did the classification arise? (212–14)

Initiate a research project on who, and with what interests, has been behind "English Only" movements.

Read Black English, like pieces from *Their Eyes Were Watching God*, by Zora Neale Hurston (1978). Use excerpts from *The Joys of Yiddish* by Leo Rosten (1968) to illustrate how difficult translation can be. Bring in

"To Tame a Wild Tongue," in which Gloria Anzaldúa (1987) argues that Chicano Spanish, a border language, "is not incorrect. It is a living language . . . a patois" (55). Suggest that the difference between a language and a dialect is dialects do not have armies.

At a neighborhood youth center, participants chose the slogan "Slang *Is* Proper" for *United Youth of Boston*:

> If it wasn't in slang, it wouldn't be a teen newspaper. It would be the *Herald* or the *Globe*. It would be weird, man.
>
> Yeah, like the *Globe* would say, "He used a .38-caliber gun in self-defense." We'd say, "He tried to shoot me, so I pulled out my joint first."
>
> People hear slang, they should read in slang.
>
> If you was raised in the South, you talk slang.
>
> If I'm talking to the president, I'm not gonna say, "Yo, what up, dog?" But I'm not talking to the president here.

Speaking A Second Language Have students write their reactions to the ideas expressed here.

Sometimes in a new language, one can say new things. Or avoid painful memories, as in the case of Holocaust survivors born in Germany or Austria, some of whom choose not to speak in the language of their childhood. Perhaps more often, there are things that a new language *cannot* express:

> To express yourself, your feelings, memory, problems, mood, all the shades of your condition, I'll never ever be able to do it the same way as in Russian.
>
> —Tatyana Mozik, *Other Colors*
> (Martin & Schreiber 1996, 39)

Ask students to consider the words of Latina educator and philosopher María Lugones (Lugones & Spelman 1983). Speaking here of women in academia, does her experience bear out in your classroom, as well?

> We and you do not talk the same language. When we talk to you we use your language: the language of your experience and of your theories. We try to use it to communicate our world of experience. But since your language and your theories are inadequate in expressing our experience, we only succeed in communicating our experience of exclusion. (575)

A Justification for Theft Use the example of the way Western historians have been able to distort Hawaiian history, relying on non-Hawaiians' ignorance of the language, to portray Hawaii as a feudal system ruled by despotic chiefs prior to becoming U.S. property. Here,

Haunani-Kay Trask (1993) writes on the evidence, in language, that no one had owned land before the Whites came.

> If the historians had bothered to learn our language . . . they would have discovered that we show possession in two ways: through the use of an "a" possessive, which reveals acquired status, and through the use of an "o" possessive, which denotes inherent status. My body (*ko 'u kino*) and my parents (*ko 'u mākua*) for example, take the "o" form; most material objects, such as food (*ka 'u mea' ai*) take the "a" form. But land, like one's body and one's parents, takes the "o" possessive (*ko 'u 'āina*). Thus, in our way of speaking, land is inherent to the people; it is like our bodies and our parents. The people cannot exist without the land, and the land cannot exist without the people. (151)

As Trask points out, "By inventing a false feudal past, the historians justify—and become complicitous in—massive American theft" (151).

Collective Themes

In time, the themes I've mentioned so far reach a stopping point. (They do often reemerge, however, weaving in and out of one another throughout the semester.) It's at this point that I suggest we pick the next theme together. Sometimes I've begun by handing out the following:

> You must be able to write what you think—and maybe what you write about your day today will be some of the same problems that the people of the world are fighting out.
>   You must be able to write what you have to say, and know that this is what matters; and I hope you can see that you can begin anywhere and end up as far as anybody else has reached. I hope you are not scared to write about what concerns you, what you know—these things matter.
>
> —C. L. R. James

We use a simple brainstorming method to select a common topic. I think it's important to explain that this is a process of letting ideas come to the surface without yet committing yourself to them. They can be considered later; at this point there's no debate or even discussion. I ask people what they want to read, write, think, and talk about over the next few weeks, and they begin calling out ideas as they come to them. By this time we've begun building a community of people who listen to each other, helping each other speak ideas into existence. It's within this context that people offer suggestions, even if slowly at first.

Someone once said that silences can be the hardest thing for a teacher to live with; we're inclined to fill them up. I agree. Yet I find if

I can hold out, the seemingly empty space almost always becomes more productive than awkward, allowing people to think, letting them know I'm serious about wanting to know what they think. To ease some of the anxiety that silence can create, as much in me as in my students, I often say, "Take some time to think," and allow the silence to continue.

My ideas of what to read and write about go into the pot, too. So far, they've never dominated, as evidenced by the fact that they're almost never chosen. I do earnestly contribute them, though. I think it's important, as I've suggested earlier, in establishing that I have a voice in the room, and that it's one of many.

I then ask that everyone vote for three of the ideas on the board. With the narrowed list that results, I ask for someone who advocates a particular topic to speak to it, so that we can consider each possibility more carefully before a final vote. This final vote is meant to elicit one common theme that interests everyone. Usually it works, but at times we've been left with two in order that everyone feel satisfied. We decide which theme to go with first and return to the other later. I've only had one group that could not choose a theme together, and as I think about it now, that makes some sense. It was the first group I facilitated for *Survival News*. The women came together to write articles for the newspaper, and many already knew what they wanted to write about. Still, among even these seemingly disparate topics, common themes emerged. Thus individual pieces were strengthened as we created groupings for the final layout and shaping of the paper. Included among them were "Our Husbands, Our Sons, Ourselves," "Poor to the Bitter End," and "Gringos, Go Home!"

Investigating AIDS and Taking Action

One of our topics at the Women's School was AIDS. Early on, I tried something that came to mind because of a mistake I'd made with an earlier theme. Having identified questions to investigate regarding rape, the group got stuck in what seemed a state of fear and anger from which it was difficult to consider new information and formulate new ideas. Ellen Berry and Elizabeth Black (1987) have written, "Losing one's bearings can act as a catalyst for growth, provided that the instructor offers 'the counterbalancing influence of supports'" (60). I didn't, and we seemed immobilized.

We agreed to abandon the topic and go on to AIDS, the second issue we'd chosen. The first day we began talking about AIDS, I sensed a similar intense feeling in the room. At that moment, I suggested we stop what we were doing and each write down our fears about AIDS. Some of us were worried about earlier blood transfusions; others, whether our partners were maintaining pledges of monogamy. As always, no one was required to share her writing, and some didn't. But for all of us, just letting the pen move and naming our fears seemed to provide a kind of catharsis that allowed us to go on.

We then returned to our initial list of questions, which included:

What is AIDS?

How do you get it?

How do you protect yourself?

Why are Black and Latino people getting it more than others?

Why isn't there a cure?

If they find a cure, will the government pay or let people die?

Is it safe to be near someone with AIDS?[2]

Each person decided which of the questions she wanted to investigate. We read articles people brought in from the newspaper, as well as pamphlets I found. It gradually became clear that the lines I'd drawn in my head between personal, political, and practical issues were blurred. After learning about self-protection, there came the question of what to do if you're a heterosexual woman who wants to use a condom and the man you're having sex with refuses. While the educational literature available on AIDS today includes many community-oriented brochures and booklets that address the range of issues that come up when AIDS is considered, the literature available at that time concealed the underlying issues. It also left untouched political questions, such as why there is no cure. And many of the pamphlets were full of "medicalese." We wended our way through dense language and attempted to puzzle out the more difficult medical questions as well as the political ones. After a few weeks, I made the suggestion that we write our own pamphlet on AIDS, one that would be easier to read and, in addition to giving some basic information, would take on the deeper questions.

The women didn't have a general perception of themselves as authoritative writers at that time, though I believe they began to in the process of writing the pamphlet. Once I made the suggestion, they jumped on the idea, and we began.

We first decided to organize the pamphlet by stating our initial questions and presenting some of the answers we found. We pulled out all the writings we'd done since we started the investigation. In most cases, more than one person had worked on a question. The writers got together and decided how to combine their writings into one, considering the most important things to say and an order for saying them. We looked back at the initial writings about our fears and decided they would set the stage for the question-and-answer section. We chose to use letters a few people had written as the cornerstone for a section titled, "A Special Note to Men." (These had been written during a discussion about condoms and the fear of talking about them with a male partner.) An in-class writing of mine became "A Note to Sisters."

The board of the Women's School gave us $100 for paper and copying. We inserted the pamphlet into the 1,100 copies of the *Philadelphia Daily News* that Mildred's son delivered and took the rest to West Philly pizza parlors, grocery stores, beauty salons, and churches.

I want to add that through this process, we recognized a link between Black and Gay oppression. This was both overtly expressed in "Why Isn't There a Cure?" and implied when the women decided to follow the suggestion of one student who said that if we were going to capitalize the word *Black*, we should also capitalize *Gay*. But all was not ideal. African Americans and gays were written about as though mutually exclusive, and the pamphlet didn't address lesbian women, due in some measure to my failure to lead an in-depth look at homophobic assumptions.[3]

"Marriage" in the Bahamas, "Date Rape" in a Women's College of Art

Making content and analysis the foundation for developing skills seems so key that I believe it's worth mentioning two more projects here.

Nan Elsasser (Fiore & Elsasser 1982) taught an all-women literacy class at the College of the Bahamas in 1979. The class picked marriage as its topic for the semester. In small groups, students created subtopics that included housework, divorce, sex, and abuse. In an article coauthored with Kyle Fiore, Elsasser describes the structure of the investigation, how she found reading materials, and the students' developing literacy skills. The semester ended with the class composing an open "Letter to Bahamian Men," published in Nassau's daily newspapers.

I read Elsasser's article when I was teaching pre-freshman composition at a women's college of art in Philadelphia, where the students felt they didn't need to know how to write. Motivation being next to nil, I was determined to find a compelling topic. Through a process similar to the one outlined earlier, we selected date rape as our theme. Some of the questions we investigated were: Why does it happen? How widespread is it? How can a woman prevent it? Where can she turn for help?[4] Inspired by Elsasser and her students in the Bahamas, I asked the women in my class if they wanted to write an open letter to the college community. There was no regularly published school newspaper, so we distributed "Moore W.A.R." (Women Against Rape) as a broadside, leaving it in conspicuous places throughout the building. Some sections were written individually, some collaboratively. It began with a typical date rape scenario, followed by a definition and some statistics, and then ideas about its cause and ways to prevent it. We ended with resources women could turn to in Philadelphia and a call for women at the college to talk about the issue. Following its publication, several students met with the dean and invited guest speakers the next semester to address collegewide audiences.

The Border Crossed Us

On occasion, I suggest a topic outside of the brainstorming process, as I did in one community college class in which there were Vietnamese, Haitian, and Cape Verdean students.

Ginoux, who is from Haiti and is a nurse's aid, spoke in class one day about the White people in the nursing home who did not want her touching them. In response, Tran, who is Vietnamese and a store clerk, mentioned the White customers who avoid letting their hands meet his when he returns their change. Several of the Haitian students reacted to his comment with surprise and suspicion, expressing openly and with evident hostility their disbelief that he had been discriminated against because of his color. This came at a point when I had been wondering how to make a bridge among the students who sat next to, and talked before and after class with, only people from their own countries.

All of the students in the class were from countries that had been under colonial rule, two by the French. I brought in historical readings and asked everyone to pick something from a country other than his or her own. Following the readings, it was the Haitian and Vietnamese students who spoke most directly to one another. "Who annihilated the Indian population of Haiti?" "Why was Haiti occupied by both the Spanish and the French?" "What is the history of slaves in Haiti?" the Vietnamese students wanted to know. The Haitian students, very familiar with their country's history, were able to answer the questions, and at least one Vietnamese student knew about the 1804 Haitian victory over the French. Haitian students asked, "What was the difference between the Japanese and the French occupations in Vietnam?" "Were the Vietnamese slaves to the French?" "Were you taught in Vietnamese in school?"[5] The Vietnamese students were also able to answer these and other questions. It's worth noting here that this was a "developmental" reading course. In general, the college faculty's expectation of the students is low, as evidenced by the simplistic text many choose and the multiple-choice exit exam given. Yet the participants of this class dug in without hesitation to difficult readings and responded to the opportunity to demonstrate expertise.

To begin this kind of discussion, pull out a world map and simply ask students what they notice as they scrutinize it. Many will be struck by the notations "UK," "Fr" and "USA" under small islands throughout the South Pacific, Caribbean, and elsewhere. Ask if any of the students come from countries formerly colonized. Of course, current maps won't indicate this.

As you read and discuss colonization, create a large-size world map and fill in the information the class finds important about each country you discuss. Along the way, draw arrows to signify the connections you see and double lines to mark the contrasts. Be sure to also jot small notations so the group remembers later what the specific connections and differences are. You might ask students to use these connections and differences as the basis for a writing. This process, too, can point to future research in which the class wants to engage.

Finally, write the following on the board: "We didn't cross the border. The border crossed us." Then structure a research project that looks into the creation of the border between Mexico and the United States. Ask students to respond to Daniel Ellsberg's observation that "*Newsweek* would have us believe that boundaries are drawn by Mother Nature."[6]

A Curriculum on Immigration: Redefining Multiculturalism, and a Move Toward Solidarity

I've mentioned earlier that I want to use techniques that help students create their own meanings out of an experience or a text, without assuming I know what that meaning will be. I think I come close to that now, and much of Chapters Four and Five focused on this. But what I want further is to question the very conditions of that meaning making itself, both for my students and for myself.

I recently completed a teachers' guide to accompany a documentary series of radio interviews with women immigrants to Boston.[7] Many of the students who will listen to *Other Colors* (Martin Schreiber 1996) are not themselves immigrants. In the current climate of anti-immigrant hysteria, nonimmigrants often talk using a homogeneous "us" and "them." The guide asks: What happens when the borders are crossed or when the "us" have parents who are "them"? How is it that many White people regard a White South African immigrant as "same" and a Latina immigrant as "different"?

> I don't think that people will consider that I am American. When they saw me they ask, "Where are you from"? . . . Can I go to the White people and say, "Where you from?" I never say that, or the White

people themselves, they never ask each other "Where you from?" but if they saw me, "Where you from? Vietnam? Chinese?"[8]

—Saly Pin-Riebe, *Other Colors*

The irony of that for me is because I'm White there's always been the assumption that I'm the same.

—Susan Brown, *Other Colors*

Other Colors attempts to loosen binary oppositions. The danger that comes from viewing the world as composed of either/ors is that there is *always* an Other whose identity is different from one's own. While Mariana Castillo speaks in the following quote from *Other Colors* of experiences in the lesbian community, many immigrant women are engaged in a similar play between acceptance and exclusion in each of the communities in which they move.

I couldn't be open as a lesbian in Venezuela. Because the culture is not ready to deal with homosexuality. But here the shock was I couldn't connect with a culture that would accept my own way of being but rather emphasized the differences. "You are Latina, I am White, therefore what we share is that we're lesbians, but very clearly, this is your own territory and this is mine." That's painful. That was very painful to me.

Other Colors is meant to illuminate some of the experiences and perspectives of women immigrants and at the same time show that cultures interweave and all of our identities are permeable and subject to change at various moments. Susan Brown is a White woman from South Africa. On the tape, she says,

Even though my parents and my teachers and the whole system in which I grew up really tried to obliterate black culture from my daily experience, it did filter through.

But many people born in the United States regard immigrants as Other, and racism is exploding in neighborhoods, worksites, and classrooms. Prejudices among immigrant communities can also be intense. *Other Colors* is based on the belief that an acceptance of the ambiguity of categories will loosen racism, as well as tensions that exist among members of different ethnic and cultural groups. None of this is meant to deny that those acknowledged as White benefit from White-skinned privilege, while people of color are the target of individual prejudice, institutionalized racism, and sometimes violence. It's also important to say that this is not an argument for assimilation or erasure of difference, but rather for a recognition of the ways in which we all jump across and between cultures.

A White woman listening to *Other Colors* wrote about the shifting position of immigrants for her: "Hearing the tapes made me realize immigrants are people. They have a voice. They're not just 'immigrants.'" In addition, categories of race have come into question. Another White student asked me, "What race are you? I mean, people wouldn't go up to you and say, 'Hey, White girl.' You're Jewish, right? So what's your race?" When I answered, "White," she said, "No, you're not." She seemed to be struggling with classifications that are becoming less clearcut to her.[9]

Other Colors reexamines current notions of multiculturalism. The term *multicultural* is typically used to describe a situation in which individuals of different cultures coexist. Multicultural curricula are created to help students appreciate diversity. But in their celebration of difference, they sometimes end up inadvertently reinforcing stereotypes and divisions. And in their evocations of harmonious pluralism, they ignore issues of power and a social structure that supports domination based on class, sexuality, gender, and race. With regard to undocumented immigrants, the fact remains that Mexicans are hunted down while Canadians are given little attention.

In a view of multiculturalism presented here and in *Other Colors*, there is a recognition that the borders between cultures are not rigid. Multiculturalism exists within individuals; we see it when Native American students in the Southwest adopt hip-hop clothes and gestures, when Honduran women living in Boston identify as both Black and Latina, when Chicana lesbians feel at home in the worlds of their families and in lesbian communities and at the same time, feel exiled in both. New Mexico college student J. Flores-Williams (1994) writes,

> The issue [of identity] becomes . . . clouded . . . if your last name is Williams, you look Caucasian, but grew up going to your *abuela's* house every Sunday morning for *menudo*, while the adults talked Spanish so you couldn't understand what they were saying. (63)

Flores-Williams' childhood positions were similar to that of Native American writer Michael Dorris (1994):

> Everybody I encountered in literature simply was unequivocally who they were . . . Where were my role models? Where was Helen, Half-Breed Hunkpapa of Houston, or Murray, the Mixed-Blood Maverick, leaping conflicting ethnicities in a single, effortless bound? Look, up in the sky! It's both a bird and a plane! It's Super-Combo! (52)

Henry Louis Gates (1991b) talks of culture as "porous, dynamic and interactive, rather than the fixed property of particular ethnic groups" (37). Speaking of dance, for example, he points out, "Judith Jamison,

Alvin Ailey, and Katherine Dunham all excelled at 'Western' cultural forms, melding these with African-American styles to produce performances that were neither, and both . . . Indeed, the greatest African-American art can be thought of as an exploration of that hyphenated space between the African and the American" (38).

Poststructuralism encourages us to look at the hyphenated space we all inhabit, the ways we, ourselves, are living in borderlands. The idea is to acknowledge where experiences among people are different without overlooking the ways we are the same. One of the central tensions in education lies in finding a way to remain culturally sensitive without accepting ethnic and racial stereotypes. One way to avoid stereotyping or essentializing culture is to show its fluidity. As Mariana Castillo, a Venezuelan composer living in the United States, says in *Other Colors*, "Here I'm seen as a Latina, and therefore the music that I can write is probably Latin music, and if I were in Venezuela I could write Latin music or I could write a symphony for a film."

A further tension lies in recognizing that while culture, difference, and racial identity are not completely fixed, neither are they entirely fluid. High school researcher Jody Cohen (1993) writes here of her interviews with African American students:

> Tamika talks about a friend's white boyfriend who "just fit in so well with everybody." Nevertheless, when I ask whether she ever forgets he is white, Tamika and Yvonne respond, "You can't forget somebody's white!" (298)

"The Nature of Classroom Discourse Changes When Inquiry Begins" [10]

Midway through our investigations of the themes students chose at the Women's School, I felt frustrated. I saw people formulating new ideas through readings and then leaving them behind in the next discussion, contradicting the new thoughts they'd just articulated. For example, some of the women talked about the way society is set up to condone rape. But then the same women insisted that men get raped just as often as women do or that the way to stop rape is to castrate rapists; their conclusions didn't follow their assumptions. It seemed that deep-seated fears were getting in the way.

At about this same time, I was reading Eleanor Duckworth's "Teaching as Research" (1986). She raises questions for teachers about their students' thoughts:

Which ideas build on which others and how?

Which get in the way of others?

How does an idea get modified?

How does a firmly held conviction influence how a person reads an experience?

In what circumstances is a person confused by/deaf to/helped by another person's thoughts?

How does a new idea lead to new questions and vice versa? (490)

Duckworth was talking about a teacher's investigation into the way her students learn. But it seemed to me that these questions could form a guideline from which we as a group could become more self-conscious of our own processes of analysis and build on them.

I began the next class by talking about what I saw happening the previous Wednesday: people stating ideas and then backing off from them, contradicting themselves instead of integrating new thoughts into old ideas. I raised the examples I mentioned here. I brought up the notion of analysis—calling up and looking deeply at what we know—and suggested we try three things:

1. Consider our opinions based on what we've read or heard someone say and then self-consciously either strengthening or changing them.
2. Note whether or not our conclusions follow our assumptions.
3. Ask one another for clarification more often, so that we encourage one another to closely examine the sense we're making and also make sure we're really getting what others are saying.

Here again, I was influenced by Duckworth (1986), who sees one of her primary functions as a teacher to "have the students try to explain the sense they are making" (482). As she puts it, "in order to explain it they seek out more phenomena that will shed light on it" (482). I knew this was true; it's true when I explain something to someone else. The questions that arise most often in Duckworth's classes are:

What do you mean?

Why do you think that?

I don't quite get it. Is that the same as what (someone else) thought [she] saw? (486)

I suggested we use these questions in our discussions, and I demonstrated their use in the next class, pointing to each as a way to consider something more deeply.

Before class I'd wondered if a reaction to all this might be, "This isn't what we're here for." But students didn't react that way at all; rather, they seemed really engaged with the whole notion of analysis. Some felt we *had* analyzed on the day when we'd been talking about rape. One woman thought we hadn't, that we'd "only expressed our feelings, which is different."

Two weeks later I noted in my journal, "Is it my imagination or are more people saying more often, 'This may be off the subject, but . . . '?"[11] If it were true, I take it as a sign that people were becoming more geared to noting where a discussion was going and which ideas were relevant to the problem we were struggling with and which weren't. If we did go off the subject, it was more consciously. It was precisely a lack of this kind of cohesion that I had often perceived to be a problem for us in discussions before.

As I've said, I'm not always sure that my perception of the track I think we're veering from is shared by everyone else. And undoubtedly, there are other perfectly reasonable tracks that I don't perceive as such. I once tape-recorded a Women's School discussion on condoms. My idea was for us to look at the transcript as a group to see (1) where everyone thought we started to really analyze something, (2) where we got off track, and (3) where we were expressing contradictions. However, I didn't finish transcribing the discussion till the semester was nearly over, and then it seemed too late to go back over the condom discussion. In retrospect, I'm sure we still could have done it. I think that for all of us, it had been a pivotal discussion. Several of the women faced very painful personal conflicts, and each of us took risks in revealing ourselves to each other. Using Duckworth's questions might have helped us become more self-conscious about what we were learning in that discussion.

Expanding Ideas and Questions: Strategies to Structure the Inquiry

Each of the strategies here has been chosen for its ability to open a dialogue among participants and encourage expansive thinking on the issues raised in class. They also make room for more students to fully participate in the group discussion, which becomes richer as a result. Many stimulate reading and writing.

Please note that many of the strategies in this and the following sections may be used either with the class as a whole or in small-group format, depending on the needs of the group at a given moment.

What Do You Know?

A good start to picking a theme apart is to ask each student to divide a piece of paper into two columns, listing everything he knows about the topic on the left-hand side. Then, while he sits back and reviews his list, ask him to jot on the right side of the paper everything he wants to know. Some of the things students know may be based on misinformation or stereotypes. If the topic is immigration, for example, nonimmigrants may include something like "Most immigrants are on welfare." Ask them if there's anything on the left side of which they're not actually sure. If so, ask them to turn these into questions for the column on the right. Sometimes we go through this process collaboratively, sometimes individually. In either case, activating what we know has helped point us to what we don't.

Sometimes we make a composite list of the things in everyone's right-hand column and then decide on an order for investigating the questions. This ordering process creates further items for the "Want to Know" list, because as we explain the relationships we perceive between ideas, we also see further gaps.

As a way to demonstrate that no category is given, we go back and reorder/regroup as the class moves through the theme, reframing the way we view it, whether the topic is immigration or the U.S. invasion of Haiti.

After reading and research, return to the collective list of questions raised in "What Do You Know?/What Do You Want to Know?" and look at which you answered, what new ones arose, and which of the things once believed are now called into question. You can then create a group strategy for investigating the questions that remain. What else does the class want to read? Who will read what? Is there someone students might interview?

Clustering

Ask each student to draw a large circle on his paper, placing the topic in the center. Then ask that each jot down other words he thinks of, as ideas shooting out from the circle. You can do individual clusters, a collective one on the board, or individual ones to stimulate the collective. Here again, you may wish to take the ideas and, as a class, categorize them.

Fast Details

Try using the fast details activity described in Chapter Four as a way to encourage expansive thinking about your topic. This activity ends with a first draft response to the theme. After students write, facilitate a discussion on the ideas that came up. These drafts can be looked at again following further investigation into the topic.

Agree/Disagree/Not Sure

Several times now I've used this exercise when we begin digging into a topic about which there are many myths. Most recently, I used it to examine stereotypes about Native Americans. In the past, it's helped us look at gay sexuality and myths about welfare.

Hand out a few large note cards to each student. Ask each to write several things he has heard about the topic—whether he thinks they are true or not—or several things he believes. Collect all the cards and divide the class into small groups. Give each group several statements to which to respond with "Agree," "Disagree," or "Not Sure," coming up with a group decision on each. Needing to negotiate a group decision facilitates active listening and speaking and thus collective reflection. Instead of note cards, you can hand out large-size sticky notes. Give each group a sheet of flip chart paper with columns for "Agree," "Disagree," and "Not Sure." Participants can then position the sticky notes as they make decisions. Then come back to the large group and facilitate a discussion on each statement.

An alternative way to structure this exercise is to bring in your own statements on immigration or immigrants titled "Myths and Facts," and information to back them up. Post signs in three corners of the room with "Agree," "Disagree," or "Not Sure." Read the first statement and ask students to move to the sign that reflects their own responses. Then ask for a volunteer or two under each sign to articulate the reasons for their position. Following this, anyone can switch to another corner if persuaded by what someone else says. You might contribute any information you think still needs to be shared.

You can also combine the two variations above. Begin with your own statements and then ask students to contribute some.

The following is a set of statements regarding immigration. If you use this kind of "Myths and Facts" format, be prepared for students to challenge the statistics you provide. The prevailing ideology has become so normalized that information to the contrary can seem heretical. As mentioned in Chapter Three, this is an opportunity to look at how "facts" are constructed and used to support specific ends. Which, and whose, interests are served by a belief that immigrants take jobs away from U.S.-born citizens? This exercise highlights the relationship between knowledge and political goals, as much as it argues for or against truth.

The italicized statements are those you would read before students move, and the bulleted items contain information you may want to contribute to the resulting discussion. Please note that the research here is current as of 1996. You may wish to research your own statistics to be sure they are up-to-date.

1. *Black people came to the United States only as slaves.*
   - In addition to the forced migration of Africans as slaves, many Black people immigrated to the United States in the 1920s from Jamaica, Trinidad, and other parts of the West Indies.

2. *Except for Africans forced into slavery, other immigrants came to this country of their own free will.*
   - Early in the 1800s, thousands of Chinese were brought to the United States as indentured servants.

3. *The current level of legal migration to this country is about three million a year, or 1.2 percent of the total U.S. population.*
   - In fact, the current level is one million, or 0.4 percent of the total population. Undocumented immigrants number approximately two hundred thousand to three hundred thousand a year.
   - According to the 1990 U.S. census, the total immigrant population in the country was 8 percent. One and one-half percent of the total U.S. population was made up of undocumented immigrants.
   - Despite the hysteria created by advocates of Proposition 187 in California, the number of undocumented immigrants entering that state each year has remained approximately 0.3 percent of the total population for the past twenty years.
   - Of the 17.5 million political refugees recognized by the United Nations worldwide, less than 1 percent find asylum in the United States.

4. *Immigrant children generally do not do well in school. The exception to this rule are the children of Asian immigrants.*
   - Children of immigrants are as likely to graduate or drop out from high school as children of parents born in the United States.
   - In a study of Salvadoran, Guatemalan, and Nicaraguan children who came to this country as undocumented immigrants, one-half were on the honor roll, despite also working fifteen to thirty hours a week.

5. *The U.S. government can't afford to provide health care, education, and other social services to immigrants. Immigrants need to pay their share.*

- Overall, immigrants pay twenty-five to thirty billion dollars more per year in taxes than they consume in services. Each immigrant, over his or her lifetime, pays fifteen to twenty thousand dollars more in taxes than he or she receives in government benefits.
- In cities and neighborhoods where immigrants are concentrated, spending by immigrant consumers makes up a significant portion of the economy.
- Most undocumented immigrants actually use few services because they are afraid of being caught by immigration authorities. While undocumented, less than 0.5 percent of immigrants who gained legal status under the 1986 amnesty program had received food stamps or AFDC (the most well-known public welfare program at the time). Less than 1 percent had received other public assistance benefits, including general relief, Social Security, supplemental Social Security, workers' compensation, or unemployment insurance.
- Many immigrants without documentation also avoid taking advantage of needed services because they are afraid it will hurt their chances of becoming a citizen. They can, in fact, be denied permanent residence based on their likelihood of becoming a "public charge," which is evaluated, in part, on whether they have used public benefits in the past.

6. *Few immigrants to the United States end up on welfare.*
   - This is true. Working-age, nonrefugee immigrants are less likely than U.S.-born counterparts to be on welfare. Much of the general increase in welfare benefits to immigrants goes to refugees, who are immediately eligible for a range of public assistance upon arriving in the United States. Important note: A study by the University of Texas at Austin found that refugees who initially take advantage of public aid ultimately achieve greater economic independence.
   - The granting of refugee asylum in this country is often based on foreign policy bias. For example, a 1985 class action suit found that 97 percent of those from El Salvador and Guatemala who were seeking asylum from political repression had been denied refugee status, while 84 percent of those from Nicaragua were approved. At the time, the U.S. government supported the governments of El Salvador and Guatemala and was actively engaged in warfare against the Sandinista government of Nicaragua.

7. *Speaking in support of federal legislation denying welfare benefits to most immigrants, U.S. Representative Bill Archer (R–Texas) said, "My*

ancestors and most of our ancestors came to this country not with their hands out for welfare checks." It's true that very few European immigrants to the United States received public assistance when they arrived earlier this century.

- In fact, during the largest wave of European immigration to the United States, more than 50 percent of all the people on welfare were immigrants. Today, only 9 percent of immigrant families receive welfare.

8. *Immigrant workers are too intimidated to organize for better conditions or join union efforts.*

- Certainly some are, but many today continue a long history of immigrant labor activism. These are just a few examples: In California, the Justice for Janitors campaign resulted in widespread unionization in Los Angeles among predominantly immigrant workers. In 1991, Mexican and Salvadoran workers at an auto racing equipment company in Los Angeles voted to join the International Association of Machinists, creating the largest manufacturing election victory in thirty years. In San Francisco, the Asociación de Trabajadores Latinos (Latino Workers Association) organizes "know your rights" workshops for day laborers and is advocating for an increased minimum wage, and La Mujer Obrera organizes immigrant women in the garment factories of El Paso, Texas.

9. *Immigrants create jobs for U.S.-born citizens.*

- Statistics indicate that the larger the immigrant population, the larger the employment gains for natives.
- Immigrants add twice as many jobs to the country as a whole than do those born here, through the creation of new businesses, spending, and by raising the productivity of U.S. companies.
- According to several studies, immigrant workers have saved the furniture, garment, and shoe industries in Southern California and textile industries in Los Angeles, New York, and San Francisco from leaving the United States, because of the availability of immigrant labor and the low wages paid to immigrant workers.
- Reductions in wages and loss of jobs are more often a result of trade deficits and manufacturers relocating overseas than immigration.
- Between 1970 and 1980, seventy-eight thousand new jobs were created in Los Angeles by immigrants who work and those who spend money in businesses that are largely supported by immigrant communities.

- In New York State, immigrants own more than forty thousand businesses that create tens of thousands of jobs and boost the economy by three and a half billion dollars.

10. *Since 1989, the poorest immigrants to arrive in the United States have come from Asia.*
    - According to the 1990 U.S. census, immigrants from the former Soviet Union are among the poorest, as well as the least employed—far more so than immigrants from Asia or Central America.

11. *Immigrants aren't learning English.*
    - Almost all children of immigrants, and the majority of adults, can speak English after a few years in the United States.
    - Throughout the country, there is an average wait of months or sometimes years to enroll in an adult English class.

12. *The most likely person to be abused by INS/Border Patrol agents is a U.S. citizen of Mexican origin.*
    - The U.S. Border Patrol regularly practices abuse against U.S. citizens of Mexican origin and other legal residents, as well as undocumented immigrants.
    - Of the fifty-one complaints of Border Patrol abuse received by the San Diego American Friends Service Committee U.S.-Mexico Border Program in 1993, forty-one were from U.S. citizens, legal residents, or visitors with permits.
    - In the past twenty years along the U.S.-Mexico border, dozens of Mexicans have been shot and killed and dozens more wounded by U.S. Border Patrol agents, with beatings numbering in the hundreds. Not one agent has been convicted for shooting and killing a Mexican.[12]

As a way to integrate the new information, you can follow up this activity by asking students to reflect on the following questions in writing: How does this new information fit in with what you already knew? Does it agree with what you thought before, or have you revised your ideas? Most importantly, what surprised you?

A Beginning Look at the Origins of Prejudice

Trying to talk someone out of a deeply held belief, such as homophobia, can be frustrating, at best. More effective is asking the person to look at the source of the belief. Before looking at homophobia or myths about gay people, you may want to use a variation on the guided imagery described in Chapter Four. Ask students, "What do you first remember hearing or learning about lesbians, or about gay men?" In this exercise, ask everyone to close her eyes. Not everyone will; that's okay. Ask the following very slowly, allowing plenty of time for people to reflect on each question. (They can be adapted to examine other beliefs, as well.)

How old were you? Maybe you were six or eight. Younger? Older?

Where were you? At home? In school? Somewhere else? Get an image of the place.

Who was around? Your parents? Grandparents? Sisters or brothers? Friends? A teacher? Picture the person or people nearby.

What were these people saying? To whom were they talking?

Even if you're not sure you can recall a *specific* incident, what do you imagine you first heard in reference to lesbians or gays?

You may not know exactly, but what do you *think* you thought or felt at the time?

Ask everyone to open her eyes and quickly jot down the event that came to mind, or ask for verbal responses.

In the ensuing discussion, ask each student how the event she's describing might relate to current perceptions.

Reexamining Beliefs and Relationships: Additional Strategies

These exercises give everyone a chance to reconsider their initial ideas, changing or strengthening them.

Dyads

After an exercise, or at any point during a discussion, ask people to pair up with someone nearby. Give everyone three to five minutes each to just talk about what she's heard so far. The listener's job is to simply encourage the speaker to keep talking, without interrupting her. You can use these dyads also while watching a video, stopping it at some point to encourage reflection on what you've seen so far and deeper engagement with what's to follow.

Dialogue Journal Groups

Dialogue journals provide an opportunity for students to jot down ideas about what they've heard or read and have other students respond to them. To begin, create small groups of three or four students each. Ask everyone to take a new sheet of paper and jot down reactions to whatever happened in class that day or week. Students in each group then pass their papers clockwise once. Each person takes the reaction in front of him and jots a response to it. Then students pass the papers clockwise once again. Now each student has a sheet of paper containing two people's comments, to which he responds. After passing papers a final time, everyone responds to three comments. After the final round, give each group a folder into which to place the papers.

The important thing about dialogue journals is to keep them going over several weeks or more. Whenever the time feels right, have students move into their journal groups and begin. Students may initially think this exercise makes no sense, since they can easily *talk* to the members of their group. Let them know that dialogue journals often allow for ideas to emerge in a way that discussion doesn't. And in the end, each group has a record of the thinking that's gone on during the semester. This activity also ensures that students who don't participate verbally will be an equal part of the written conversation.

Note: Tell students you'll be collecting the folders from time to time, to get a sense of what's on everyone's mind.

Redoing the Cluster

Take the same words you clustered earlier and recluster them, comparing the ideas you form to the previous ones.

Revising Drafts

Have students pull out initial drafts of writing done before inquiry into the theme began. Ask if, after reading or hearing what they have, anyone would want to change his first or last sentence. Ask those who do to see if a changed premise or conclusion means they need to revise anything in the middle.

Another way to initiate a second draft is to simply ask, "How would you revise your writing based on what you have heard?"

As students move their initial writings through several drafts, ask them to talk with the class about the ways their ideas are changing.

A Student-Created Role Play

Ask the students to come up with characters and a scene that represent a dilemma central to your theme. For instance, if the theme is "Our Children's Schools," they may come up with a scene in which community members have a meeting with the neighborhood school's principal regarding needed improvements in the bilingual program. Once they've got a fairly fleshed-out central issue and a scene, let a few participants begin creating a dialogue. If they get stuck at any point, you might ask, "Anyone want to help out?" Then others can call out suggestions or even take over a role.

At some point, you might also freeze the action and ask everyone to take a piece of paper and write what she imagines will happen next. Let them know a few lines could suffice, or they may need a page—it doesn't matter. You can gauge by looking about the room, but three or four minutes is usually enough time to allow for this writing. Now use these writings as the basis for further discussion. A role play can also be turned into a fotonovela—a story told in photographs with balloon captions—in ESL and literacy classes.

Comparing Descriptions and Summaries: Class, Gender, and Race

Divide the class into small groups, and assign each group a different character from a multicultural reading, audiocassette, or videotape. Ask the group members to list words that describe the person, and then compare the descriptions among the groups. What do these descriptions reveal about class, gender, and race—or about our notions of the same? Alternatively, as suggested in the previous chapter, have each student write his own summary of a text. In sharing these, help students examine the histories, values, and knowledge that shaped them.

Interviewing

There are many times when it makes sense to ask students to interview one another or someone outside the class regarding your theme. If the topic is immigration, for example, students might interview family members regarding the way gender influences immigration experiences or the way culture changes over generations. The following interview guidelines were prepared by broadcast journalist Tatiana Schreiber for the *Other Colors* teachers' guide (Martin & Schreiber 1996).

Interview Guidelines

- Create a list of questions. Which would get a yes or no answer only? How can you change the question to get more information or encourage the interviewee to express an opinion?

- It helps to ask about specific examples or stories as a follow-up to a general response. If the person being interviewed says, "I really liked it when I first got here," follow up by saying, "Can you give an example of something you really liked?" Try asking, "What was most surprising about . . . ?" "What was the worst disappointment in . . . ?"

- Always tell the person you are interviewing that he doesn't have to answer any question if it seems too personal. What seems all right to you might not feel comfortable to someone else.
- Begin with your own list of questions during the interview, but remember to listen to what your interviewee is saying, and ask related questions. Don't be afraid to let go of your prepared questions if what the interviewee is talking about is more interesting than what you had planned to ask.
- It can make the person being interviewed feel more at ease if you start by saying, "I have a lot of questions I want to ask, but if there are other things you want to talk about, please feel free to go ahead and say what *you* think is important."
- On the other hand, this is your chance to indulge your curiosity! Think about what you really want to know but never had a chance to ask anyone before—then do it!

As an added step, have the interviewer show her write-up to the interviewee for the latter's reaction, with this twist: ask the interviewer to then reflect on the ways her own interests and ideas might have influenced what she chose to include and exclude. (38)

Facilitating Rich Discussions

There are things not mentioned elsewhere in these chapters that help me create fuller discussions—ones in which more students participate and examine a topic from more angles. The following are a few of the strategies that help facilitate this. While several might seem obvious, I find sometimes it's easy to forget to use them!

- Encourage students to ask one another and you for clarification when they need it. (Of course, modeling this will help.) In this way, we are more likely to really tune in to what others are saying, and we also encourage the speaker to closely examine her or his own ideas.
- Pay close attention to the ways participants relate to a discussion. Discussion can seem to wander all over the place and often we make decisions about which track to follow. But I've found times when, while I've assumed someone was taking us off on a tangent, the speaker saw her contribution as definitely linked to the discussion at hand. It's just that I wasn't seeing the link. Cynthia Ellwood wrote that, as a White teacher in a culturally diverse Milwaukee school, she had to understand that what her students see and know

"may rationally be different from what I see and know" (1991, 3). Rather than cutting some voices off, I try to provide opportunities for people to expand on the sense they're making. All teachers have moments when we think discussions are going offtrack, and they can. But ask yourself sometimes whether your perception of the track is shared by your students. Does what you perceive to be off the subject in fact relate in a way you didn't immediately see?

- If you find you're immediately talking after each person speaks, remind yourself to allow students to engage with one another. If this isn't happening spontaneously, help turn the class into a group whose members relate to one another, not just to you, by relating what one speaker says to what another has said. When it seems right, take questions addressed to you and return them to the group.

- Allow the silence. Silences can be the hardest thing for a teacher to live with. Yet if we can hold out, the seemingly empty spaces almost always become more productive than awkward, allowing people to think, letting them know we're serious about wanting to know what they think, and producing important contributions. To ease some of the anxiety that silence can create—as much in us as in our students—you might want to say, "Take some time to think," and allow the silence to continue. Related to this, don't be too quick to cut off a brainstorming session. Even if it seems to be winding down, be sure to allow a little extra time for additional ideas to come out. Almost inevitably, more will.

- If someone speaks in generalities, ask if she can speak from experience, as a way to be specific.

- To bring out the beliefs that underlie an opinion, ask what it is the speaker finds convincing in the viewpoint he is advocating.

- Sometimes when a discussion becomes particularly heated, yet confusing at the same time, an effective strategy is to ask everyone to stop and just write whatever is in her head at that instant. Not only does it help refocus the discussion, but some of the most reflective writing can emerge at these moments.

- If discussion suddenly stops after you ask a question, try something like, "Maybe my question doesn't get at the real issues. What do you think we really should be talking about here?" or "What seems to be the central issue right now?"

- If someone dominates the conversation, try interrupting with, "Thank you. We'll try to come back to what you're saying. But let's stop here and see what other people are thinking." Another effective strategy is to simply—or simultaneously—shift your position in the room. As you move to another corner, participants' gaze will move with you, taking in other people in the room. Encourage new participants by moving toward them as they begin to speak.

- If someone brings up a misconception, stop and ask how the group or specific individuals might check into whether the statement or assumption is true. While we all make on-our-feet decisions about what to interrupt and what to let pass during a discussion, letting certain things stand can be dangerous.

- Probe for more. Something as simple as "Say more about that" or "What are your questions?" (instead of asking students *if* they have any) or "I'd like to invite someone who hasn't spoken yet to join the discussion" helps expand discussions, so that more students participate in a conversation which examines the topic from more angles.

- Linger over the issues raised. Asking simply, "What happened to-day?" gives both the teacher and students various perspectives on what occurred as a result of listening to and discussing a topic. This technique is especially helpful for me when the question elicits en-couraging things about a class in which I focused only on the small disasters. It's different from asking the more common, "What was most useful today? What was least helpful?" The difference is sub-tle, yet the more open the question, the wider becomes the range of responses.

From there, you can use more specific questions. For example, you might try asking students what major themes emerged during the class and also contribute what you perceived them to be. The following questions also give everyone a chance to more deeply consider what we heard:

"What did you find most persuasive or convincing today?"

"Does what you heard today jibe with what you thought before, or have you revised your ideas?"

"What beliefs were reinforced, or changed, or broadened as a result of what we did today?"

"What surprised you?"

"Are you realizing anything about (immigration, sexual harass-ment, racism) and its effect on you?"

"Has a new idea led to a new question? A new question to a new idea?"

"What seems important that we haven't yet talked about?"

The key is to use anything you come up with that allows you to slow down and linger over a topic.

A Postscript on The Power of a Group

I was in New York City the winter of the Gulf War and went with a friend to an antiwar speak-out at the Riverside Church. Like most people, I was absorbed by the war at the time. But I was also absorbed in the four-day institute I was to begin facilitating the next morning. The hall was jam-packed when we arrived. Though I'd been tired when we left the house, I felt immediately energized and drawn in by the crowd and its faces—many those of older, seasoned activists. But as speaker after speaker took to the podium, my mind wandered back to the institute and the materials I still needed to organize. Then Daniel Ellsberg came to the microphone. The first thing he did was ask us a question: "When I arrived tonight and heard [the moderator] announce the news of the latest peace proposal, I felt like dancing! I don't get that feeling often these days, and I wanted to embrace it. But hardly anyone applauded when the announcement was made, and I want to know why." He looked around the room and waited for an answer, and everything changed in that moment. The individual reasons that people hadn't responded to the announcement, most to do with an expectation that the United States would reject the proposal, aren't what's important now. What's important is what his question *did*. People stood up and spoke in that cavernous room, and many of us in our seats turned to one another for the first time, murmuring agreement or dissent. As Ellsberg then responded to what he had heard, many of us continued reacting with the people sitting near us.

U.S. Representative Major Owens spoke next. He said he'd heard that 20 percent of the U.S. population was against the war, and then he asked how many people lived in New York City. "Seven million," came the shouts. "And what is 20 percent of seven million?" "A lot!" "And what if over one million people went out right now and stopped traffic in New York City in opposition to this war?" Owens then began his talk. It was now 10 P.M. I forced myself to leave, counting on my friend to relay other enthusiastic outbursts by the group. He did, the minute he got home. A large group had left the hall and headed directly to Times Square to hold a demonstration. Now, I have been to many political events about many compelling issues over many years. We might sign a petition, put money in a hat, or place our names on a volunteer sign-up sheet. But I have *never* been part of an audience that got up out of our chairs to stage an action then and there. I believe it's because

Ellsburg turned us into a group, and Owens then built on it. Do the same thing in your classroom, and it could lead anywhere.[12]

Notes

1. It's possible, but frustrating, to try to follow through on a theme in a coherent way in a program that has a policy of admitting students at any time during a semester. Some programs reject this policy in favor of a preregistration period and a cutoff date for admitting new students. While administrations complain that it's unfair to ask people to wait till the next semester, every teacher I know knows it's unfair to current students and him- or herself to keep trying to include people who haven't been part of shaping what the class has developed into. The pressure to admit students at any time often comes, in reality, from funders who mandate class size. In evaluating grant proposals from adult literacy programs, one state's department of education deducts points for those without a rolling admission policy because it means that they have a higher number of vacant slots. This issue has come up in discussions among teachers who have organized a union or are in the midst of trying to.

2. From "Class Notes, Philadelphia, Folder One."

3. For ideas on challenging homophobia in the classroom, see materials available from GLSEN (Gay, Lesbian, Straight Educators Network), 122 W. 26th Street, New York, NY 10001. See also *Radical Teacher* #45 on lesbian/gay/queer studies.

4. From "Class Notes, Philadelphia, Folder One."

5. From "Class Notes, Philadelphia, Folder One."

6. From a speech given at the Riverside Church, New York City, 7 February 1991.

7. *Other Colors: Stories of Women Immigrants* (Martin & Schreiber 1996) includes audiotaped interviews and a teachers guide. For ordering information, write to: Other Colors, PO Box 12355, Philadelphia, PA 19119.

8. More and more, there is a recognition that White has often been seen by White people as an invisible, normalized backdrop against which all people of color stand out. At some point in your discussion of immigration, you may want to ask the group about this. For example, if you used the fast details activity based on the word *race*, did White students list words indicating a belief that only people of color are characterized by race?

9. From "Class Notes, New Mexico Folder."

10. From preface to D. Goswami and P. Stillman (1987).

11. From "Class Notes, Philadelphia, Folder One."

12. Information from: *Proposition 187 Organizing Manual*, published by Albuquerque Border City Project; "Stereotypes Dead Wrong on Immigrants, Stats Say," *The Denver Post*, 12 February 1995; *Poverty and Welfare Among Immigrants in California*, published by the Tomás Rivera Center; *Myths and Facts: Immigration*

and the U.S., published by the Coalition for Immigrant and Refugee Rights and Services; C. Tactaquin, "What Rights for the Undocumented?" *Report on the Americas* XXVI (1) 1992; "Immigrants: Building the Union Yesterday and Today," *Solidarity* December 1994; "News Item," *Solidarity* July 1995; "Barbarians at the Border," *Network News: Newsletter of the National Network for Immigrant and Refugee Rights* VII (1) 1994; and "Immigration Quiz: Myths and Facts," *Philadelphia Public School Notebook* September 1995.

Epilogue

When my daughter was a newborn, and I was out of the house alone, someone would often say something like "Mom's day out?" with a little wink. Of course, my partner, who shared equally in our daughter's caregiving, never got a reaction to being out and mobile without his child. There were lots of other examples of this double standard, and part of me experienced amazement, even outrage, that in 1997 it still existed. But another part of me—not a small part—felt guilty in those moments. When Nomi was still very young, I went one Saturday morning to a coffee shop to do some writing for a research project in which I was involved. I was sitting with my cup and my sweet roll and my papers covering the table when a woman with a baby made her way to a table nearby. As she was getting settled, I made funny faces at the baby and asked the woman how old she was. When she said, "Five months," I told her I had a baby the same age. "Well, where's your baby?" she asked. I stuttered and mumbled, "At home." I don't even know what this woman really meant by her question, but within an instant, I felt there was something wrong with being at this coffee shop, writing, without Nomi. Moments like these got to me in ways I didn't expect. Twenty-five plus years is a lot of time spent in feminist consciousness raising. But the discourse of motherhood won't let go. I have deconstructed it on a conscious level backward and forward. But what remain are the emotional entanglements, tied, no doubt, to a struggle to identify with and also distance myself from my own mother as primary caregiver, not to mention social structures that make the fragile balance between motherhood and work impossible at times. The point is, we all live at this nexus of internalized discourses, unconscious fears and desires, and social and political constraints. That's why working with my students through a deconstruction of how the school system failed them isn't enough!

Just before sitting down to write this conclusion, I visited in Cleveland with three friends from junior high school, two of whom I hadn't seen in twenty-five years. We began talking about what we remembered about each other, and immediately all three recalled that I was into "causes." Surprised, I asked them what they meant. Jan said, "Like pollution." They also remembered me talking back to disrespectful teachers, particularly the home economics teacher who humiliated us by making us model the awful things we sewed. I have no memory of that either. But the surprising thing about all this is that my three closest friends weren't into causes or talking back. I kept wondering where this influence came from. In telling the story to a friend when I returned home, I suddenly remembered wearing a black arm band to school in eighth grade when the students were killed at Kent State. And then I remembered that the arm band came from an antiwar moratorium that my father took me to at the university where he was teaching. And then I remembered that, as a rabbi, my father supported conscientious objectors during the Vietnam War.

I haven't recognized this legacy because, for other reasons, I wanted to distance myself from my father. The idea that he had liberal politics and acted on them is not the story I've told myself. In fact, I've sometimes thought the reason I became a feminist was in reaction to my father's treatment of my mother. And maybe I did, but there's also this other piece I left out. It's a piece of who he was and who I am. And I need it now especially as I worry about the difficult parts of my own childhood I don't want to pass on to my daughter. The picture turns out to be more complicated; there are more parts of it I can embrace. Writing isn't the only way to get to these other stories, the paradoxes poststructural and psychoanalytic thought teaches us to be open to, but it *is* a way—to get new visions on our experiences and to tell our stories. That's why writing and publishing are two of the most powerful things we can offer the people in our classrooms.

This is clearly an autobiographical work, yet I can't swear all of the things are true. How I make sense of them—how we all make sense of our work and lives—is maybe what this book is really about. It was never intended as a search for perfection, and my own contradictions are evident. I wanted to question the taken-for-granted, to illuminate the struggle, the complexity of teaching, and a deeper level of change we're not getting to. The emphasis on publication in the previous chapters extends to us as teachers. We need more and more to publish our reflections of who we are in the classroom and what we want to achieve.

The answer to why we haven't achieved more as progressive teachers is not located in the students, which I think critical pedagogy does not fundamentally realize. The image of "the illiterate" as dysfunctional, insinuated again and again by both critical pedagogy and mainstream literacy campaigns, weaves its way through theory, classroom technique, funding appeals, and student outreach. It's fundamental; it's deep; and until it changes, no new pedagogy can emerge.

As for poststructural ideas, I think the most powerful thing about them is that they challenge the notion that the world is unified and based on an inherent order, thus making room to envision very different worlds. Along the way toward working for them, I hope this book is useful.

References

Albuquerque Border City Project. 1994. Fund-Raising Appeal. Albuquerque. November.

Albuquerque Literacy Program. 1994. *Celebrating Community Voice: A Guide for Training Volunteer ESL Tutors in Participatory Literacy*. Albuquerque, NM.

Amidei, N. 1992. "Test Your Welfare I.Q." *Survival News* Summer/Fall: 21.

Amott, T. 1993. "The War on Welfare: Clinton's Carrots and Sticks." *Dollars and Sense* November/December: 12–15, 32–34.

Anzaldúa, G. 1981. "Speaking in Tongues: A Letter to Third World Women Writers." In *This Bridge Called My Back: Writings by Radical Women of Color*, ed. C. Moraga & G. Anzaldúa, 165–74. Watertown, MA: Persipone Press.

——— 1987. *Borderlands/La Frontera: The New Mestiza*. San Francisco, CA: Aunt Lute Books.

Armitage, D. 1994. "Demanding Exhibition Explores Disease of Racism." *Albuquerque Journal* 22 May: G6.

Association for Community-Based Education. 1988. *Literacy for Empowerment: A Resource Handbook for Community Based Educators*. Washington, D.C.

Atwell, N. 1987. *In the Middle: Writing, Reading, and Learning with Adolescents*. Portsmouth, NH: Heinemann–Boynton/Cook.

Auerbach, E. R., & N. Wallerstein. 1987a. *ESL for Action: Problem Posing at Work*. Reading, MA: Addison-Wesley.

———. 1987b. *ESL for Action: Problem Posing at Work, Teacher's Guide*. Reading, MA: Addison-Wesley.

Aviles, E., & M. Banks. 1992. "On the Question of Race." In *Redescubriendo America*, ed. A. Ramos, D. Menkart, G. Belli & L. Holmes-Bonilla. 67–68. Washington, D.C.: Network of Educators on the Americas.

Ayers, W. 1990. "Classroom Spaces, Teacher Choices: A review of *Among School-children*." *Rethinking Schools* 5 (1): 3, 16.

Bakhtin, M. M. 1986. *Speech Genres and Other Late Essays*. Ed. C. Emerson & M. Holquist. Austin: University of Texas Press.

Baldwin, J. & Y. Cazac. 1976. *Little Man, Little Man: A Story of Childhood*. New York: Dial Press.

Belliveau, M., C. Marchant, & I. Yankwitt. 1995. *Unmasking Face to Face: A Workbook on Welfare*. New York: Stanley M. Isaacs Neighborhood Center.

Benjamin, J. 1987. *The Bonds of Love: Psychoanalysis, Feminism, and the Problems of Domination*. New York: Pantheon Books.

Berlak, A. C. 1996. "Teaching Stories: Viewing a Cultural Diversity Course Through the Lens of Narrative." *Theory Into Practice* 35 (2): 93–101.

Berry, E., & E. Black. 1987. "The Integrative Learning Journal (or, Getting Beyond 'True Confessions' and 'Cold Knowledge')." *Women's Studies Quarterly* XV (3 & 4): 59–64.

Berthoff, A. E. 1981. *The Making of Meaning: Metaphors, Models, and Maxims for Writing Teachers*. Upper Montclair, NJ: Boynton/Cook Publishers.

———— 1982. *Forming, Thinking, Writing*. Portsmouth, NH: Heinemann–Boynton/Cook.

Bhabha, H. 1983. "The Other Question: Homi K. Bhabha Reconsiders the Stereotype and Colonial Discourse." *Screen* 24 (6): 18–36.

Bleich, D. 1991. "Reading from Inside and Outside One's Community." In *Practicing Theory in Introductory College Literature Courses*, ed. J. M. Cahalan & D. B. Downing, 19–35. Urbana, IL: National Council of Teachers of English.

Boston Adult Literacy Fund. 1991. Fund-Raising Letter. March.

Brady, J. 1994. "Critical Literacy, Feminism, and a Politics of Representation." In *Politics of Liberation: Paths from Freire*, ed. P. L. McLaren & C. Lankshear, 142–53. New York: Routledge.

Bush, B. 1989. "No Liberty Without Literacy." *Gannett Foundation Magazine* Summer: 6, 22.

Butler, J. 1990. "Gender Trouble, Feminist Theory, and Psychoanalytic Discourse." In *Feminism and Postmodernism*, ed. J. Nicholson, 324–40. New York: Routledge.

———— 1993a. *Bodies That Matter: On the Discursive Limits of "Sex."* New York: Routledge.

———— 1993b. "A Skeptical Feminist Postscript to the Postmodern." In *Postmodernism Across the Ages*, ed. W. Readings & B. Schaber, 233–37. New York: Syracuse University Press.

Calkins, L. 1983. *Lessons from a Child*. Exeter, NH: Heinemann Educational Books.

Central Manchester Caribbean English Project. 1986. *Triangular Minds: Black Youth on Identity*. Manchester, England: Manchester Free Press.

Chavez, A. 1991. "A Home Away from Home." *United Youth of Boston* June/July: 9.

Chetwynd, H., L. Manicom, S. Murphy, & L. Yanz. 1992. *Women Educating Women to End Domestic Violence*. Toronto, Canada: Popular Education Research Group.

Christensen, L. 1992. "The Father I Never Knew." *New Youth Connections* April: 18.

Clark, V. A. 1991. "Developing Diaspora Literacy and Marasa Consciousness." In *Comparative American Identities: Race, Sex, and Nationality in Modern Text*, ed. H. J. Spillars, 40–61. New York: Routledge.

Clifford, J. 1984. "Cognitive Psychology and Writing: A Critique." *Freshman English News* 13: 16–18.

———— 1991. "The Reader and the Text: Ideologies in Dialogue." In *Practicing Theory in Introductory College English Literature Courses*, ed. J. M. Cahalan & D. B. Browning, 101–11. Urbana, IL: National Council of Teachers of English.

Cohen, J. B. 1989. Review of *The Bonds of Love: Psychoanalysis, Feminism, and The Problem of Domination*, by J. Benjamin. *Zeta Magazine* 2 (4): 76–78.

Cohen, J. 1993. "Constructing Race at an Urban High School: In Their Minds, Their Mouths, Their Hearts." In *Beyond Silenced Voices: Class, Race, and Gender in U.S. Schools*, ed. L. Weiss & M. Fine, 289–308. Albany: State University of New York Press.

Coles, G. 1987. *The Learning Mystique: A Critical Look at "Learning Disabilities."* New York: Fawcett Columbine.

Cosme, M. 1995. "Married with Children." *United Youth of Boston* Spring: 8.

Crimp, D. 1992. "Portraits of People with AIDS." In *Cultural Studies*, ed. L. Grossberg, C. Nelson, & P. Treichler, 117–33. New York: Routledge.

de Courtivron, I. 1993. "The Body Was His Battleground: A Review of *The Passion of Michel Foucault*," by James Miller. 10 January *New York Times*: 1, 29–30.

deLeón, A. 1990. "The Answer That Stares You in the Face." *Free My People* 1 (5): 1.

Delpit, L. D. 1988. "The Silenced Dialogue: Power and Pedagogy in Educating Other People's Children." *Harvard Educational Review* 58 (3): 280–98.

———— 1994. "Seeing Color: A Review of White Teacher." In *Rethinking Our Classroom: Teaching for Equity and Justice*, ed. B. Bigelow, L. Christensen, S. Karp, B. Miner, & B. Peterson, 130–32. Milwaukee: Rethinking Schools.

Didion, J. 1980. "Why I Write." In *The Writer on Her Work*, ed. J. Sternburg, 17–25. New York: W. W. Norton & Co.

Dorfman, L. 1992. "Cracks in the Edifice: Postmodernist Critique of Public Health." Nonpublished manuscript. San Rafael, CA: Marin Institute.

Dorris, M. 1994. "Mixed Blood." *Hungry Mind Review* Fall: 52.

Douglass, F. 1968. *Narrative of the Life of Frederick Douglass an American Slave*. New York: New American Library.

Duckworth, E. 1986. "Teaching as Research." *Harvard Educational Review* 56 (4): 481–95.

———— 1991. "Twenty-Four, Forty-Two, and I Love You: Keeping It Complex." *Harvard Educational Review* 61 (1): 1–24.

Ebert, T. 1991. "The 'Difference' of Postmodern Feminism." *College English* 53 (8): 886–904.

Edelsky, C. 1991. *With Literacy and Justice for All: Rethinking the Social in Language and Education.* New York: Falmer Press.

Ellwood, C. 1991. "An Urban Teacher Talks to Teacher Educators: Why We Need Ethnic Studies in Teacher Preparation Programs." *Rethinking Schools* 5(3): 3, 18.

Ellsworth, E. 1989. "Why Doesn't This Feel Empowering? Working Through the Repressive Myths of Critical Pedagogy." *Harvard Educational Review* 59 (3): 297–324.

———— 1992. "Teaching to Support Unassimilated Difference." *Radical Teacher* 44: 4–9.

Evans, A. 1991. "If Teens Could Talk." *United Youth of Boston* June/July: 1–2.

Fiore, K., & N. Elsasser. 1982. "'Strangers No More': A Liberatory Literacy Curriculum." *Harvard Educational Review* 44 (2): 115–28.

Fish, S. 1980. *Is There a Text in This Class?* Cambridge, MA: Harvard University Press.

Flax, J. 1984. "Mother-Daughter Relationships: Psychodynamics, Politics and Philosophy." In *The Future of Difference,* eds. H. Eisenstein & A. Jardine, 20–40. New Brunswick, NJ: Rutgers University Press.

Flax, J. 1993. *Disputed Subjects: Essays on Psychoanalysis, Politics, and Philosophy.* London: Routledge.

Flores-Williams, J. 1994. "Understanding Bi-Cultural Reality." *La Herencia del Norte* Summer: 63.

Freire, P. 1978. *Pedagogy in Process: The Letters to Guinea Bissau.* New York: Seabury Press.

———— 1985. *The Politics of Education: Culture, Power, and Liberation.* South Hadley, MA: Bergin & Garvey Publishers.

———— 1993. *Pedagogy of the Oppressed.* New York: Continuum.

———— 1996. *Pedagogy of Hope: Reliving Pedagogy of the Oppressed.* New York: Continuum.

Freire, P., & D. Macedo. 1987. *Literacy: Reading the Word and the World.* South Hadley, MA: Bergin & Garvey Publishers.

Freire, P., & D. Macedo. 1993. "A Dialogue with Paulo Freire." In *Paulo Freire: A Critical Encounter,* eds. P. McLaren & P. Leonard, 169–76. New York: Routledge.

Fulwiler, T. 1987. *The Journal Book.* Upper Montclair, NJ: Boynton/Cook Publishers.

Gallop, J., & C. Burke. 1984. "Psychoanalysis and Feminism in France." In *The Future of Difference,* ed. H. Eisenstein & A. Jardine, 106–21. New Brunswick, NJ: Rutgers University Press.

Gates, H. L. 1986. "Writing 'Race' and the Difference It Makes." In *"Race," Writing, and Difference,* ed. H. L. Gates, 1–20. Chicago: The University of Chicago Press.

———— 1991a. "'Authenticity,' or the Lesson of Little Tree." *The New York Times* 24 November: 25–30.

———— 1991b. "The Debate Has Been Miscast from the Start." *Boston Globe Magazine* 13 October: 26, 36–38.

Gee, J. 1988. "The Legacies of Literacy: From Plato to Freire Through Harvey Graff." *Harvard Educational Review* 58 (2): 195–212.

Goldberg, N. 1986. *Writing Down the Bones*. Boston, MA: Shambhala.

Goswami, D. & P. Stillman. 1987. *Reclaiming the Classroom: Teacher Research as an Agency for Change*. Upper Montclair, NJ: Boynton/Cook.

Gwaltney, J. 1980. *Drylongso: A Self Portrait of Black America*, New York: Vintage Books.

Haraway, D. J. 1991. *Simians, Cyborgs, and Women: The Reinvention of Nature*. New York: Routledge.

Henriques, J., W. Hollway, C. Urwin, C. Venn, & V. Walkerdine. 1984. *Changing the Subject: Psychology, Regulation, and Subjectivity*. London: Methuen.

Hirshon, S. 1983. *And Also Teach Them to Read: The National Literacy Crusade of Nicaragua*. Westport, CT: Lawrence Hill & Co.

hooks, b. 1989. *Talking Back: Thinking Feminist, Thinking Black*. Boston, MA: South End Press.

———— 1994. *Teaching to Transgress: Education as the Practice of Freedom*. New York: Routledge.

Hurston, Z. N. 1979. "How It Feels to Be Colored Me." In *I Love Myself When I Am Laughing . . . and Then Again When I Am Looking Mean and Impressive,* ed. A. Walker, 152–55. Old Westbury, NY: The Feminist Press.

Hurston, Z. N. 1987. *Their Eyes Were Watching God*. Urbana, IL: University of Illinois Press.

Ifill, V. 1987. "Untitled." *Hear My Soul's Voice: Writings by the Jefferson Park Writing Center* VI: 20.

Jacobson, K. 1994. *Embattled Selves: An Investigation into the Nature of Identity Through Oral Histories of Holocaust Survivors*. New York: The Atlantic Monthly Press.

James, D. L. 1990. "Doing the System Shuffle." *Step by Step: Creative Expression by West Virginia Youth* Fall: 10.

Jamieson, K. H. 1992. *Dirty Politics: Deception, Distraction, and Democracy*. New York: Oxford University Press.

Jay, G., & G. Graff. 1993. "Some Questions About Critical Pedagogy." *Democratic Culture* 2 (2): 1, 15–16.

Johnson, B. 1985. "Thresholds of Difference: Structures of Address in Zora Neale Hurston." In *"Race," Writing, and Difference*, ed. H. L. Gates, 317–28. Chicago: The University of Chicago Press.

Johnston, P. H. 1985. "Understanding Reading Disability: A Case Study Approach." *Harvard Educational Review* 55 (2): 153–77.

Jordan, J. 1985. *On Call: Political Essays*. Boston, MA: South End Press.

Kahn, K. 1973. *Hillbilly Women*. New York: Avon Books.

Katz, M. L. 2000. Private Correspondence.

Kohl, H. 1991. *I Won't Learn from You!: The Role of Assent in Learning*. Minneapolis: Milkwood Edition.

Kozol, J. 1978. "A New Look at the Literacy Campaign in Cuba." *Harvard Educational Review* 48 (3): 341–77.

Krivak, A. J. 1992. "Tales of Brave Ulysses: A Reflection on AIDS Ministry." *America* 472–73.

Lather, P. 1992. "Post-Critical Pedagogies: A Feminist Reading." In *Feminisms and Critical Pedagogy*, ed. C. Luke & J. Gore, 120–37. London: Routledge.

Le Sueur, M. 1982. *Worker Writers*. Albuquerque, NM: West End Press.

Lippard, L. 1990. *Mixed Blessings: New Art in a Multicultural America*. New York: Pantheon Books.

——— 1992. "The Color of the Wind." *Crosswinds* IV(VIII): 18–20.

Lorde, A. 1984. *Sister Outsider*. New York: Crossing Press.

Lugones, M., & E. V. Spelman. 1983. "Have We Got a Theory for You! Feminist Theory, Cultural Imperialism, and the Demand for 'the Woman's Voice.'" *Hypatia* 1 (1): 573–81.

Lytle, S. L. 1990. "Living Literacy: Rethinking Development in Adulthood." Revised version of "Living Literacy: The Practices and Beliefs of Adult Learners," presented at American Educational Research Association Annual Meetings, Boston, MA, April.

Macedo, D. 1993. "Literacy for Stupidification: The Pedagogy of Big Lies." *Harvard Educational Review* 63 (2): 183–206.

Mahoney, M. A., & B. Yngvesson. 1992. "The Construction of Subjectivity and the Paradox of Resistance: Reintegrating Feminist Anthropology and Psychology." *Signs* 18 (1): 44–73.

Martin, D. 1975. *Reappraising Freire: The Potentials and Limits of Conscientization*. Master's thesis, University of Toronto, Toronto, Canada.

Martin, J. F. 1991. *Surviving the '90s: Alcohol, Other Drugs, and HIV/AIDS. Health Education for English as a Second Language and Adult Literacy Programs*. Waltham, MA: Mount Auburn Hospital Prevention and Training Center.

Martin, R. 1986. "A Conversation with Ira Shor." *Literacy Research Center Newsletter* 2 (1): 1, 6–7.

——— 1989. "Listen to a New Word: Publishing from the Grassroots." *Focus on Basics* 2 (2): 5–7.

——— 1991. "Listen Up: Youth, Writing, and Resistance." *Resist Newsletter* 237: 1–7.

——— 1993. *Neighbors Talk in Roxbury, Dorchester, and Jamaica Plain*. Jamaica Plain, MA: Neighbors Talk Publishing Committee.

Martin, R., & T. Schreiber. 1996. *Other Colors: Stories of Women Immigrants.* Albuquerque, NM: Other Colors Project.

Martinez, D. 1994. *Mother Tongue.* Tempe, AZ: Bilingual Press/Editorial Bilingue.

Massachusetts Adult Basic Education Directory. 1993. March.

Mayher, J. S. 1990. *Uncommon Sense: Theoretical Practice in Language Education.* Portsmouth, NH: Heinemann–Boynton/Cook.

Morley, D., & K. Warpole. n.d. *The Republic of Letters: Working Class Writing and Local Publishing.* London: Comedia Publishing Group.

Murray, D. M. 1985. *A Writer Teaches Writing.* Boston, MA: Houghton Mifflin.

Nash, A. 1993. "Pro-Worker Job Training." *Labor Page* 58 (October/November): 4–5.

Naylor, G. 1982. *The Women of Brewster Place.* New York: Penguin Books.

Neely, B. 1986. "Sister." *Essence Magazine* April: 56–64.

Neely, B. 1990. "Spilled Salt." In *Breaking Ice: An Anthology of Contemporary African-American Fiction,* ed. T. McMillan, 56–64. New York: Penguin Books.

Nuttal, C. 1982. *Teaching Reading Skills in a Foreign Language.* London: Heinemann Education Books.

O'Neill, K. 1991. "Telling the Wild Truth: A Review of *Wild Mind: Living the Writer's Life,*" by Natalie Goldberg. *Sojourner* May: 15–16.

Orbach, S., & L. Eichenbaum. 1987. "Separation and Intimacy: Crucial Practice Issues in Working with Women in Therapy." In *Living with the Sphinx: Papers from the Women's Therapy Centre,* ed. S. Ernst & M. Maguire, 49–67. London: Women's Press.

Orner, M. 1992. "Interrupting the Calls for Student Voice in 'Liberatory' Education: A Feminist Poststructuralist Perspective." In *Feminisms and Critical Pedagogy,* ed. C. Luke & J. Gore, 74–89. New York: Routledge.

Penley, C. 1992. "Feminism, Psychoanalysis, and the Study of Popular Culture." In *Cultural Studies,* ed. L. Grossberg, C. Nelson, & P. Treichler, 479–500. New York: Routledge.

Perez, H. 1989. "Students Praise Their Tutors." *Students Speaking Out* 3 (2): 2.

Rich, A. 1979. *On Lies, Secrets, and Silence.* New York: W. W. Norton.

Riggs, M. T. 1995. *Black Is . . . Black Ain't: A Personal Journey Through Black Identity.* San Francisco, CA: California Newsreel.

Rockhill, K. 1988. "E-MAN-Ci-Patory Literacy: An Essay Review of *Literacy: Reading the Word and the World.*" P. Freire and D. Macedo. *Canadian Women Studies/Les Cahiers de la Femme* 9 (3 & 4): 113–15.

Roman, L. G. 1993. "White Is a Color! White Defensiveness, Postmodernism, and Anti-Racist Pedagogy." In *Race, Identity, and Representation,* ed. C. McCarthy & W. Crichlow, 71–88. New York: Routledge.

Rosten, L. 1968. *The Joys of Yiddish.* New York: McGraw Hill.

Rural Community Education Cooperative. 1987. *Claiming Our Economic History*. Jellico, TN: Mountain Women's Exchange.

Russell, M. G. 1983. "Black-Eyed Blues Connection: From the Inside Out." In *Learning Our Way: Essays in Feminist Education*, ed. C. Bunch & S. Pollack, 272–84. Trumansburg, NY: Crossing Press.

Sanchez-Tranquilino, M., & J. Tagg. 1992. "The Pachuco's Flayed Hide: Mobility, Identity and *Buenas Garras*." In *Cultural Studies*, ed. L. Grossberg, C. Nelson, & P. Treichler, 556–70. New York: Routledge.

Schutte, O. 1993. *Cultural Identity and Social Liberation in Latin American Thought*. Albany: State University of New York Press.

Shor, I. 1980. *Critical Teaching and Everyday Life*. Boston, MA: South End Press.

Shor, I., & P. Freire. 1987. *A Pedagogy for Liberation: Dialogues on Transforming Education*. South Hadley, MA: Bergin & Garvey.

Simon, R. 1984. "Being Ethnic/Doing Ethnicity: A Response to Corrigan." Response to Philip Corrigan's remarks during Race, Ethnicity, and Education: Critical Perspectives. Symposium. Toronto, Ontario, Canada.

Simon, R., & D. Dippo. 1987. "What Schools Can Do: Designing Programs for Work Education That Challenge the Wisdom of Experience." *Journal of Education* 169 (3): 101–16.

Snyder, C. 1984. "Analyzing Classifications: Foucault for Advanced Writing." *College Composition and Communication* 35 (2): 209–16.

Spelman, E. 1988. *Inessential Woman*. Boston: Beacon Press.

Stanley, W. B. 1992. *Curriculum for Utopia: Social Construction and Critical Pedagogy in the Postmodern Era*. Albany: State University of New York Press.

Struhl, K. 1979. "Teaching Socialist Ethics at Co-Op City." *Radical Teacher* 12 (March): 12–16.

Stuckey, J. E. 1991. *The Violence of Literacy*. Portsmouth, NH: Boynton/Cook Publishers.

Survival News. 1992. "Everybody's News." A special issue. Summer.

Tan, A. 1991. "Mother Tongue." In *Best American Essays 1991*, ed. J. E. Kaplan & R. Atwan, 196–202. Boston: Houghton-Mifflin Co.

Tate, C. 1984. *Black Women Writers at Work*. New York: Continuum.

Todorov, T. 1984. *Mikhail Bakhtin: The Dialogic Principle*. Minneapolis: University of Minnesota Press.

Tompkins, J. 1990. "Pedagogy of the Distressed." *College English* 52 (6): 653–60.

———. "Pedagogy of the Distressed: Comment and Response." *College English* 53(5): 599–605.

Tracy. 1991. "Growing Up Lesbian." *Teen Voices* Spring: 13.

Tracy, M., & M. L. Campbell. 1993. Exchange of letters in *The Women's Review of Books* X (8): 4–5.

Trask, H. 1993. *From a Native Daughter: Colonialism and Sovereignty in Hawaii*. Monroe, ME: Common Courage Press.

Walker, A. 1974. "In Search of Our Mothers' Gardens: The Creativity of Black Women in the South." *Ms.* May: 67.

Walkerdine, V. 1985. "Dreams of an Ordinary Childhood." In *Truth, Dare, or Promise: Girls Growing Up in the Fifties,* ed. L. Heron, 63–77. London: Virago.

——— 1994. "Femininity as Performance." In *Education Feminism Reader,* ed. L. Stone, 57–69. New York: Routledge.

Wallace, M. 1992. "Negative Images: Towards a Black Feminist Cultural Criticism." In *Cultural Studies,* ed. L. Grossberg, C. Nelson, & P. Treichler, 664–71. New York: Routledge.

Washington, M. H. 1980. *Midnight Birds: Stories by Contemporary Black Women Writers.* Garden City, NY: Anchor Books.

Watson, G. 1989. "Boston Agonizes Over Student Violence." *New York Times* 28 October: 8.

Weiler, K. 1991. "Freire and a Feminist Pedagogy of Difference." *Harvard Educational Review* 61 (4): 444–74.

West, C. 1992. "The Postmodern Crisis of the Black Intellectuals." In *Cultural Studies,* ed. L. Grossberg, C. Nelson, & P. Treichler, 689–705. New York: Routledge.

——— 1993. Preface to *Paulo Freire: A Critical Encounter,* ed. P. L. McLaren & P. Leonard. New York: Routledge.

Wheeler, J. 1992. "Voice." In *Aboriginal Voices: American Indian, Inuit, and Sami Theater,* ed. P. Brask & W. Morgan, 37–43. Baltimore: Johns Hopkins University Press.

Williams, G. H. 1995. *Life on the Color Line: The True Story of a White Boy Who Discovered He Was Black.* New York: Dutton.

Williams, S. A. 1978. Foreword to *Their Eyes Were Watching God.* Urbana, IL: University of Illinois Press.

Williamson, J. 1981/1982. "How Does Girl Number Twenty Understand Ideology?" *Screen Education* 40: 80–87.

Wolfe, M. 1986. "Writing, Testing, Reading." *New York City Writing Project Newsletter* Summer: 2–6.

Index

3 798